DOCUMENTS ON GOVERNMENT
AND THE ECONOMY

RESEARCH IN THE HISTORY OF ECONOMIC THOUGHT AND METHODOLOGY

Founding Editor: Warren J. Samuels (1933–2011)
Series Editors: Jeff E. Biddle, Ross B. Emmett and
Marianne Johnson

Recent Volumes:

Volume 28A: Research in the History of Economic Thought and Methodology: A Research Annual; Jeff E. Biddle and Ross B. Emmett; 2010

Volume 28B: English, Irish and Subversives among the Dismal Scientists; Nigel Allington, Noel Thompson; 2010

Volume 28C: Economic Theory by Taussig, Young, and Carver at Harvard; Warren J. Samuels, Marianne Johnson; 2010

Volume 29A: Research in the History of Economic Thought and Methodology: A Research Annual; Jeff E. Biddle and Ross B. Emmett; 2010

Volume 29B: Research in the History of Economic Thought and Methodology: Frank H Knight in Iowa City; Ross B. Emmett; 2011

Volume 29C: Wisconsin, Labor, Income, and Institutions: Contributions from Commons and Bronfenbrenner; Marianne Johnson and Warren J. Samuels; 2011

Volume 30A: Research in the History of Economic Thought and Methodology: A Research Annual; Jeff E. Biddle and Ross B. Emmett; 2012

RESEARCH IN THE HISTORY OF ECONOMIC THOUGHT AND
METHODOLOGY   VOLUME 30-B

DOCUMENTS ON GOVERNMENT AND THE ECONOMY

EDITED BY

MARIANNE JOHNSON

*Department of Economics, University of Wisconsin-Oshkosh,
Oshkosh, WI, USA*

United Kingdom – North America – Japan
India – Malaysia – China

Emerald Group Publishing Limited
Howard House, Wagon Lane, Bingley BD16 1WA, UK

First edition 2012

Copyright © 2012 Emerald Group Publishing Limited

British Library Cataloguing in Publication Data
A catalogue record for this book is available from the British Library

ISBN: 978-1-78052-826-7
ISSN: 0743-4154 (Series)

ISOQAR certified
Management Systems,
awarded to Emerald for
adherence to Quality
and Environmental
standards ISO 9001:2008
and 14001:2004,
respectively

Certificate Number 1985
ISO 9001
ISO 14001

INVESTOR IN PEOPLE

CONTENTS

LIST OF CONTRIBUTORS

Margaret Albert   Department of Liberal Arts and International
                         Studies, Colorado School of Mines, Golden,
                         CO, USA

Brady J. Deaton   Department of Food, Agricultural and Resource
                         Economics, University of Guelph, ON, Canada

Marianne Johnson   Department of Economics, University of
                         Wisconsin-Oshkosh, Oshkosh, WI, USA

David M. Levy   Department of Economics, George Mason
                         University, Fairfax, VA, USA

Martin E. Meder   Department of Economics, University of
                         Wisconsin-Oshkosh, Oshkosh, WI, USA

Sandra J. Peart   Jepson School of Leadership Studies, University
                         of Richmond, Richmond, VA, USA

Warren J. Samuels   Deceased, Department of Economics, Michigan
                         State University, East Lansing, MI, USA

David Schweikhardt   Department of Agricultural, Food and Resource
                         Economics, Michigan State University, East
                         Lansing, MI, USA

James Sterns   Department of Food and Resource Economics,
                         University of Florida, Gainesville, FL, USA

Patricia Aust Sterns   Department of Environmental and Global
                         Health, University of Florida, Gainesville, FL,
                         USA

INTRODUCTION

Much of this volume of *Research in the History of Economic Thought and Methodology* considers the contributions made by Warren J. Samuels to economic methodology, law and economics, and the history of economic thought. A brief biographical profile of Samuels is provided in the Volume 30A this year. Samuels established the A volume of *RHETM* as a place for longer articles, detailed book reviews, and other documents that did not fit into the standard journal article format. Later, the B and C volumes were created to preserve and publish archival document. Samuels remembers that "a goodly number of items...[were] given to me by Ed Witte in May/June 1957 when he was trying to lighten his load as he retired; I graduated [at] the same time...the original obstacle I faced was that some of our teachers and students [were] fearful of embarrassing themselves. I can assure you that this problem has not materialized" (Samuels by email, May 18, 2011).

Samuels took editing work seriously and considered it "something of a career in and of itself, that is, apart from my own research and writing" (Samuels 1998, p. 3); in fact, in addition to *RHETM*, he edited the *Journal of Economic Issues* for 10 years. As part of this second career, Samuels built an impressively extensive library in economics and related fields, including significant archival documents, many of which have been published in *RHETM*. While some were from his time at the University of Wisconsin, Samuels also collected numerous documents – from individuals and from used book stores – including a set of typed and bound notes from Frank W. Taussig's economic theory course at Harvard from 1921. These were recently published in Volume 28C of this journal. Samuels laid out his vision for the continued operation of the journal:

> It would be wonderful if between us all, hopefully joined by others, we were able to collect, edit and publish a number of volumes of archival materials, especially, but not limited to, the institutionalism that Ely, Commons, Perlman and others established, of which we were the primary beneficiaries. As some of you may know... I established an annual which began with one volume a year and now is a three-volume annual, *Research in the History of Economic Thought and Methodology* where two volumes have been generally devoted to archival materials from Ely, Commons, and Perlman, as well as from non-institutionalists, and from other universities, the Chicago School. (Samuels by email May 18, 2011)

The papers and documents in this collection adhere to this vision. They include one of the last pieces that Samuels was working on, an examination of property as a function of politics, based on archival documents contributed to Heinrich von Treitschke. In addition, we publish notes from Samuels' Economic Role of Government course, and an analysis of economic liberals as quasi-public intellectuals by David M. Levy, Sandra J. Peart, and Margaret Albert. The latter includes a collection of archival documents related to economics in the public sphere by Rose Wilder Lane, Ludwig von Mises, T. N. Carver, including ones published in *The Economic Sentinel* and *Economic Council Review of Books*.

Marianne Johnson
Editor

REFERENCE

Samuels, W. J. (1998). Journal editing in the history of economic thought. *History of Economics Review*, 27(Winter), 3–5.

ECONOMIC LIBERALS AS QUASI-PUBLIC INTELLECTUALS: THE DEMOCRATIC DIMENSION

David M. Levy, Sandra J. Peart and Margaret Albert

Rose Wilder Lane Instructing Congress.

Documents on Government and the Economy
Research in the History of Economic Thought and Methodology, Volume 30-B, 1–116
Copyright © 2012 by Emerald Group Publishing Limited
ISSN: 0743-4154/doi:10.1108/S0743-4154(2012)000030B004

POLICY AND PROCEDURE IN PUBLIC DEBATE

How do we understand a one-sided controversy? In the 1940s, the teachings of technical economists were attacked by public intellectuals. The best-known controversy occurred when the "individualist" public intellectuals, Rose Wilder Lane and V. Orval Watts, wrote against the new generation of Keynes-influenced textbooks. The economists did not respond to the attacks publicly. The controversy is remembered only as a one-dimensional attack over policy, the scope of government activity. If it were that simple then its consequence would be largely personal, destroying the market for the first of the Keynesian textbooks (Lorie Tarshis's) and presenting the second (Paul Samuelson's) with a de facto monopoly. Once, however, we start to distinguish among the targeted textbooks, this all-inclusive policy orientation is not helpful (Levy & Peart, 2011). Moreover, there is another economist with a rather different political point of view, Ludwig von Mises, who also was attacked publicly by the same individualists but who, unlike his Keynesian contemporaries, replied in private.

A one-sided public controversy requires us to think about how to interpret quasi-public intellectuals, those who although attacked in public do not respond the same way. We propose to make the counterintuitive case that in an important dimension, that of democratic procedure, von Mises and the younger Keynesians were closer to each other than to the individualists. In particular, for von Mises and the younger Keynesians, their commitment to liberal democracy was prior to their policy advocacy. We offer a series of texts, some unpublished and others merely very difficult to find, presented in chronological order as a way to recover the dimensions in which the attack on the liberal economists occurred.

Tarshis and Samuelson differed in how to visualize the economist's role in the economy. Tarshis wrote his book supposing the economist to be inside the American economy urging reforms through democratic means. Samuelson's economist is harder to place, since his model covers both democracies and totalitarian states (Levy & Peart, 2011). This illusiveness allowed him to write prudently in an attempt to avoid Tarshis's fate. In remembering the episode, Samuelson tells us that he wrote carefully to avoid controversy, so perhaps the little joke that accompanied Watts's review that Samuelson was "playing peek-a-boo with the reader" was not unfair. We'll discuss this aspect of the controversy as individualists versus modern liberals.

Von Mises's policy recommendations are unlikely be confused with his Keynesian contemporaries. Consequently, Lane's and Watts's attack on von Mises's views allows us to distinguish between an attack on government involvement in the economy and an attack on democratic commitments to bring about policy changes. The question of where the economist is in an economic model is important to understanding von Mises. His economist cannot be distant from the society to have an impact. Following Max Weber, he holds that economic science is value-free in a more austere sense than we observe in the recent practice of economists. Von Mises's economist can only advise his fellows in his capacity as citizen and voter. We'll discuss this in terms of individualists versus classical liberalism, viewing von Mises as the greatest Manchester School liberal of his generation (Simons, 1944). To bring home the seriousness of the attack, we shall reprint a defense of von Mises's position against Watts's charge that by favoring democracy, von Mises was in violation of the oath of allegiance to the American Constitution he took to obtain citizenship.

The third aspect of the conflict of individualists comes with those who became the moving spirits on the Mont Pelerin Society (MPS). It is harder to describe this debate ideologically if only because the views of the participants changed so much in the decades that followed. In the 1940s, for example, George Stigler was a Knightian with deep egalitarian commitments (Levy & Peart, 2008). We'll refer to this controversy as individualists versus neoliberalism without presupposing that classical and neoliberal are all that different in the topics under debate in that period. One fragment of the conflict, published by Dan and Claire Hammond (2006), shows in the mutual unhappiness between Watts (then the staff economist of the Foundation for Economic Education [FEE]) and Milton Friedman and George Stigler over their views on equality expressed in *Roofs or Ceilings?* Watts's name comes up again when we learn that F. A. Hayek was required by American funding sources to include him in the MPS (Steiner, 2009, p. 190). Lane continually attacks Hayek's views in her letters to Jason Crane, one of the funders of the MPS (Lane & Crane, 1973). One indication of the complexity of the debate shows in the letter reproduced below in which Watts, in his position of the FEE staff economist, wrote to von Mises deploring von Mises's pro-democratic views. In the letter, Watts compares with alarm von Mises's democratic views and Friedman and Stigler's egalitarian views.

THE TEXTBOOK CONTROVERSY

The textbook controversy began with Lane's 1947 review of Tarshis's *The Elements of Economics* in Merwin K. Hart's *Economic Council Reviews*. A large political campaign followed to purge Tarshis's book from college campuses. The 1950 review by Watts of Samuelson's *Economics* and other economics textbooks in *Economic Council Reviews* seems to have had no negative impact on those texts's sales. Indeed, the net effect of the reviews was to destroy the viable alternative to Samuelson's text and so influence the history of modern economics. Historians as well as the participants have long been puzzled by this outcome (Colander & Landreth, 1995,

1998; Elzinga, 1992; Samuelson, 1997). Tarshis's and Samuelson's ideologies are very similar, so why would one text's market be destroyed and another pass through unharmed? One clue to their fate is that Tarshis's text embraces democratic reformism, something largely absent from Samuelson's, and made him more vulnerable to a political attack (Levy & Peart, 2011).

Locating the attack on Tarshis is complicated by the fact that Hart and Lane's views are so different.[1] A contemporary antifascist writer of some note who wrote under the name "John Roy Carlson" thought it perfectly obvious that Hart was a pro-fascist anti-Semite (Carlson [Derounian], 1946), a judgment that we find in Samuelson (1997). While the "fascism" might be debated, the anti-Semitism really can't be.[2] The two who knew Hart rather well and shared his anti-collectivism denounced his anti-Semitism. Isaac Don Levine's (1950) attack was flamboyant, public and reportedly costly,[3] while Robert LeFevre's (1999, p. 220) was cautiously posthumous. On the other hand, Lane's views puzzled "Carlson" because they seemed to be from an older world. Nonetheless, his description of her anarcho-capitalist position comes through unfiltered, and the observation that if you wrote her a letter, you'd get a long response:

> [H]er lengthy letters made little sense. Her extreme individualism and extreme *laissez-faire* attitudes have seemingly alienated her from events in the world. ... She describes her philosophy as the 'restrained anarchy of capitalism.' ... She's even got it in for the Danbury Conn., Public Service Commission, which regulates the number of taxicabs ... (Carlson [Derounian], 1946, p. 282).

So what does a "fascist" anti-Semite have in common with an anarcho-capitalist? The answer comes in the texts below: an aversion to democratic action. It is not clear whether Hart coined the slogan that America was "a republic not a democracy," but we find him using it in the 1940s long before it became a staple of the John Birch Society worldview. Hart's influence in the John Birch Society was considerable.[4]

The first needful thing is to take Lane's review seriously. This is very hard to do since she wasn't a professional economist and she was a very popular writer (Samuelson, 1997). As far as we know, none of the economists she attacked made her defend her interpretation in public. From all of this it is all-too-easy to impute incompetence. However, her interpretation of Tarshis was sharply challenged in the correspondence kicked off in the anti-Tarshis campaign. In response to a challenge from the provost of Cornell University, she claims that her review of Tarshis's book received a remarkable endorsement. This paragraph is extracted from the letter we reproduce below:

> In so far as Provost Adams's letter is derogatory to me and to my review of this book, while I would not want to print this without Professor Schumpeter's express permission I think I may say that he read the review and expressed even enthusiastic concurrence with it as an

accurate appraisal from a non-technical point of view. He said that he himself would not use
its phraseology but he thought it even remarkably accurate as a fair and unbiased judgment of
the book by one who is not a trained economist. Professor Joseph Schumpeter of Harvard has
perhaps the highest standing among economists in this country and Europe.

Although the letter from Joseph Schumpeter to which she refers has not been
published and may not have survived, we find little reason to doubt that it was
real. (Arthur Diamond cautions that Lane may have overinterpreted Schumpeter's
customary graciousness.) As "Carlson" testifies, she wrote *long* letters and when
we read them it is clear that she discusses other correspondence in them. For
instance, her letters to Jasper Crane includes a discussion of her correspondence
with von Mises in a totally candid manner (Lane & Crane, 1973). Had not the
Lane–von Mises correspondence survived, we could recover their positions if not
the reasons for these positions from the Lane–Crane correspondence.

The Plotters should be required reading before attempting the Tarshis controversy because it helps identify the participants. The most extensive response
to Hart, who passed the letter on to Lane, comes when Frank Gannett wrote the
provost of Cornell University. It is perfectly clear why a letter from Gannett who
owned a chain of newspapers in upstate New York would be taken seriously in
Ithaca (Carlson [Derounian], 1946, p. 297).[5] It is also the case that some of the
people to whom the letters were addressed knew all about Hart and Lane from
reading *The Plotters*.[6]

INDIVIDUALISTS AND VON MISES

Tarshis's democratic reformism was shared by Ludwig von Mises whose first
American book, *Omnipotent Government* (von Mises, 1944), was instrumental
in beginning his correspondence with Lane. The fact that von Mises and Tarshis
would urge their fellow citizens to act in different manners is what allows us to
separate the policies they endorsed from the process they endorsed to implement
these policies. Mises's commitment to democracy and public opinion is two-
fold. First, his liberalism is enormously close to John Stuart Mill's, which helps
explain why Mill was the only "socialist" he took seriously (Levy & Peart, 2008;
Peart, 2009). The letter of October 15, 1949 is remarkably clear in laying out the
importance of public opinion in von Mises's view. Second, von Mises held that
since economic science was value-free, he could not make unconditional recommendations for policy on the basis of his role as economic scientist from outside
society. Recommendations could only be made in his role as citizen and voter
inside society. There is nothing in von Mises's system that allows him, qua economic scientist, even to propose Paretian improvements let alone Kaldor–Hicks

improvements. He must speak qua citizen in a democracy. Whether this is hopelessly old-fashioned, or the way forward after the "failure" of new welfare economics, depends upon one's point of view. There is a reason why Henry Simons begins his widely noted review of *Omnipotent Government* this way:

> Professor Mises, patriarch of the modern Austrian school, is the greatest living teacher of economics – if one may judge by the contributions of his many distinguished students and protégés. (Simons, 1944, p. 192)

Lionel Robbins was, of course, one of the great economists to whom Simons referred and Robbins was never convinced that new welfare economics of either the Kaldor–Hicks or the Paretian variety solved the problem of mixing fact and value.[7]

Action as citizen in a democracy drew Lane's fire at von Mises both in her review of *Omnipotent Government* and their subsequent correspondence (Doherty, 2007; Hülsmann, 2007, p. 860). However, by reading Lane's reviews of both von Mises and Tarshis, along with Lane's correspondence, we can see that action as citizen in a democracy is a central issue for Lane in her quarrel with the two schools of economic liberals regardless of their specific policy proposals.

When Lane accused Tarshis of paganism, as we read below, those who knew her *Discovery of Freedom* (Lane, 1993 [1943]) would recognize that she is using a term for those who believe in direction by authority. She doesn't use the word "pagan" to describe von Mises's views but she does question his sincerity in his anti-socialism! He does, after all, believe in democratic government. Watts's view that von Mises's democratic views put him in violation of his oath of allegiance to the Constitution should not be disregarded as an outlying eccentricity. Indeed, the belief that socialism grows out of democracy is something that has a very hardy life. Lane's "Stalin" remark in her final letter to von Mises reminds us that the past is another country, suggesting we should purchase a dictionary before we visit it.

INDIVIDUALISTS VERSUS NEOLIBERALS

American individualists were important if for no other reason than they had links to resources, and the MPS, now taken to be the center of neoliberalism, required resources to function (Mirowski, 2009). Hart's Economic Council had an office in the Empire State Building, a point noted with derision in some correspondence in the anti-Tarshis campaign. This campaign served as a fund-raising opportunity judging from the donations that it generated. Well before the MPS began, it was resources such as these that allowed the economic publicists at the Los Angeles Chamber of Commerce to develop FEE.[8] Leonard Read is the name which the official history remembers. Read was not an economist, but Watts was. Behind Watts there is another economist, of far greater importance.

Very little is known about this period of the individualist movement. Perhaps the greatest puzzle is the role of the last of the great 20th century free-market social Darwinists in economics, T. N. Carver. Carver, although largely unknown today, was a figure of considerable stature as one might expect from his position of chair at several departments at Harvard, president of the American Economic Association, and confidant of President Hoover.[9] Six years before Watts reviewed Samuelson's text, Samuelson himself had described Watts's book that he was reviewing as the voice of Carver (Samuelson, 1944). Then Samuelson could presume Carver's views were known. A quick search in Google books – vice "fool killer" table – will turn up a chart that can function as a sufficient statistic of Carver's view of the worth of ordinary people.[10]

We have no reason to believe that Watts shared this aspect of Carver's views. Nonetheless, as late as April 1945 in a Los Angeles Chamber of Commerce publication, Carver was writing kind hypotheticals about Hitler's population control methods. Carver's earlier views were completely unconditional (Levy & Peart, 2009). Because we have never seen a reference to the Carver pamphlet, we include a few pages of Carver's attack on the free movement of people. It is perhaps worthy of our remark that we obtained our copy from the library of the late Percy Greaves, who was long associated with FEE. The cover has his embossed ownership mark clearly visible.[11]

If one passes over the social Darwinist episode in American individualism and economics in an embarrassed silence, as historians of economics have done until relatively recently, then one misunderstands what Hayek did by building the MPS out of the greatest opponents of social Darwinism in the economics profession, Knight and von Mises (Levy & Peart, 2009). When Watts writes as staff economist to von Mises to express his unhappiness about von Mises's democratic views, he juxtaposes these views to Friedman and Stigler's defense of income equality. The correspondence of Watts with Friedman and Stigler over their FEE pamphlet *Roofs or Ceilings?* has been published (Hammond & Hammond, 2006). The FEE discussion over von Mises's democratic views is noted by Hülsmann (2007, pp. 857–859) but without the context provided by the FEE unhappiness with the Friedman and Stigler's Knightian views.

When Watts reviewed Samuelson's *Economics* for Hart's *Review*, he was no longer at FEE. He had been replaced by Harper, who wrote in defense of von Mises's views. Although much is unclear about the collision between European liberalism and the individualism in America before the arrival of Hayek and the rise of the Chicago School, what is visible provides a background to the debates over democracy in the MPS that have been the subject of much recent attention

(Mirowski, 2009). Perhaps, if the correspondence of Schumpeter and Lane were located, we would be able to see more deeply into the antidemocratic positions of the time.

Hayek, most modestly, claimed that Knight and von Mises were the two central intellectual figures of the MPS. In the context of the time, both Knight and von Mises stood out among the opponents of collectivism as flamboyant liberals of a very classical sort. They were both strong advocates of democracy and opponents of social Darwinism. Don Patinkin (1973) has written how radical Frank Knight appeared to his students. Even so, by the time Patinkin studied at Chicago (1941–1947), advocacy of social Darwinism and eugenics in free market circles was vanishing and with this so passed the memory of Knight's argument with Carver and the gospel of efficiency and survival (Levy & Peart, 2009).

The phrase that appears in the Hart's *Economic Council Letter* that Lane sent von Mises, "America is a Republic not a Democracy," still has traction today in some political circles. Her disapproval of von Mises's democratic views is noted in Lane's correspondence with Crane (Lane & Crane, 1973), but her correspondence with von Mises lays out just how much is at stake for their worldviews. Lane's appeal to the views of W. Röpke in her final letter to von Mises reminds us that the MPS had many members with remarkably heterogeneous views on democracy, and some of these views changed over time. Hayek's views, for example, are extremely complicated. He worked for decades to develop an *explanation* of the basis of tyranny of the minority, the traditional democratic problem of factions, and late in his life proposed to cure it with the oldest of all known majoritarian institutions, election by lot (Peart & Levy, 2011).

ROBERT LEFEVRE'S INTERPRETATION

In his posthumously published autobiography, an associate of both Watts and Lane who had worked for Merwin Hart, Robert LeFevre, describes his experience listening to Watts's economics and reading Lane's *Discovery of Freedom* in dramatic religious terms. His insight may help us understand the conflict between individualists and utilitarian liberals, regardless of whether the liberalism is a classical version articulated by von Mises or a modern one espoused by Tarshis.

First, we quote the discussion of both Watts and Lane reported in Carl Watner's biography of LeFevre. The biography is a condensation and augmentation of the then unpublished autobiographical manuscript, a version we are told that LeFevre approved before his passing (Watner, 1988, p. 236):

> It was the first time Bob had actually studied free market economics, and he was amazed how Watts stated the realities of human action in language that everyone could understand.

The principles Watts set forth were essentially the same principles taught by the "I Am [*sic*]," only in lay terms. Watts also explained that the basic free market principles he was teaching were only taught at a few places in the country. Read's Foundation for Economic Education was probably the foremost organization in the world with respect to free market education. Such teachings were not to be found on any American university campus.

…

Bob was fascinated with books like Rose Wilder Lane's *The Discovery of Freedom* and other materials he obtained through the Foundation for Economic Education. Mrs. Lane's book simply got under his skin. One of her main themes was that human energy is under the control of the individual human being. It was as though she reinforced Daddy Ballard's preaching that each person is in control of himself. The mainspring of human progress, she said, was the removal of political restrictions from the individual. It was only when human energy was uninhibited by outside political forces that human progress went forward. (Watner, 1988, pp. 136, 137)

The value of Watner's contribution, who was able to talk with LeFevre as he was working on the manuscript, is evident if we compare this account with the less informative but much longer version in the unedited autobiography. The basic story is there along with much gossip but not LeFevre's judgment of the identity of Lane's views and of "Daddy" Ballard's (LeFevre, 1999, Vol. 2, pp. 166–167).

LeFevre's long, colorful involvement with the Ballards and the "I AM" movement is detailed in both versions of his autobiography. As *United States v. Ballard*, 322 U.S. 78 (1944), marks the border the Supreme Court has set between free expression of religion and criminal fraud, rarely have scholarly accounts taken the "I AM" movement or the Ballards seriously as religion or teachers. However, Catherine Albanese's recent documentation of the length and breadth of what she calls the American metaphysical religion offers a context for "I AM" as something other than simple fraud. This is important; even if the Ballards were fraudsters, we still need to explain why their doctrine attracted believers among sincere people. The Ballards, in Albanese's account, offer a variation on a well-known theme in which the believer finds God and the ability to bend matter and time (Albanese, 2007, pp. 467–470). It is perhaps sufficient to note that the Ballards's "ascendant master" was an 18th century alchemist of some notoriety.

In this context, we should read what Watts, late in his life, wrote in a preface to an edited collection of free market economic essays. For what purpose, he asks, was the volume put together?

The student should keep always in mind, however, that the primary purpose and use of these studies is personal, not political. The aim is not to change votes or governments, but to release the individual's will and ambition from the shackles of unfounded fears and false hopes. (Watts, 1967, p. iv).

The utilitarianism to which von Mises adheres (von Mises, 1949) is an old version in which the "greatest happiness of the greatest number" was interpreted in terms of the well-being of the majority. Moreover, the utilitarians of the classical period, Jeremy Bentham, James Mill, as well as John Mill himself, were completely clear that the greatest happiness principle was equivalent to the Golden Rule of Christianity (Peart & Levy, 2005). Neither von Mises nor his utilitarian masters nor their Christian partners offered the greatest happiness principle as energizing enlightenment to the believers. A utilitarian Christian might well have a more expansive concern for distant people; indeed, the traditional criticism of the coalition of the "dismal science" and Exeter Hall (Peart & Levy, 2005) is precisely that they do, but that's as far as it goes.

Watts and Lane on the other hand are offering a doctrine in which concern for other people is satisfied by teaching them this energizing enlightenment. Once they believe they can free themselves, this freedom brings sufficient energy to create public order without political activity. Indeed, political activity is a barrier to this energizing enlightenment. At the end of his career, Watts may be reaching back to Carver's teaching that the "best" religion is one which energizes the most (Carver, 1912). Watts got into trouble at the beginning of his career when, as a teaching assistant at Harvard, he was chastised by his superiors for assigning what they thought was Carver's mix of economics and religion (Watts, 1954).

If LeFevre is right in placing Watts and Lane in the same belief system as the "I AM" movement, and Albanese is right about the "I AM" movement as something in the wider gnostic worldview, then we have insight into the quarrel between liberals and individualists. Max Weber explained the conflict between Christianity and Gnosticism long ago. Here is Frank Knight's translation of the critical passage:

> In contrast with the ascetic religion of salvation of India and its defective action upon the masses are Judaism and Christianity, which from the beginning have been plebeian religions and have deliberately remained such. The struggle of the ancient church against the Gnostics was nothing else than a struggle against the aristocracy of the intellectuals. (Weber, 1927 [1923], p. 363)

This is an episode in the long argument between intellectual experts and ordinary people. The shared modesty of von Mises and Tarshis tells us how liberalism constrains real experts in their role as public intellectuals.

THE COALITIONS OF THE 1960s

Successful political movements are built from coalitions. Consequently, collapsing debates to one dimension, albeit useful for polemical purposes, hides coalition. Coalition is unnecessary if a political movement can be restricted to the like-minded. From the existence of a coalition we can impute, on noncontroversial rational choice grounds, the result that the desired reform could not have been affected without trades. If you can have something for nothing, why would you pay for it? Coalitions exist when the dimensions of agreement are regarded by the participants themselves as more important than the dimensions of disagreement. Democratic movements in Britain began with the antislavery movement, at foundation a coalition between Christian evangelicals and utilitarian political economists, "Exeter Hall" and the "dismal science" as Thomas Carlyle taught us (Peart & Levy, 2005).

In the 1960s we can discern the makings of two coalitions out of the debates of the earlier decades. A potential coalition, one that only scholars have noticed, could have been formed around those who believe that procedure is prior to policy. What unites James Buchanan and John Rawls is their shared liberal commitment that procedure is prior to policy, a visualization of politics as exchange, not pillage (Peart & Levy, 2008).

One effective coalition was built around the participants in the debates in the 1940s. Perhaps most retrospectively successful of such ventures was the short-lived educational institution founded by LeFevre in the Rampart Range of the Rocky Mountains of Colorado, the Freedom School and Rampart College. It was this venture that brought LeFevre into working contact with both Lane and Watts. The world might laugh at this venture in large part because of the foibles, failings, pretensions, and the poverty of the proprietors. A log building at the school was called "Rose Wilder Lane Hall" to remember the time she personally made the mortgage payment to keep the school functioning for another month.[12]

What hasn't been seen is the intellectual power of the coalition set in motion. Here from an earnest school booklet of 1964 that informs the potential students of the pickup time and place of the school station wagon is a two-page announcement of how the status quo will be challenged. Those who are inclined to smile at the pretension found on the first page – an unfamiliar Greek coinage, "phrontistery," was given to the new project of this unaccredited establishment in the Colorado mountains – might wait until it is revealed who it was who proposed to accomplish this challenge to the status quo.[13]

If one knows neither the seriousness of the debate between Lane and Watts with von Mises nor the mutual unhappiness between Watts and Friedman, one would not appreciate what is so remarkable about this gathering. It was through this ferment, we learn from Ronald Hamowy's definitive *Encyclopedia of Libertarianism*, that Charles Koch passed on his way to help remake the world of American politics (Doherty, 2008). What one does not learn from the *Encyclopedia* is that this faculty was recruited by a young student of Hayek from the Committee on Social Thought (Watner, 1988, p. 208). Nearly 50 years later that student, Hamowy himself, would publish the definitive edition of Hayek's *Constitution of Liberty*

A Freedom School Project

The Phrontistery is a major step in an expanding educational venture.

What is a Phrontistery (PHRON' TISTERY)? The Greeks used the word to indicate A PLACE FOR THINKING. It was occasionally used disparagingly by those bystanders who feared a challenge to the intellectual status quo.

The intensive two-week summer courses at the Freedom School of necessity provide a condensed period of study touching lightly on various aspects of the humanities. The six-month Phrontistery now underway will provide exploration in depth in such fields as economics, political theory, history, philosophy and biochemistry as they relate to human liberty.

At this place for thinking, eleven distinguished professors will serve as visiting lecturers. From November 1, 1963, to May 1, 1964, nineteen selected students (from eight states and two foreign countries) will concentrate their efforts to correlate and develop new material for textbooks and a curriculum for a proposed liberal arts college. The roster of distinguished professors is available upon request.

The Phrontistery.

Dean of the Phrontistery
V. Orval Watts, Ph.D.
Northwood Institute
Midland, Michigan

Assistant Dean
Robert J. Smith
Completing graduate thesis
under Dr. Ludwig von Mises

Oscar W. Cooley, M.S.
Ohio Northern University
Ada, Ohio

Arthur A. Ekirch, Jr., Ph.D.
The American University
Washington, D.C.

Milton Friedman, Ph.D.
University of Chicago
Chicago, Illinois

F. A. Harper, Ph.D.
Institute for Humane Studies
Stanford, California

Bruno Leoni, Ph.D.
University of Pavia
Turin, Italy

James J. Martin, Ph.D.
Deep Springs College
Deep Springs, California

Ludwig von Mises, Ph.D.
New York University
New York, New York

G. Warren Nutter, Ph.D.
University of Virginia
Charlottesville, Virginia

Sylvester Petro, Ll.M.
New York University
New York, New York

Gordon Tullock, J.D.
University of Virginia
Charlottesville, Virginia

Roger Williams, Ph.D.
University of Texas
Austin, Texas

Phrontistery Professors.

(Hayek, 2011 [1960]) with thousands of his master's scholarly gaps patched. One can change the world best if one does not care much who gets the credit.

TECHNICAL NOTES

The Lane–von Mises correspondence is found in the Grove City College Archive. All of Lane's letters held there are typed and dated. There is also one handwritten note penned to a May 1, 1947 issue of the *Economic Council Letter*, which puts forward the National Economic Council's position that America is a republic not a democracy. They are what von Mises received. All of von Mises's letters in their holding are file copies that respond to her letters. None of them are signed. Two of his are typed and two are handwritten. (His handwriting is very easy to read. His autographs from the late 1960s in our possession are marvels of penmanship.) We include two letters from Lane's employer at the National Economic Council (Merwin Hart) to von Mises as well as three reviews that Lane published in the *Economic Council Review of Books*. There is another letter in the Grove City College Archive that seems out of place so we have not printed it. In it the author, whose name we cannot read, tells von Mises that he (?) heard from "Fritz Hayek" that von Mises was in New York.

Watts's letter to von Mises, F. A. Harper's response to Watts's unlocated manuscript, and Read's letter to Lane are found in the Grove City College Archive FEE collection. We thank Grove City College for permission to reprint the correspondence for which they own the copyright.

The correspondence concerning the Tarshis texts is found in the University of Oregon Division of Special Collections and University Archives in the Merwin K. Hart Collection.

A collection of the *Economic Reviews* that published Lane's review of Mises's and Tarshis's books as well as Watts's review of the new generation of textbooks is found in Lane's collection in the Herbert Hoover Presidential Library. The correspondence with regard to Lane's *Economic Reviews* is not in their holdings. Whether it can be recovered at this date is a matter of Knightian uncertainty. The one hope is that she will tell her correspondents what others have written to her.

The Carver pamphlet and the Freedom School Bulletin are in our possession.

ACKNOWLEDGMENTS

We are grateful to the Grove City College Archive for the correspondence relating to Ludwig von Mises and to the University of Oregon's Division of Special

Collections and University Archives for correspondence relating to the Tarshis controversy. We thank them both for granting us permission to reprint. We are grateful to Cornell University's Provost for permission to reprint Provost Adam's letter. Permission to include excerpts from the writings of Rose Wilder Lane has been granted by the copyright owner, Little House Heritage Trust. The Herbert Hoover Presidential Library provided copies of the *Economic Council Reviews.* We thank Arthur Diamond for help with Joseph A. Schumpeter's correspondence. Conversations with David Colander have led to a rethinking of the paper. Ronald Hamowy may forgive us if we spoil his joke. Jane Perry and David Ortiz-Escobar helped with the proofreading. We would like to thank the Pierre F. and Enid Goodrich Foundation and the Earhart Foundation for support for the research. An afternoon's conversation with Richard Ware helped us understand some critical connections. We are responsible for any errors that follow.

NOTES

1. One can simplify by shining a light on Hart while keeping Lane in the shadows, e.g., Schlesinger (1949, p. 206): "A man named Merwin K. Hart wrote to every member of the boards of trustees of colleges using *Elements of Economics,* an economic text written by Professor Lorie Tarshis of Stanford University. An enclosed review denounced the book for its exposition of the doctrines of Lord Keynes and identified Keynesianism as a form of Marxism. Hart's letter had an immediate effect. Organizations of small businessmen passed resolutions in his support. Trustees and alumni wrote outraged letters to college presidents. Yet who was Merwin K. Hart? His record had long been known to students of the American proto-fascist demimonde. ... in a speech before Harvard's Free Enterprise Society, he inveighed against the Marshall Plan and 'the international Jewish group which controls our foreign policy.'"

2. The specialists at the FBI reported the fascism as an allegation not as a fact: "The earliest reference to Lindbergh's political activities in FBI files is in fact related to Merwin Hart, whom the Bureau described as 'the alleged promoter of an American Fascist movement'." (Wallace, 2003, p. 252)

3. Murray Rothbard (2007 [1991], p. 150) claimed that fear of angering the financial backers of Hart kept Don Levine from appearing on the editorial board of the first version of the *Freeman.*

4. Moser (2005, pp. 164, 165) offers reason to believe that Hart's influence has been underestimated. Moser does not study the textbook controversy.

5. A letter from Lane to Herbert Hoover (March 5, 1948) brings him up to date on the campaign and tells him that the "fight still rages" and Cornell has experienced a drop in donations. (Herbert Hoover Presidential Library)

6. Hart's characteristic response to those who cited *The Plotters* was to refer to passages in John T. Flynn's *The Smear Terror* to discredit "Carlson" (Flynn, 1947, pp. 17–26). The careful reader of *The Plotters* would know of the close working relationship between Hart and Flynn. *The Smear Terror* appeared initially in the *Chicago Tribune,* printed in pamphlet form with John T. Flynn as publisher and distributed by Hart's Economic Council. (Moser, 2005, p. 172)

7. Robbins's role in preparing the ground for von Mises's migration to America can be better appreciated now that the Henry Hazlitt archive is now online. Hazlitt, who wrote a stream of articles

and reviews that featured von Mises's ideas, seemed to have learned of von Mises's importance in the revival of European liberalism through correspondence with Lionel Robbins in 1934. Robbins's letter of November 30, 1934 may be the critical moment. Robbins's remark that von Mises's book is the best thing in social sciences for the last 25 years points to Robbins's great edition of Wicksteed's 1910 *Common Sense of Political Economy*. Retrieved from http://www.hazlitt.ufm.edu/index.php?title=DOC18151_3. pdf&gsearch=lionel%20robbins. Accessed on April 10, 2012.

8. Here are some amounts, as reported by Walter Winchell, which went to Hart's National Economic Council (*Washington Post*, June 13, 1950, p. B11): "Top Contributors to Hart's Council: William Volker Charities Fund, H. W. Luhnow, President (1947–1949, $15,250); James H. Rand, President Remington Rand (1947, $500); S. H. Kress & Co., C. M. Punk, Treasurer (1948–1949, $1000); J. I. Case Co., F. A. Wirt, Advertising Manager (1949, $1000); Lone Star Cement, R. A. Hummel, President (1947–1949, $5750); Pure Oil Company, H. M. Dawes, Chairman (1948, $1000); Sears Roebuck & Co., Robt. E. Wood (1943–1949, $16,000); Brewing Corporation of America, J. H. Bohanon, President (1945, $3000); General Motors, Donaldson Brown, Vice Chairman (1945, $5000); National Steel Corporation, F. M. Stesse, Vice President (1945, $5000); Eastern Air Lines (1945, $5500); Republic Steel Corporation, T. F. Patton, Vice President (1945, $10,000); John J. Raskob (1937–1949, $4500); Texas Company, Jas. Pipkin, President (1949, $2700); Empire State, Inc. (1949, $500); Carter Carburetor Company (1949, $1000); Lammot du Pont (1945–1947, $16,000); Irenee du Pont (1945–1947, $7912.94)."

The du Pont contribution was challenged by the IRS, so the court case allows Winchell's numbers to be checked in one instance: "Lammot du Pont was denied a refund of approximately $17,000 in Federal income taxes in an order today by Federal Judge Richard S. Rodney. The collections figuring in two combined suits were made in 1945 and 1946. Du Pont asserted contributions made to the National Economic Council, headed by Merwin Hart, were for business purposes and should have been allowed by the Collector of Internal Revenue as business-expense deduction. Judge Rodney ruled the funds were contributions or gifts." (*New York Times*, May 4, 1951, p. 27)

These numbers suggest how Hart, single-handedly with a $25,000 contribution, would be able to pay for the 1945 Congressional staff work to analyze the 84 volumes of testimony on events leading up to the attack on Pearl Harbor. As Moser (2005, p. 169) tells the story, the House majority dumped the documents supposing that a resource-constrained minority staff would not be able to handle the work load.

9. The Henry Hazlitt archive provides a window on this period. Hazlitt never abandoned his admiration for Carver. One finds Hazlitt expressing debt to Carver and the note to the publisher about the background of his 1951 novel. Retrieved from http://www.hazlitt.ufm.edu/index. php?title=DOC8571_39.pdf&gsearch=carver. Accessed on April 10, 2012.

Hazlitt complains in his September 30, 1963 column "Books for America" that the economics book list put out by the White House Library has nothing by Carver. Hazlitt's unhappiness with the inclusion of Frank Knight's *Ethics of Competition* and not *Risk, Uncertainty and Profit* is both odd (the "miscellaneous" essays were selected by unnamed "former students" [Milton Friedman, George Stigler, and Alan Wallis!] and informative given Knight's hostility to the larger enterprise of efficiency ethics inside which Carver's enterprise is embedded. Retrieved from http://www.hazlitt.ufm. edu/index.php?title=DOC3158_12.pdf&gsearch=carver. Accessed on April 10, 2012.

10. Hart and Carver overlapped at Harvard. Was there a connection? Hart's emphasis on the importance of "human energy" reads much like Carver (Levy & Peart, 2009). "As the world has long noted, sometimes not without envy, the liberty our Fathers won released in America the greatest aggregate amount of human energy that history has ever known. It is not alone that men became physically free. Their spirit became free. Their minds, their hopes, their ambitions, their vision were unchained" Hart (1944, p. 687). Was Carver's influence still at Harvard when Samuelson moved from

Chicago? We sent a paper to Samuelson in mid-2009. We received a brief response telling us that he did not have enough life left to read our paper. We marvel at the courtesy that obligated him to give up some life to write to tell us this.

11. World Cat finds only two copies in public holdings. One is at UCLA and the other at the New York Public Library.

12. The 1965 Freedom School brochure is in the Henry Hazlitt archive. A picture of "Rose Wilder Lane Hall" can be found at http://www.hazlitt.ufm.edu/index.php?title=DOC1620_9.pdf&gsearch=ro se%20wilder%20lane%20hall. Accessed on April 10, 2012.

13. Evidently, the coinage was considered eccentric even by the relaxed Freedom School criterion as it does not appear in the 1965 brochure. The only occasion on which "phrontistery" occurs in the Henry Hazlitt archive is a 1964 lecture by Gordon Tullock.

REFERENCES

Archival material

Grove City College Archives.
Herbert Hoover Presidential Library.
Henry Hazlitt Archives. Retrieved from http://www.hazlitt.ufm.edu/index.php/Main_Page. Accessed on April 10, 2012.
University of Oregon Division of Special Collections and University Archives, Merwin K. Hart Collection.

Printed material

Albanese, C. L. (2007). *A republic of mind and spirit: A cultural history of American metaphysical religion*. New Haven, CT: Yale University Press.
Carlson, J. R. [A. Derounian]. (1946). *The plotters*. New York, NY: Dutton.
Carver, T. N. (1912). *The religion worth having*. Boston, MA: Houghton Mifflin.
Colander, D. C., & Landreth, H. (Eds.). (1995). *The coming of Keynesianism to America: Conversations with the founders of Keynesian economics*. Cheltenham, UK: Edward Elgar.
Colander, D. C., & Landreth, H. (1998). God, man, and Lorie Tarshis at Yale. In O. Hamuda & B. B. Price (Eds.), *Keynesianism and the Keynesian revolution in America* (pp. 59–72). Cheltenham, UK: Edward Elgar.
Doherty, B. (2007). *Radicals for capitalism: A freewheeling history of the modern American libertarian movement*. New York, NY: Public Affairs.
Doherty, B. (2008). LeFevre, Robert (1911–1986). In R. Hamowy (Ed.), *Encyclopedia of libertarianism* (pp. 287–288). Thousand Oaks, CA: Sage.
Elzinga, K. G. (1992). The eleven principles of economics. *Southern Economic Journal, 58*, 861–179.
Flynn, J. T. (1947). *Smear terror*. New York, NY: John T. Flynn.
Freedom School. (1964). *1964 bulletin*. Colorado Springs, CO: Freedom School.
Hammond, D. & Hammond, C. (2006). *Making Chicago price theory: Friedman–Stigler correspondence 1945–1957*. London, UK: Routledge.

Hart, M. K. (1944). Another truth that is self-evident: Liberty, the essential foundation of American life. *Vital Speeches of the Day, 10*, 687–690.

Hayek, F. A. (2011 [1960]). *The constitution of liberty*. R. Hamowy (Ed.), Chicago, IL: University of Chicago Press.

Hülsmann, J. G. (2007). *Mises: The last knight of liberalism*. Auburn, GA: Von Mises Institute.

Lane, R. W. (1993 [1943]). *The discovery of freedom: Man's struggle against authority*. San Francisco, CA: Fox & Wilkes.

Lane, R. W., & Crane, J. (1973). *The lady and the tycoon: The letters of Rose Wilder Lane and Jasper Crane*. Caldwell, ID: Caxton.

LeFevre, R. (1999). *A way to be free: The autobiography of Robert LeFevre*. Culver City, CA: Pulpless.

Levine, I. D. (1950). The strange case of Merwin K. Hart. *Plain Talk, 4*(February), 1–9.

Levy, D. M., & Peart, S. J. (2008). George J. Stigler. In L. Blume & S. Durlauf (Eds.), *The new Palgrave's dictionary of economics* (2nd ed.). New York, NY: Palgrave. doi:10.1057/9780230226203.1570

Levy, D. M., & Peart, S. J. (2009). *F. A. Hayek and the leadership of the Mont Pèlerin Society: Transition to a new liberalism*. Prague, Czech Republic: International Leadership Association.

Levy, D. M., & Peart, S. J. (2011). Soviet growth and American textbooks: An endogenous past. *Journal of Economic Organization and Behavior, 78*, 110–125.

Mirowski, P. (2009). Postface. In P. Mirowksi & D. Plehwe (Eds.), *The road from Mont Pèlerin: The making of the neoliberal thought collective* (pp. 417–455). Cambridge, MA: Harvard University Press.

Moser, J. E. (2005). *Right turn: John T. Flynn and the transformation of American liberalism*. New York, NY: New York University Press.

Patinkin, D. (1973). Frank Knight as teacher. *American Economic Review, 63*, 787–810.

Peart, S. J. (2009). We are all "persons" now: Classical economists and their opponents on marriage, the franchise and socialism. *Journal of the History of Economic Thought, 31*, 3–20.

Peart, S. J., & Levy, D. M. (2005). *The "vanity of the philosopher": From equality to hierarchy in post-classical economics*. Ann Arbor, MI: University of Michigan.

Peart, S. J., & Levy, D. M. (2008). The Buchanan-Rawls correspondence. In S. J. Peart & D. M. Levy (Eds.), *The street porter and the philosopher* (pp. 397–416). Ann Arbor, MI: University of Michigan.

Peart, S. J., & Levy, D. M. (2011). F. A. Hayek's sympathetic agents. In A. Farrant (Ed.), *Hayek, Mill and the liberal tradition* (pp. 39–56). London, UK: Routledge.

Perelman, M. (2007). *The confiscation of American prosperity: From right-wing extremism and economic ideology to the next great depression*. New York, NY: Palgrave Macmillan.

Rothbard, M. (2007 [1991]). *The betrayal of the American right*. Auburn, GA: von Mises Institute.

Samuelson, P. A. (1944). Do we want free enterprise? [review of Orval Watts]. *The Annals of the American Academy of Political and Social Science, 236*, 198–199.

Samuelson, P. A. (1997). Credo of a lucky textbook author. *Journal of Economic Perspectives, 11*, 153–169.

Schlesinger, A. M. (1949). *The vital center: The politics of freedom*. Boston, MA: Houghton Mifflin.

Sennholz, M. (1993). *Leonard E. Read: Philosopher of freedom*. Irvington on Hudson: NY: Foundation for Economic Education.

Simons, H. C. (1934). *A positive program for laissez-faire*. Chicago, IL: University of Chicago Press.

Simons, H. C. (1944). Omnipotent government [review of Ludwig von Mises]. *The Annals of the American Academy of Political and Social Science, 236*, 192–193.

Steiner, Y. (2009). The neoliberals confront the trade unions. In P. Mirowksi & D. Plehwe (Eds.), *The road from Mont Pèlerin: The making of the neoliberal thought collective* (pp. 181–203). Cambridge, MA: Harvard University Press.

Von Mises, L. (1944). *Omnipotent government: The rise of the total state and of total war.* New Haven, CT: Yale University Press.

Von Mises, L. (1949). *Human action: A treatise on economics.* New Haven, CT: Yale University Press.

Wallace, M. (2003). *The American axis: Henry Ford, Charles Lindbergh and the rise of the Third Reich.* New York, NY: Macmillan.

Watner, C. (1988). *Robert LeFevre: "Truth is not a half-way place."* Gramling, SC: The Voluntaryists.

Watts, V. O. (1952). *Away from freedom: Revolt of the college economists.* Los Angeles, CA: Foundation for Social Research.

Watts, V. O. (1954). When a preacher wasn't wanted! *Christian Economics, 6*(January), p. 4.

Watts, V. O. (1967). Preface. In V. O. Watts (Ed.), *Free markets or famine* (pp. iii–vi). Midland, MI: Pendell Company.

Weber, M. (1927 [1923]). *General economic history.* F. H. Knight (Trans.). New York, NY: Adelphi.

TEXTS

We provide the texts as we have found them, in chronological order, with the briefest of annotations. We begin in 1944 with Lane's note to von Mises about her excitement that Yale was publishing his books. We end in 1950 with a note from Leonard Read scolding her for her final letter to von Mises. There is, we hasten to add, so much we don't see.

We reprint only a portion of Carver's pamphlet for the *Economic Sentinel.* We will provide scans of the whole pamphlet upon request for anyone who wishes to see the full original.

We reprint Watts's reviews of the textbooks in their original form even though they are available in Watts's 1952 *Away from Freedom* because the phrase that Samuelson remembered – "playing peek-a-boo with the ------" – is not found in the reprinted version. Samuelson on one occasion remembered Watts's remark as "playing peek-a-boo with the Commies" (Colander & Landreth, 1995, p. 172) suggesting that there was only a crude ideological issue, although on an earlier occasion he remembered the passage as "playing peek-a-boo with the reader" (Perelman, 2007, p. 25). At this date, we have no hope of finding out whether Watts was responsible for the little snippets in which the phrase appears or whether this was Lane's addition.

The material within square brackets is generally our addition. We have left the spelling and assertion of facts as we find them, rarely calling attention to problems with the editorial [*sic*]. On one occasion the printing errors enter the correspondence as when Lane calls von Mises's attention to the fact that in the review of *Human Action,* her attempt to use his "praxeology" was thwarted by the *Review's* production department, which (generally) replaced it with "praxiology." On occasion the error is so remarkable that it strains credulity that a professionally printed periodical would let it pass. The "Bible's Eleven Commandments" is one such. There are a few others that merit the note that we see this too and that really is what is written. Scans are available upon request.

[Lane and von Mises on *Omnipotent Government*]

R 4, Box 42
Danbury, Connecticut
June 29, 1944

My dear Dr. von Mises,

The Yale University Press has given me your address, so that I might write to thank you for giving Americans your true books.

You know, as well as I, the great value of such books, and how few they are. It is only to please myself that I try to express to you the gratitude of an American for your service to my country and, I am sure, eventually to the whole world's population.

Though your description of recent events and the present situation in Europe, and your analysis of their causes, seem to me accurate and penetrating (since they agree with my own observations and thought!) and I suppose that your view of conditions in this country isn't immediately cheering, still we know that truth must prevail because it is true. Meanwhile, your books are invaluable to the increasing number of Americans who are beginning actively to work on the sound basis of libertarian principles, and it is only a minimum courtesy to thank you for them.

Doubtless you are in touch with Sir Ernest Benn's Society of Individualists in London. I do not know how well informed you are of similiar [*sic*] movements in these States. You will not mind my sending you some of their various publications, from time to time, in the hope that some of them may be interesting news to you.

With every good wish
                    Yours sincerely,

                    Rose Wilder Lane / ASL

[Von Mises's Response to Lane's June 29, 1944 letter]

It gives me great satisfaction to see my book appreciated by an author of your rank and merit.

I do hope that our endeavors will not be futile and that people will one day find the way forward to the true principles of liberty. And I must confess, your letter has infused in me a dose of optimism in this regard.

I thank you very much for your intention to send me publications on the pro-individualist movements in this country. I will read them with great attention.

This September the Y[ale University Press] will publish a small book of mine on B[ureaucracy]. I hope it will interest you no less than O[mnipotent] G[overnment].

The Foundation for Economic Education, as is well known, grew out of the Los Angeles Chamber of Commerce. Very little has been written about the Los Angeles Chamber of Commerce in that era that can help us understand the debates. Perhaps the place to begin is Mary Sennholz's uncritical biography of Leonard Read. She links T. N. Carver and Orval Watts to Read:

> Leonard's favorite instructor whom he tried to engage again and again was Thomas Nixon Carver, Professor of Political Economy at Harvard for twenty-two years. But Professor Carver was in such great demand for summer sessions and seminars and his honorarium correspondingly high, that the Western School could rarely afford him. Professor Carver recommended his young disciple, Dr. V. Orval Watts ... [he] proved to be so popular with his students, so direct and dynamic in his lectures, that he became the Western School's favorite instructor. When Leonard became General Manager of the Los Angeles Chamber, Dr. Watts followed him as Economic Counsel and the first full-time economist employed by a chamber of commerce in the United States. They formed an outstanding team, instituting many free-market courses in Los Angeles and other cities in California. Read and Watts became close confederates in the cause of freedom, working together and comforting each other about the course of events. (Sennholz, 1993, p. 59)

Sennholz writes that Watts was on the senior staff at the Foundation for Economic Education. (p. 77)

According to Watts's entry in *Who's Who in America* (1956–1957), he was economic counsel for the Los Angeles Chamber of Commerce from 1939 to 1946 and "econ. Editor" for FEE from 1946 to 1949. This explains why his 1950 review of the new generation of economics textbooks does not carry a FEE address. So, did Leonard Read's "close confederate" last only three years at FEE?

Samuelson's 1944 review of Watts's *Do We Want Free Enterprise?* suggests why one would distance Watts from the larger liberal tradition:

> In his first chapter the writer sets forth an ant-colony philosophy of life in which atomistic competition replaces instinct as a motivating force, but in which the end of activity is not comfort and material well-being so much as "striving and achieving." The popularity of the much maligned New Era slogan, "A chicken in every pot, a car in every garage," is only one of many historical instances which suggest that intelligent conservatives will avoid resting their case on such a philosophy of life. (Samuelson, 1944, p. 199)

It is important to remember how deeply Samuelson had been influenced by the Knightians at Chicago. The liberalism that group was most dramatically articulated in Henry Simon's *Positive Program for Laissez Faire* (Simons, 1934). Had he lived, Simons would have been central to the MPS.

The next few pages, a simple reproduction from the Los Angeles Chamber of Commerce pamphlet, give reason why it is important to distance a Carver-influenced movement from the liberal tradition. Carver's attack on the laissez-faire tradition in terms of the movement of people is completely clear in his defense of planning of a country's demography. Immigration restriction is a central tenant of the eugenic movement (Peart & Levy, 2005).

Cover of the Carver Pamphlet.

CHAPTER IX [PAGES 44–52]

Wholesale immigration of wage workers or an abnormally high birth rate among them can make full employment impossible.

No matter how friendly our government may be toward industry and labor, and no matter how rapidly our industries may expand, they cannot be expected to solve the unemployment problem for the whole world. Other countries must solve their own problems of unemployment and not dump them on us. That is, they must not send their surplus workers to us. Our labor market could be glutted in spite of all that our industrialists could do if we were to let down the bars and admit all the immigrants that cared to come. The more our industries expand and the higher the wages, the more eager the workers of backward countries will be to come here. Much as we may sympathize with them, our first duty is to our own workers.

But should we not lend a helping hand to those backward countries? Certainly, but the best thing we can do for them is to show them how a country can solve its own problem of unemployment. So long as they can send their unemployed to us, they will have no adequate motive for reconstructing their economic systems. Our most humane policy toward them is, first, to serve notice on them that they must take care of their own unemployed, and, second, to show them by our own example that it can be done.

But we need not expect the backward and overpopulated countries to appreciate our example. They will resent the prosperity and the high standard of living which we exhibit. They will call us a dog in the manger. They will demand the privilege of sharing the wealth which we are producing and consuming. They will urge that "the earth is for all," and "we are all equally God's children." If we submit to their pleas or threats, we are lost. Under unrestricted immigration, America will become an Asiatic colony as it once became a European country.

If our immigrants were mainly scientists, inventors, investors, managers and enterprisers, they would not glut the labor market but would help to make more jobs for our workers. But when they are mainly manual workers they increase the number of job-seekers more than they increase the number of jobs. These are the immigrants who could defeat our best plans for full employment.

INTERNATIONAL TRADE IN MEN, COMMODITIES

The economic laws that govern international trade in men parallel those that govern international trade in commodities. Where international migration is unrestricted, each nation tends to export that of which it has, not an absolute, but a relative surplus, and to import that of which it has a relative lack. No nation has ever had an absolute surplus of men of high talent and training. But a nation where enterprise is free and education universal will always have a relative surplus of that valuable resource as compared with a nation where enterprise is restricted and education limited to a few. Consequently, men of training and talent will tend to move from the one country to the other.

Every country, including ours, has an absolute surplus of men of low talent and poor training, that is, of unskilled workers. But a country with poor schools and aristocratic restrictions will always have a greater surplus than a country with democratic liberty, free enterprise, and large expenditures for education. Consequently, where free migration is permitted, the stream of worker migration will flow toward the latter country.

Under our "quota system," the flow of immigration to this country is somewhat restricted. This restriction has done more for American labor, but not for labor racketeers, than any other piece of legislation during the last half century. Had it not been for this restrictive legislation, we would have been flooded with immigrant labor following World War I.

However, the quota system does not apply to the western hemisphere. In other words, there is no legislation to prevent a tide of immigration from flowing in from low-standard areas and classes of the western hemisphere. This flood has been held back since 1930 by an order, issued by President Hoover, instructing American consular officers to refuse visas to prospective immigrants who might displace native workers. Until this beneficent order is rescinded, it will help to protect the American worker against a dangerous form of competition.

LEAST PLANNING WHERE MOST NEEDED

But, immigration from Heaven has much the same effect on the labor market as that from other countries. The high birth rate among recently arrived immigrant workers, and those not so recently arrived, tends also to congest the labor market. Men of low mentality also tend to have large families and to keep up a large supply of unskilled labor. With low mentality goes a lack of prudence and of disposition to plan families. Here, where we need planning the most, is where we plan the least.

Every military adventurer, eager for a large supply of cannon fodder, has urged large families among the poor. There may have been politicians who, from no higher motives, preached the same doctrine. For similar reasons, foxes might urge larger families among rabbits. It is certainly the wrong way to solve the problem of unemployment.

Those high-minded but ignorant people who urge either free immigration or a high birth rate among the poor will be more to blame for any unemployment that may exist than are the industrialists or the government. After all, when you come to think of it realistically, what reason can one give why industry should be held responsible for employing all the workers brought into existence as the result of moral exhortations to have larger families?

Among those who are capable of exercising prudence in the planning of their families, a high standard of living is an effective safeguard against overpopulation. A high standard of living exists wherever no man will marry or undertake the support of a family until he is reasonably certain of being able to provide his family not only with necessaries, but some comforts and luxuries as well. To be specific, if no one will marry until he can afford an automobile, or feel sure of being able to, it is fairly certain that no children will be legitimately born except in families that can afford automobiles. The same proposition can be repeated with respect to any other article of luxury.

HOW LABOR MARKET CAN BE GLUTTED

But among men of low mentality, there is no effective standard of living because there is no prudential planning. Multiplication of numbers among them is a biological rather than a rational or a moral process. Unless controlled, their progeny, in time, can glut any labor market and defeat any attempt to create full employment.

However, a high birth rate among people of high mentality would have the opposite effect on the labor market. It would work like the immigration of such people from foreign countries. That is, it would balance our population, fill the ranks of job-makers rather than of job-seekers, and increase the demand for manual labor. Birth control means an increase of the birth rate among the highly capable as well as a lower birth rate among the least capable members of society. Such comprehensive planning would do much to solve the problem of providing full employment.

In all this welter of discussion of economic planning, scarcely a word has been uttered by any planner on the important subject of population planning. Yet the population problem is fundamental. Our own governments, Federal, State and local, interfere, it is true, but in the wrong way. They actually subsidize the breeding of unemployables by various systems of indiscriminate relief.

No one who studies the subject seriously will dispute the fact that, until Asiatics were excluded, we were in danger of being inundated by millions of oriental coolies. Those unhappy countries had and still have more people than they can take care of and were ready to dump their surplus populations on our shores. After they were excluded, and before the quota system of restriction was adopted, the sources of our immigration were shifting from northwestern Europe to southeastern Europe and western Asia. Areas with lower and lower standards of living were displacing areas of higher standards as sources of our population.

FACTS NO PLANNER CAN DISPUTE

When we restricted immigration from Europe, western Asia and Africa by the quota system, we left wide open the doors for low-standard immigrants from the western hemisphere and the Philippines. In addition, there is the tendency of our poorest people to have more children than they can support and educate. So long as people who lack intelligence continue to spawn others who lack intelligence, we shall have more of such people than we can possibly employ at good wages.

These are facts which no economic planner can dispute. We must foresee that when conditions improve so that there are more jobs to be had they will be filled to a large extent by immigrants from countries with low standards of living and large families. We must understand that no other form of economic planning can do much to eliminate poverty until we stop importing poverty, and that we can't employ all of our own people until we stop giving their jobs to the unemployed whom other countries send us. Why do not our economic planners begin their planning where it is most needed and where it will do the most good?

Several reasons suggest themselves. One is that our economic planners do not take time to think about population problems, or, if they think at all, they think that it is impossible to do anything about such things. Still another is that they think that population is a matter of Divine Providence rather than the emotions, the passions and the ignorance of men. A less commendable reason is the desire for an abundance of cheap cannon fodder, but this is probably confined to military adventurers and imperialists.

A still less commendable reason is the desire for an abundant supply of cheap labor which means mass poverty. This reason should be, but unhappily is not, limited to a narrow-minded type of employer who seems to think that men exist so that industry may expand rather than that industries should expand so that men may live more abundantly.

AIMS OF PLANNED POPULATION

The most contemptible reason of all is the desire to see unemployment and poverty increase until there is enough discontent to produce a revolution. This desire is probably confined to those temperamental rebels who can see nothing good in the present economic system, and who are, therefore, willing to see suffering increase under it until the masses are driven to desperation. Then our revolutionists will have their inning.

A scientific population policy is one which (a) maintains the optimum ratio between population and land (including all natural resources); (b) maintains the optimum ratio among all kinds of labor, or the optimum distribution of the working population among all occupations.

It would avoid the terrific overpopulation such as one sees in certain old countries of the Orient. It would also avoid the terrific occupational congestion which one sees in every country, including our own.

The man-land ratio, which Sumner and Keller, in their great work on "The Science of Society," treat as one of the fundamental social problems, has given the world more trouble than any other. Strong races have, in the past, maintained a favorable man-land ratio by taking more land when they needed it. They maintained a favorable ratio between population and land, not by planning their population but by planning their campaigns of conquest. Their planning was of the imperialistic sort for the acquisition of more land for their teeming populations. They at least had far-reaching plans for solving the fundamental problem of the man-land ratio. In this respect they were, on the intellectual, if not on the moral side, far ahead of any of our present-day economic "planners."

Democratic countries are inclined to repudiate that method of solving the population problem. Besides, the civilized countries seem to have reached a deadlock. They have become so jealous of one another as to make it impossible for any of them to extend its colonies. Until this deadlock is broken, the easy solution of the population problem by conquest and colonization is impossible. The alternative solution is to keep population within bounds. That requires population planning.

CONTINENT OF AFRICA LIES OPEN

If the various nations of the white race could break the deadlock by declaring a truce among themselves and permitting conquest and colonization, it would spell the doom of some of the weaker races. These races – weak in the sense of being backward in the technology of war – would go the way of the Tasmanians, the American Indians and other weak races. The whole continent of Africa and the Amazon Valley lie open – awaiting the development of the technology of cooling, as northern regions, a few centuries ago, awaited the development of the technology of heating.

But Africa is populated. The full power of that continent to absorb European colonists would require the extinction of the natives. It remains to be seen whether

Europe will be ruthless enough to avail herself of the full opportunity. She may prefer to preserve the natives as cheap laborers, and to use Africa as an outlet for surplus capital rather than as an outlet for surplus labor, keeping her own laboring populations in Europe to glut the labor market and supply cheap labor at home.

On the whole, the probability seems remote that the optimum man-land ratio can be much longer maintained, even by the superior fighting races, by the simple expedient of taking more land. The United States especially seems unfitted, both by geographical position and temperament, for a career of expansion by conquest and colonization. A change in population policy seems forced upon us by our own unwillingness to embark on a career of ruthlessness toward weaker people.

There are no habitable regions now unoccupied. In fact, there never were – within historic times. Even the American continent was inhabited about as densely as it could be by men who made their living by hunting and fishing. They had to be dispossessed of their hunting grounds in order that Europeans could have fields to plow and plant. According to the standard of tillers of the soil, the continent was, of course, sparsely populated; but not according to the standards of their predecessors who preferred to hunt and fish. The tillers of the soil, who wanted the hunting ground of the hunting tribes for plow land, had one unanswerable argument – they were able to take it. The same argument still exists for those who are unscrupulous enough to use it. The weaker races survive because of the moral scruples of the stronger races.

LABOR SUPPLY MAY BE DANGEROUS

The term "moral scruples" may be inaccurate. The landless and propertyless masses of Europe and America may find it easier to take land and property from their richer fellow citizens than to take land from the weak races in distant parts of the earth. This is a suggestion which property owners would do well to ponder. Their desire for an abundant supply of cheap labor may be their own undoing. This may come about in a "most exquisitely constitutional manner" by simply voting heavier and heavier taxes on property for the benefit of the propertyless. It may also come by violence if, as the result of a planless population, manual workers continue to multiply out of all proportion to the need for them. It is easy to show that the propertyless masses would merely be killing the goose that lays the golden eggs; but, even so, the property owners should consider whether they want to be the goose or not.

For a very few of the mechanically gifted nations, commerce may, for a time, take the place of colonization. England, for a century and a half, profited enormously by this method. She bought raw materials from newly opened and sparsely populated regions, worked those raw materials into finished products, sold the finished products to other countries, and lived on the profits of the transaction. That opportunity is being closed, first by the number of rivals that are trying to play the same game; second, by the narrowing of the areas of sparse population; and, third, by tariff barriers. From now on for Europe and America, it is a choice of war for colonial and commercial expansion, population planning, or mass poverty such as one sees in the Orient where neither of the first two policies has been followed.

RUSSIA'S STUPID POPULATION BOAST

Communism is no cure or preventive. Where family responsibility is removed, there is no prudential or automatic check on the rate of multiplication. Russia boasts, with fatuous stupidity, that her population can double every 30 years. If that could go on, she would have more than a billion people in 90 years. Of course, her population will not reach such limits – although it is physiologically possible – for the simple reason that she cannot support so many people from her own soil without reducing her standard of living. It is physiologically possible to breed at that rate, but it is economically impossible to support the resulting population. Long before that number is reached, her hungry hordes, reduced to a common level of poverty by her excess population and her communism, will want more land. They will see comparative plenty in capitalistic countries and will demand an opportunity to share in it. Europe will once more stand with her back to the Atlantic, fighting for her existence against the hungry hordes from the East.

With us, in the United States, the problem of maintaining a favorable man-land ratio is not acute, and is easily solved. With our present standard of living, coupled with our family system which tries to hold parents responsible for the support of their own children, our birth rate is not likely to be so high as to result in overpopulation by natural increase. So long as we were bringing in millions of immigrants with a low standard of living and a consequent high birth rate, we were not free from that danger. Such danger of this kind as remains arises from two sources. First, there is the fact that we may still bring in from western hemisphere countries considerable numbers of individuals who have low standards of living and high birth rates. These can still swell our numbers and lower our quality, besides perpetuating and aggravating our race problems. There is the further fact that people of low mentality cannot have a standard of living like that of people of high mentality and will therefore multiply according to their animal impulses and not according to any standard of family building.

POPULATION CONGESTION IS U.S. PERIL

However, our real danger is not that of overpopulation but of congestion. Population congestion is of two sorts, local and occupational. Local congestion can be relieved by the simple process of moving people from congested areas to sparsely populated areas. A sparsely populated area does not mean an area where the population per square mile is low, but where the ratio of the number of people to the number of opportunities to make a living is high. A desert region may be overpopulated even though there are fewer than one person per square mile.

The relief of local congestion is so easy as to cause us little perplexity. The difficult problem is that of occupational congestion. To relieve a congested occupation, now that conquest and colonization are out of fashion, requires statesmanship of a high order. In fact, it is, and must be, until the problem is solved, the chief problem of statesmanship. Moreover, it must be confessed with shame, few of our statesmen have ever shown any interest in this problem, and, what is worse, those who have attempted to grapple with it have not received much popular support. The popular political pastime seems to be to hurl maledictions at employers for not employing more men at higher wages, or at the economic system as a whole for not providing work for all whom blind biological forces can bring into existence.

The first and most obvious step is to reduce all immigration quotas to the lowest possible terms and to extend the quota system to the western hemisphere and the Philippines. That will leave us free to provide employment for the natural increase of our own population.

The next thing to do is to provide opportunity for and enforcement of parental responsibility. It is sensible and humane to avoid bringing into the world congenital defectives and to discourage them from inflicting the curse of a burdensome life upon future generations of their own kind. In one respect, Hitler was more rational than most contemporary government "planners." He agreed with them that government should guarantee jobs or a livelihood to everyone. However, he saw, as they did not, that in order to make good on this guarantee, government must take over the corresponding responsibility for parenthood and decide who might or might not be born. His policy of sterilizing defectives is a logical part of a governmental policy of social security and "planned" economy.

FAMILY PLANNING IS ESSENTIAL

The third thing to do is to extend the knowledge of birth control to the poorer classes that they may plan their families as the more well-to-do classes have always done. Family planning is an essential part of sound population policy. When family building, among all classes, displaces a mere biological urge as a source of population, the population problem, in both its quantitative and its qualitative aspects, will be solved. The optimum man-land ratio will be maintained and the congestion of the lower economic occupations will be relieved.

Birth control and family building mean larger families among the highly capable and successful as well as smaller families among the less capable and less prosperous. The differential birth rate is an important factor in the congestion of the manual trades and the routine occupations, and the deficit of creative workers, especially in the field of industry.

A fourth thing to do is to lend every possible encouragement to industrial enterprise. This must include a frank recognition of our indebtedness to the man who can make two jobs grow where one grew before.

A fifth thing to do is to enlarge and improve our system of popular education as rapidly as is psychologically possible. The school has been the chief agency for the relief of occupational congestion. It thins out the workers in the lower ranks and increases their numbers in the higher ranks of industry.

This should have relieved occupational congestion where it is greatest. It would have done so long ago if we had not undone the beneficent work of our schools by our efforts to create an oversupply of cheap labor – an industrial reserve army of unemployed. We have kept up this industrial reserve army by importing ignorance and brawn from countries with low standards of living, by encouraging large families among the poor, by breeding morons and other defectives.

Having been guilty of all these stupidities we now have the effrontery to pretend that we don't know why there are so many unemployed.

We reproduce the first part of the issue of the *Economic Council Review of Books* of November 1945 (Vol. II, No. 10), which contains Lane's review of *Omnipotent Government*.

Recurrently during the recorded human experience on this planet, people have produced a surplus of wealth, more than enough to keep themselves alive and sufficient to support an organized State and its rulers. Invariably these rulers have used their subjects in war, extending their rule over a larger number of persons. Historians call this process "the rise" of that State, and from ancient Ur, Chaldea, Assyria, Egypt, Rome, to modern Spain, France, Germany, this "rise" has been followed by a disaster called "the decline and fall" of that State.

In the past this so-called rising and falling has occurred in a time-period of centuries, therefore it had been beyond the reach of general observation. Only the scholars have seen it recorded on clay tablets, fallen monuments, ruins of cities and fragments of parchment. They have always studied the phenomenon with deepest interest and they are still trying to account for it.

On the assumption that the gods controlled men, they could attribute the rise and fall of States only to the favor, wrath, or caprice of the gods. Science, arising lately, abolished the gods. Modern scholars therefore assume that something else controls mankind, and during the past two centuries they have ascribed the rise and fall of States to climate, race, coal-mines, the discovery of America, the rise of machines, the disappearance of the American frontier, and simply to Natural Law. Assuming that Natural Law controls men, the view is that the State is a living organism which, like all forms of life, is born, is young, matures, and naturally grows old and dies.

These scholarly views, popularized by professional thinkers, permeate modestly practical minds to an extent that may surprise you. For instance, everyone knows that Americans are husky, hustling, prosperous, hopeful and full of vitamins because America is young. If you pack up your troubles in your old kitbag and smile, boys, smile, the cause of your doing so is the union of these States in 1789; an Icelander can't do that, Iceland was founded in 930. At the same time, of course you know that these United States matured, abruptly, in 1933; therefore Wendell Phillips's remark, "The cardinal principle of our national life is that God gives every man the sense to manage his own affairs," is no longer true. It was true before the American frontier disappeared, but now the American economy is mature. The adult economy removes from my skull the brain which God formerly placed there, and gives someone else the sense to manage my affairs. Why does an adult economy do this? Because it is so complex.

All this seems quite clear to the Walter Lippmanns and Charles Beards, but it isn't to me. I am not an intellectual, and somewhere along their line of reasoning I ask myself: Do they have sense enough to raise a hill of beans?

Of course they do not raise a hill of beans. These professional thinkers do nothing but think; the rest of us support them in comfort and leisure for that sole purpose.

Now, under their noses, is the answer to a question that thinkers have tried to answer for thousands of years. Here is the first complete example in history of the rise and fall of a State. Germany has risen and fallen within the memory of living men. The whole span of Germany's existence as a State covers 75 years. The records of every action and event in its brief history are recent, complete, detailed, indisputable, and easily accessible.

Thirty-two years ago, Americans were admiring Germany to the point of worship. American scholars and students went to Germany as Moslems go to Mecca. At the crest of the greatest popular adulation that an American President has ever excited, the adored Teddy rose even higher when the Kaiser of Germany received him as a guest. American professional thinkers were chorusing incessantly, "Germany is fifty years ahead of us in social legislation." Look at Germany now.

If this catastrophe were the bankruptcy of General Motors, business men would learn from it not to follow the policy adopted by the directors and stockholders of General Motors. If it were a plane crash, experts would find the flaw in the plane's construction or control, and designers or pilots would learn from it not to repeat the error. This is the "fall" of a State, the wreck of a civilization, the end of Europe. What is the cause of this disaster, precisely? What was the flaw in the German State? What policy did Germans adopt; what course did they pursue, that Americans must not follow if the United States are not to repeat the German catastrophe?

These seem to me to be obvious and reasonable questions. Surely it is the job of scholars and of the numerous American professional thinkers to answer them. If they do not answer such questions, I cannot conjecture of what use they are, nor why other Americans should support them in leisure to think.

My own modest job at this moment is to report to readers of this Review whatever sources of such useful information I may be able to find in books. I have not found, yet, that American professional thinkers are doing any thinking about these questions. As an aid to unprofessional thought I can offer at present only two books, both by Germans.

Professor Ludwig von Mises's *Omnipotent Government: The Rise of the Total State and Total War,* is indispensable. Every American should make it a permanent addition to his library, for reading and rereading.

Professor Mises is a scholar in the sound tradition of European scholarship and he is an economist; this is to say that he is a liberal, an opponent of socialism. For 26 years he taught economics at the University of Vienna and at the Graduate School of International Studies in Geneva. He is still living; in this country, of course. He saw the development of the German catastrophe from its beginning and, in economic terms, he describes it accurately and sensibly. Don't let his being an economist discourage you; he does not write the socialist jargon that stymies any rational mind trying to cope with the economics course in American colleges. He writes clearly, often brilliantly.

This book explains the economic fallacy that leads men to create the total State, total war, and total disaster to the State and to themselves. A sensible child can understand Professor Mises's explanation, of the reason why the economic tyranny now called "administrative law" destroys a productive economy and, of course, the State that a productive economy supports. Even Mr. Eric Johnston, were he to read this book, might possibly grasp the reason why "administrative law" and free enterprise can be combined only as the lion and the lamb can be.

Professor Mises sums up his admirable exposition of these facts in two sentences: "The choice for mankind is not between two economic systems. It is between capitalism and chaos."

He gives the reader, also, a sketch of Germany's short political history, showing that the Germans chose chaos when they did not support the German liberals. Of course he uses the word, "liberal" correctly. The German liberal movement was the farthest eastern reach, in 19th-century Europe, of the revolutionary idea that came from Philadelphia: All men are born equal and endowed by their Creator with inalienable liberty.

Unfortunately, Professor Mises himself is a victim of the confusion into which this declaration threw European political thinking. In economics he is absolutely sound, but in politics he is bewildered. The result is that this book is comparable to a blueprint of an automobile chassis drawn by an engineer who thoroughly understands the transmission system but isn't quite certain whether the power comes from the gas tank or the steering gear.

For the whole crux of the matter is the structure of the State – the means and methods of restricting the police power of men in public office in a manner that will permit the energy of other men to work in producing and distributing wealth.

Professor Mises describes the German experience which, as he says, "demonstrates the impracticability of hereditary absolutism." If he sees that this experience demonstrates the impracticability of tyranny *per se,* he does not say so. He implies vaguely that the antithesis of hereditary absolutism is democracy, without defining the word "democracy." The definition, of course, is majority absolutism.

He seems to have the delusion, prevalent in Europe since the time of Alexis de Toqueville [*sic*], that the United States of America are a democracy. He should read the Constitution of the United States and the Federalist Papers which explain why the Constitution was designed to prevent democracy here, and the causes of the fact that, as Madison wrote, "democracy is as short in its life as it is violent in its death."

The flat self-contradictions in Professor Mises's political thinking will flabbergast you. For example: "The State, if properly administered, is the foundation of society, of human co-operation and civilization. It is the most beneficial and useful instrument in the endeavor of men to promote human happiness and welfare. But it is not God. It is simply compulsion and coercion; it is the police power."

One must admire the last two sentences as an achievement in realism, for a European (as they would be for a Japanese) born in a society based on belief in the Divine Right and near-Divinity of Royal blood. But the first two sentences merely transfer the idea of Divinity to a policeman. This is the political fallacy that leads men to create Hitlers and Stalins. The self-evident truth is that the Creator endows every person with non-transferable life, liberty, and ability to seek his own happiness, and doubtless Professor Mises himself does not require a policeman to compel him to do so. The function of the State actually is to stop anyone who uses compulsion and coercion to interfere with this natural human endeavor. Since, for this purpose, the State must be police force, it is "dangerous, and must be watched like fire," as Washington said. Police force can no more be the foundation of society than fire can be the foundation of a house.

Such political errors sprinkle the pages of this book. "For the sake of domestic peace, liberalism aims at democratic government." Not at all; liberalism aims at restricting the State to its useful function. "It [this liberal aim] failed because the world abandoned both liberalism and capitalism." But the world has never had liberalism and capitalism; this world-revolutionary effort has hardly begun, and it has not failed; it has merely encountered reaction against it in Europe and Asia. "Every nation is prepared to believe." But nations do not have minds and souls; only a person can think and believe. "It is obvious that every constitutional system can be made to work satisfactorily when the rulers are equal to their task." Stuff and nonsense! It is equally obvious that any motor car can be run satisfactorily, with or without pistons and steering gear, if the driver is equal to his task.

These political fallacies, running through this book, side by side with rational economic thinking and an accurate report of events in Europe, add to the book's value for the discriminating American reader. Far more fully than the author supposes, he has explained the cause of the German reaction which produced total war and destroyed Germany and Europe. The basic failure was in the lack of rational political thought, and this book admirably displays that lack.

I urge you, therefore, to get this book and keep it; read it and reread it. It is essential to an American's education today. And while you're about it, get Professor Mises's *Bureaucracy*, a little book which disposes of a lot of current nonsense. It explains why bureaucrats are what they are, and why it does no good to change bureaucrats in the middle of bureaucracy.

Lane's unhappiness with von Mises's democratic views was shared by Watts who was then employed by the Foundation for Economic Education. Watts handled the correspondence with Milton Friedman and George Stigler over their rent control pamphlet. Some of the unhappiness in that exchange (Hammond & Hammond, 2006) is visible in the letter to von Mises.

It will be noticed in F. A. Harper's report, Watts accused von Mises by violating his oath of allegiance with his pro-democratic views, a point which is not made by Watts in the correspondence we reprint. Watts did not long remain in the employ of FEE. He was no longer at FEE when he reviewed Samuelson's *Economics* and the other modern texts for Hart's *Economic Council Review*. He had been replaced by Harper whose response to a longer, unlocated Watts attack on von Mises's democratic views we reproduce following Watts's letter.

[Foundation for Economic Education Letterhead]

December 9, 1946

Dr. Ludwig von Mises
777 West End Avenue
New York 25, New York

Dear Doctor von Mises:

The more I think about it the more I am worried by your apparently approba-
tory references to "democracy" in "The Age of Dictatorship."

You know that true democracy – "majority rule" – is vicious as a political
method. Furthermore, this is precisely what many or most Americans understand
by "democracy," and it is what the communists *want* them to understand by it.
The communists know that democracy is the way to destroy liberty and usher in
the "dictatorship of the proletariat." They show this by supporting every proposal
for a more democratic form of government in France. They want Americans to
believe in democracy, and unfortunately their wish has been realized.

In my opinion, therefore, it is as necessary to show the American people the
folly and menace of democracy as of interventionism, price control, social security, or fiat money.

True, some Americans use the term "democracy" loosely to mean some kind
of political utopia. But this loose use of the term arises from loose thinking, that
is, from failure to see the evils of democracy. We must not let any of our readers
go unwarned on this matter. They must not get from us the idea that democracy
is good or harmless. Democracy was never a good word like liberalism. It is a
bad word which our enemies are trying to make us think is good, so that we will
accept the evil thing. We should not fall into this trap.

"Social security" may be a good thing, if the words are used to mean some
good thing, like "law and order," or "political stability." But, as used today, social
security means a specific government program, one which you and I regard as
evil. Therefore, we would not put out a piece in which "social security" was spoken of approvingly, even though the author was using the phrase in some technical sense quite different from the popular usage. We would be afraid that unwary
readers would think we approved the thing which the word commonly means.

For the same reasons, I believe, we should avoid every appearance of endorsing
"democracy," even if we mean by it something different from "majority rule," and
even if many other people use it loosely to mean representative government.

As a matter of fact, those who recognize the evils of real democracy, seldom
use the term in an approving way. They may at first, but soon they get so tired of

explaining that they do not mean democracy when they say democracy, that they begin using terms which better convey the meaning they intend, and then they stop using democracy.

There is only one reason any person would use "democracy" in an approving way after he had seen the evil of true democracy (majority rule). That reason is political expediency. That is, he might continue using the word to curry favor with the unthinking, or to avoid antagonizing them. In other words, he would do what Friedman and Stigler did when they said, "Even for those, *like us*, who favor greater equality ... rent controls are folly." Please don't let us do it.

Democracy, as most people understand it and advocate it – government by Gallup polls – is the surest and quickest way to socialism and dictatorship. The American people need to be warned of this as much as they need to be warned of anything. Your use of the term, in an approving way (e.g. end of page 5), and your failure to denounce democracy, I believe, are as serious failures as would be an implied endorsement of fiat currency.

I hope you will give this matter your most earnest consideration. Despite my rather numerous suggestions for slight changes in form of statement, I think the article is beautifully written and one of the best "fight talks" I have read. The conclusion is a masterpiece of eloquence. I was informed, inspired and thrilled by the piece as a whole. I hope you will make it really tops by changing your tolerance or approval for democracy into outright condemnation.

Very truly yours,

V. Orval Watts

Memorandum
To: Dr. Watts   13 January 1947
From: F. A. Harper
Subject: About your "Democracy vs. Liberalism," a criticism of Mises position
on "Democracy"

The presumption of this entire discussion seems to be that Mises's definition of a
democracy indicates his opposition to:

1. A *Republic*, as a form of government
2. *Limited* government
3. *Constitutional government*, and a judiciary
4. Having "... supreme power ..." reside with "... individuals whence it springs
   and by whom it must eventually be exercised."

Each of these presumptions, it seems to me, is without foundation.

1. In expressing favor for "democracy," Mises is not thereby expressing disfavor
   for a "republic," which by definition is one form of democracy. His definition and the way he uses it in the manuscript involves the contrast between
   the broad classification of democracy, including a republic as a subclass, and
   dictatorial systems such as Bolshevism, Fascism and Nasism.
2. His definition, and the way he uses it in the manuscript, does not oppose the
   idea of limited government. The manuscript is, in fact, very clear on that point
   throughout; it is founded on antipathy toward interventionism. In using the
   term democracy, including republic, in contrast to any form of dictatorship,
   he is talking about the *place* of eventual placement of power of authority, *for
   whatever scope of operation is delegated to government* – which is another
   question.
3. In defining democracy as he did, and using it as he did in the manuscript,
   he was not expressing opposition to a constitution, and to respect for its
   mandates as interpreted, by a judiciary. Note that in talking about those
   ruled being in position to determine the mode in which power is to be
   exercised (directly by plebiscite or indirectly by election; in the form of a
   republic or other), he specified this process as applying to the *legislative
   and executive* branches only, aside from the question of a Constitution and
   a judiciary.
4. Your preference (page 5) for a system wherein "... supreme power..." resided
   with "... *individuals* whence it springs and by whom it must eventually be
   exercised" seems to fit Mises's definition and his use of the term democracy

in its context. It seems to describe his concept, in fact, much better than it does your concept as expressed on pages 2–4. For instance, there is implied in your discussion on these pages an opposition to certain changes in government _no matter what the wishes of whatever proportion of the people_; would you be opposed to the woman-suffrage amendment (page 4) if approved by 100% of the then eligible voters, or 90%, or 80%, or 70%, etc.?

Some Details:

(Page 1) Mises's definition does not contradict the responsibility of government officials to support a Constitution, as interpreted by a judiciary. A pledge to support the Constitution is not tantamount to a pledge to violate the will of the people, for it applies only where the Constitution gives clear guidance – usually of a prohibitive nature. In setting up, as you did, a conflicting choice between supporting the Constitution and obeying the will of the people, you must be presuming that the people shall not be given the right, _by any means_, to alter the Constitution. Otherwise, the will of the people may be obeyed through adherence to a Constitution that is subject to change by the will of the people, somehow.

(Page 1) There is the clear implication on this page that Mises is advocating sovereignty by the government rather than by individuals. It seems to me clearly the contrary. He is expressing favor of a system wherein government, whatever its scope, shall be of a nature where power, directly or indirectly, possibly with a Constitution somehow subject to change, shall reside with the people governed. This, he says, is in contrast to any of the forms of government where power resides in the government, operated at will by somebody or by some gang.

(Page 2) It is here implied that vestige of power with those (as in Mises's definition) means decision _solely_ by unanimous consent. This seems to me to be unfounded. It means, I would say, the right to participate in the decision, whether that question is to be settled in terms of a majority, plurality, unanimity, or whatnot (which must be specified in each instance). Nor does it imply, I would say, that _everyone_ would have to be given the right to vote, as you suggest.

(Page 1) It seems to me unwarranted to charge that the use of the phrase "those ruled" (in Mises's definition) implies collectivism – if, in using that term, you mean any of its extreme types such as communism. Strictly speaking, of course, each governmental operation is by nature a sort of collective operation within its scope – the police system, etc.; in this sense, complete absence of anything collective would be one way to define anarchy.

In the same sense as you see in Mises's statement an implication of collectivism, it would also seem that one would find evidence of "collectivism" in approving existence of corporations, or cooperatives, or arrangements between neighbors to exchange help, or the operations of a home, etc.

(Page 2) And I fail to see why Mises's definition implies that *everyone* shall vote. Is it not reasonable to concede that he means giving *the right to vote* according to some plan of eligibility? Then if you or I fail to exercise our power to vote, we do not thereby acquire any power to invalidate the results – if we do not like them.

(Top Page 3) All this implies that Mises advocated either no Constitution or a Constitution subject to easy change. I do not find that in his definition. That is a consideration outside the scope of his definition, not in conflict with it.

(Page 3) I would not agree that the value of the American Constitution "… lies in the fact that it is not easily changed, but that it thwarts the will of the majority …." I think its virtue lies in the wisdom of its content, and only because of that is there any virtue in its fixity. If its content was totally "unwise," the lack of ease of change would be of negative value. And so far as the objective of thwarting the will of the majority is concerned, the governments of Stalin, Hitler, and the former enthroned Kings seem to be fully as well adapted as any Constitutional government could ever be.

(Bottom of Page 3) The mere fact that changes have occurred in the Constitution since its origin is no evidence that the changes are unwise – unless it is also contended that the original document was the height of perfection. Is that the contention being made? Or is it now with existing amendments, so perfect that it should not be altered; if so, by means within the specifications of Mises's definition, or if not, how?

(Bottom of Page 4) By Mises's definition, I doubt if the American government has become "far more democratic than formerly." It may have become more like the Greek type of democracy and less of a republican democracy, but by his definition *both* are democracies.

(Bottom Page 5) In his definition of democracy, and in the way he uses the term generally in the text of his manuscript, I do not think Mises is violating his vow of allegiance to an American republic, as it is implied here he is doing. Nor do I think, as implied here and in the title ("Democracy vs. Liberalism"), that he is taking a nonliberal position. On the contrary, a design of government whereby power resides somehow with those ruled, directly or indirectly, with or without a Constitution, etc., is the only form consistent with liberalism. If then they use that power for some act which you or I deem unwise, it is their privilege to do so and to suffer the consequences. To prohibit them from "doing themselves any harm," by not allowing them that power, is consistent with *nonliberal* economic doctrines like price control, with nonliberal religious schemes like a "state controlled" religion, with some form of dictatorial design of government "to protect the people against self-inflicted harm."

Now we return to the correspondence between von Mises and Lane, beginning with a letter to von Mises from her employer, which we follow with Lane's note on the Hart attack on democracy, another Hart note and then serious correspondence.

[National Economic Council Letterhead]

April 24, 1947

Dr. Ludwig von Mises
777 West End Avenue
New York 25, N.Y.

Dear Dr. von Mises:

Thank you very much for sending me the pamphlet on economic planning. I shall put it with my reading for the coming weekend.

It was a great pleasure to meet you Tuesday at Mr. Hoiles luncheon and to have the opportunity of sitting next to you.

I am enclosing several of our recent publications; also a small leaflet which tells in brief something of the purposes and objectives of the National Economic Council. Our radio broadcast, which is there referred to, terminated in February.

If you would like, I shall be glad to put your name down on a small complimentary list to receive these publications. The Economic Council Letter is semi-monthly, the Review of Books, monthly, and the Council Papers come out at irregular intervals.

                                                            Very sincerely yours,

                                                            Merwin K. Hart /ASL
MKH:ec   President
Enclosures

my dear Dr. Mises — I hope that you will have time to read this because it may make more clear to you the American view of democracy.
yours sincerely Rose Wilder Lane

ECONOMIC COUNCIL LETTER

Published Semi-Monthly by

NATIONAL ECONOMIC COUNCIL, Inc.

350 Fifth Ave., New York 1, N. Y.
903 First National Bank Bldg., Utica 2, N. Y.
600 Investment Building, Washington 5, D. C.
1559 Continental Illinois Bank Bldg., Chicago 4, Ill.

Council Letter No. 166
May 1, 1947

Let's Get This Straight

ON September 19, 1940, the President of the National Economic Council, in an address before the Union League Club of New York City, remarked that the United States was planned as a republic and not as a democracy. He added:

"It is time to brush aside this word (democracy) with its connotations. It is time to return to the conception of the republic—a conception so clear that all can understand."

On September 21st *The New York Times*, in an editorial entitled "We The People," said that Mr. Hart apparently assumed that "democracy" and the American concept of government are not the same thing. It stated that Mr. Hart had enunciated a "curious doctrine" which "must have surprised his Union League Club audience."

The editorial further said, "If power ultimately resides in a universal electorate of free adult citizens—as it does in the United States—we have a democracy. If it does not, we have something else."

Now this distinction between republic and democracy is no mere quibble of words. Even a cursory examination of American history yields overwhelming evidence that the United States is not, and never was intended to be, a democracy; that the use of the word democracy to describe the United States goes back (except for scattered allusions in earlier days) only about a dozen years, and that it is the result of pure propaganda. After all, Hitler said that a lie big enough and often enough told will presently be believed.

The Chinese learned, centuries ago, that "The beginning of wisdom is calling things by their right names." When we Americans become so befuddled that most of us no longer call our very country by its right name, it is time to do something about it.

The purpose of this letter, therefore, is to tell why the United States is a republic, and why, even after the passage of certain recent laws, it is not a democracy.

* * * * *

The members of the Constitutional Convention of 1787 discussed the attributes of democracy and rejected it on the ground that it had always failed. Thus on May 31, 1787, Edmund Randolph told the Convention that the object for which the delegates had met was "to provide a cure for the evils under which the United States labored; that in tracing these evils to their origin every man had found it in the turbulence and trials of democracy. . . ."

No delegate protested this statement. The Convention was clearly in accord with it. Mr. Elbridge Gerry at about the same time told the Convention: "The evils we experience flow from the excess of democracy. The people do not want (that is, do not lack) virtue; but are the dupes of pretended patriots."

Let us remember these lines as this or that Senator or Representative in Washington comes forward with a bill to provide fresh control over, and regulation of, the American people—always, of course, with a further building up of bureaucracy, and too often with one eye on the vote in his state or district.

Alexander Hamilton, in a speech June 21, 1788, said in part:

"It has been observed that a pure democracy if it were practicable would be the most perfect government. Experience has proved that no position is more false than this. The ancient democracies in which the people themselves deliberated never possessed one good feature of government. Their very character was tyranny; their figure deformity."

Now let's go quickly back through the centuries and read a few opinions expressed by others.

Aristotle said, in 322 B.C., "A democracy when put to the strain grows weak and it is supplanted by oligarchy."

Seneca said in 63 A.D. that "Democracy is more cruel than wars or tyrants."

Montesquieu said in 1748 in *The Spirit of the Laws*, "Democracy hath two excesses to avoid, the spirit of inequality which leads to aristocracy or monarchy, and the spirit of extreme equality which leads to despotic power. . . ."

Jean Jacques Rousseau said in 1762, "If there were a nation of gods they would be governed democratically; but so perfect a government is not suitable for man."

Lane's note to von Mises on an *Economic Council Letter*.

[National Economic Council Letterhead]

June 30, 1947

Prof. Ludwig Elder [*sic*] von Mises
777 West End Ave.,
New York 25, N.Y.

Dear Prof. von Mises:

I think you will agree that the American proposals for an International Trade Organization, now being discussed in Geneva, are a direct and dangerous threat to the future of our Republic.

It seems clear that this threat must be met my [*sic*] mobilizing public opinion against it. As part of an effort to this end, I enclose [a] copy of a statement to the American people which it is my earnest hope you will feel free to sign.

The statement is being sent first to a few distinguished Americans like yourself. When it has received their signatures, we propose to send it for further signatures to men of standing throughout the nation. After that it will be released to the press in an appropriate and dignified manner as a factor in the formation of public opinion.

Hoping to hear from you soon, I am,

Sincerely,

Merwin K. Hart/ASL
President

July 5, 1947

My dear Dr. Mises,

My conscience is still bothered by my silence which consented to your remark to me at Mr. Hoiles's luncheon, that you and I are "agreed on fundamentals." At the time, it didn't seem the place or moment to talk about fundamentals. I should have said at once, however, that as an American I am of course fundamentally opposed to democracy and to anyone advocating or defending democracy, which in theory and in practice is the basis of socialism.

It is precisely democracy which is destroying the American political structure, American law, and the American economy, as Madison said that it would, and as Macauley prophesied that it would do in fact in the 20th century.

Compared to this fundamental perversion of American individualism in theory, and to the actual destruction of law, suppression of human rights, and wrecking of the Republic which result from this perversion, it's a relatively superficial fact that praise of democracy, and representing democracy as "the opposite of social-ism" is [a] Communist Party tactic in this country. Of course the reason that it is the Party tactic here is that Communists understand political theory and know what they are doing.

Everyone whom I know who knows you personally insists that you sincerely believe that you are opposed to socialism, and that you do not know what you are doing. This was my own opinion after reading OMNIPOTENT GOVERNMENT and BUREAUCRACY. It may be true. If it is, you will want to see the very incomplete list of democratic organizations, enclosed, which will faintly indi-cate to you the groups with whom you align yourself here, by your footnote in PLANNED CHAOS and your praise of democracy throughout this booklet. This is merely a question of tactics and of associates, of course; not of fundamentals.

I write this note simply to repair my omission at Mr. Hoiles's luncheon; to say that I am *fundamentally* opposed to the political theory you support and the politi-cal practice you advocate: democracy.

With all good wishes,

Yours sincerely,

Rose Wilder Lane/ASL

[Ludwig von Mises's response to Rose Wilder Lane's July 5, 1947 letter]

Dear Madam,

I did not make any remarks to you at Mr. Hoile's luncheon. It is my principle never to address any reviewer who called my writing "Stuff and nonsense." When Mr. Hoiles introduced me, I just muttered "How do you do."

I do not care whether or not you consider me sincere. I know that all communists and ex-communists are fundamentally opposed to my theories.

Yours sincerely,

LANE'S REVIEW OF TARSHIS'S *ELEMENTS*

We now leave what we are calling the first round of the Lane–von Mises discussion in July 1947 and reproduce Lane's influential review of *The Elements of Economics* from the August 1947 edition of *Economic Council Reviews* (Vol. 4, No. 8), which launched the textbook controversy. The simplest evidence of its popular success is that our copy comes from a "third printing." We wish to emphasize the paragraph that speaks to Tarshis's democratic presuppositions:

> *The Element of Economics* plays upon fear, shame, pity, greed, idealism, hope to urge young Americans to act upon this theory *as citizens*. This is not an economics text at all; it is a pagan-religious and political tract. It inspires an irrational faith and spurs it to political action. From cover to cover there is not a single suggestion of any action that is not political – and Federal. [emphasis in the original]

Taken independently of Lane's attack on von Mises's political views in *Omnipotent Government*, one might well pass over this remark as eccentric. A good reason to take it seriously is that it is quoted in the leaflet produced in the anti-Tarshis text campaign that we reproduce immediately following the review.

[From the *Economic Council Review of Books*, Vol. IV, No. 8, August 1947]

Very soon now, young Americans will be going away, or going back, to college. Their numbers will be impressive, for this is the unique country in which education is not a class-distinction. From farms, mines, slums and mansions, this country's future citizens troop into the colleges to learn how to remake the new world that we older ones remade in our time and will leave to them. So this month let's look at a textbook.

This is an odd thing to do, I know, for there is perfect trust in education. Americans anxiously supervise every detail of their children's lives, except their schooling. No matter what the cost in time, effort, self-education, they care for the children's health, habits, manners. It doesn't occur to them a school can cripple minds.

How many parents assume that anything eatable, any plaything, any companion or nurse or dentist or doctor is good? How many Big Business men pay a million dollars for rubber or steel without specifying kind or quality and with no check of deliveries to see that they are up to specifications? And how many parents, how many tax-payers supporting the schools and universities, how many endowers of education, ever look at the education? How long is it since you read a textbook?

I recommend urgently to your attention a textbook of the highest standing, endorsed by foremost educators and adopted for use this year by leading colleges: *The Elements of Economics*, by Professor Lorie Tarshis of Stanford University, published under the editorship of Dr. Edgar S. Furniss, Professor of Sociology and Dean of the Graduate School of Yale University.

There is nothing new or unusual in this textbook; I urge you to read it because it is typical. Its merit is simplicity. It teaches in everyday words the Keynesian theory that has dominated economic teaching for years, and is now orthodox in universities and powerful in Washington.

This textbook contains many lies; I mean contradictions of fact, which a competent economist knows are lies, such as (p. 53) "a hundred years ago ... great depressions, like those of recent years, were simply not known." (pp. 685, 686) "A century ago our economy ... could not have a high standard of living, but neither could it have severe depression." It contains also many lies of omission and distortion, such as emphasizing business profits without mentioning a loss, though every economist knows that 50 percent of American corporations normally show losses and nearly a third of them are in the red at the top of the biggest booms. But I have not the space to discuss this text's lies and you may read them for yourself. The importance of *The Elements of Economics* is its effective propaganda for the Keynesian theory.

Not to go into the Keynesian theory's ancient, pre-Christian theological origins, in modern economics it represents Karl Marx's theory of "the inherent contradictions of capitalism." Communists hold that these contradictions are now killing capitalism while maturing within its womb the World Commune fathered by omnipotent History. (I am not satirical; they do believe this.) The basic contradiction within capitalism, briefly, is that capitalism produces so much wealth that it causes poverty. For example: If Americans will not eat more than 100 billion loaves of bread a year, and capitalist bakeries produce 150 billion, the bakeries must close for six months and bakers starve to death while the surplus bread is eaten. This is the Marxian–Keynesian explanation of depressions.

Of course, the fact is that government's economic action directly caused every depression in this country's history, as well as the chronic depression in which nearly all mankind lived hungry and died young through all past history.

The Keynesians, however, emphatically are not communists. In the broad troop-movement of the Marxians, they advance in the center. They come to save capitalism, as Hitler rescued the Sudeten Germans and Stalin frees the Greeks. And the great value of *The Elements of Economics* is that it does not hide the Keynesian theory and methods in technical jargon; it states them in plain words.

Unfortunately, a review cannot give an adequate conception of its emotional effects, however, because these are made by implications, by assumptions, by the approach that editors call a "slant," and by innumerable repetitions. For instance, the ideas of "business firm" and "profit" are welded together by repeating "profit" in every line of pages dealing with business firms. Once, only once, Professor Tarshis writes, (p. 30) "But it must not be supposed that to seek profits is an act of villainy. ... These actions are not censured. ..." And in all fairness he says of a producer, (p. 145) "He is not necessarily more grasping than other people, although he is perhaps in a position where he can grab more successfully."

There is a play of irony, too obvious to be missed but subtle enough to flatter the adolescent who catches onto it, and there are strokes of burlesque to delight any classroom. Read the parable of the ignorant savages (p. 331) who had no banks but did have "a thing which many people consider much more important – a standard. But it was not a gold standard. It was a rock standard." "... their dollar bills were inscribed, 'Will Pay to the Bearer on Demand One Dollar in Rock.'" You'll roar with laughter at their ridiculous dismay when their boulder rolled into the sea and there was no measurement of money. (Standard weights and measurements are silly, aren't they?) Then brighten your day with mirth over the absurdity of a government's paying its debt, (p. 518) and leave the classroom chanting:

"And now the budget's balanced,
Retrenchment is the hero.
On either side is entered
A solitary Zero."

I cannot do justice to this textbook's charm for the immature. I cannot convey the impact of its grave passages upon their deepest and best emotions. And I have no space to give to the bits of old propaganda that decorate its main theme, such as the charge that corporations own patents to suppress them, thus preventing progress – and, somewhat illogically, that inventions eliminate jobs and starve workingmen; the attacks on advertising as economic waste; the many variations of "10 percent of the people own 90 percent of the wealth" which was a lie in the 1880s and is even further from truth now.

Dr. Furniss writes in his introduction, "This book contains the best that the expert economist has to offer regarding the economic problems of our times, …" and that it will equip the student "to take an active part as a citizen in the determination of policy in economic matters." The text at once (pp. 2, 3) arouses the enthusiasm for this task "we set a certain high standard … for our economy. We expect it to deliver the goods. … And when it fails to do so, we attempt to discover the causes of these failures and to correct them. …"

"How then do we want our economy to operate? … We want as large an output as possible. But it is not enough that the total output be at the maximum permitted by our resources and technical knowledge. That output must be distributed in a way that satisfies us. We do not want all of the output to go to ten people, leaving nothing for the rest. We want everybody to have a fair share of what is produced." (p. 8) "We have seen enough of the effects of unemployment, of inflation, of war, of depression, and of poverty." "… only if these conditions are remedied can ordinary people have material well-being." (And try to find a college student who has ever heard that capitalism is the first and only economy in which ordinary people wear shoes; that ours is the first and only country in which ordinary people have never starved to death by thousands in famines. Try to find one; you'll be surprised.)

First, the student compares our economy with the Russian. He sees (pp. 28, 29) "one striking difference. In our economy, there are millions of independent business firms. In the Russian economy, the private business firm does not exist. … We have said that the business firm is the basic unit in a capitalist economy. Its importance derives from the fact that decisions about output, price, the level of employment, the methods of production, and a great number of other things that influence our economic well-being are made within the individual firm. … When prices rise, they do so because the managements of business firms have decided to raise them. In a capitalist economy there is no overall government planning board which determines the total output of an industry, the prices it will charge, or the level of employment. …

"In the Russian economy the decision to produce, let us say, 20 million tons of pig iron is made by the Central Planning Board, which presumably takes into account the needs and resources of the Russian economy before it comes to a decision. The same board determines how many automobiles to produce, how many pairs of socks to manufacture, and how many acres to put into wheat." (Of course, the Central Planning Boards of France and Spain dictated the acres of wheat in the Mississippi Valley 200 years ago; there was little wheat, few socks, and no automobiles.) "In our economy no such institution exists. ... In a socialist economy, important questions of output, price, employment are planned collectively. In a capitalist economy, these decisions are made separately by individual firms."

This contrast is impressed by repetitions throughout the book. (p. 29) "... the firm is owned by private individuals. The determination of how much to produce, or of the price to be charged for the product, is made with one interest in mind – that of the owner. The owner's interest is to secure as large a profit as possible out of the business firm, ..."

(p. 185) "There should be no confusion about who changes prices. It is easy to gain the impression that prices are changed by 'the forces of competition,' or 'the laws of supply and demand,' or 'inflation,' or 'deflation.' Indeed, a full-page advertisement, sponsored by an important business firm – " [Sorry, I haven't space for this.] "The implication is that prices are not made by man; ...." "This is absurd, though it is easy to see why the firm which printed this advertisement was eager to shift the blame for higher prices away from itself to some acceptable scapegoat. Prices are raised or lowered because some men decide to raise or lower the price they charge." "... they are no more compelled to do so than you are compelled to read this sentence." "... it will be well worth while to remember this general truth."

(pp. 237, 238) "... our economy ... seems to resemble an enormous jigsaw puzzle rather than a well-designed bridge. ... A jigsaw puzzle in which each piece determined its own size, color, and shape with no regard to the total design would seem to be nearer the truth. ... The United States Steel Corporation may decide to supply 30 million tons of steel ingots. ... The Free Sewing Machine Company may decide to manufacture 35,500 sewing machines. ... In a capitalist economy, each firm arrives at its own decisions. ..."

"In contrast to our planlessness, a socialist economy has its Central Planning Board ... to insure that there is some sort of balance. ... The pieces of the jigsaw puzzle are all cut by plan, and while the pattern may not be perfect, at least it is intended to be. But in a capitalist economy ... there is no Central Planning Board that tells General Motors how many automobiles to produce or General Foods how much cereal to package."

All these comparisons lead irresistibly to the final conclusion, (p. 686) "the ways by which the whole pie can be made larger are not available to any single group within the economy. Labor or farmers by themselves cannot do a great deal to create prosperity. To do so takes considered, and concerted, action by the whole economy. That is a fact which simply must be faced."

Of course, two or three facts and a little arithmetic would show Professor Tarshis that the Central Planning Board which he urges so plausibly upon trusting ignorance cannot possibly exist in a modern economy. I offer him the simplest indication of this impossibility:

In these States now, about 50,000,000 workers produce some 8 million different articles, sold and bought in 140 metropolitan markets. Costs, and therefore economical prices, inescapably vary for all these products and in all these places. To price these products economically, therefore, require 140 times 8 million equations: 1,120,000,000 equations. (Plus a few more equations for those products, such as candy bars, whose manufacturers figure average costs and equalize prices in all markets.) To determine equitable price-wage relationships, Professor Tarshis might classify the 50 million workers, roughly, into 1,000 groups. (This would be tough on workers, especially new ones, who didn't fit the groups, but never mind them.) The Board will then have to work out only 1,000 times 1,120,000,000 equations.

Assuming that an accountant can – and, in a government bureau, would – figure out one of these complicated equations every sixty minutes, a Central Planning Board of 50,000,000 accountants, established in 1937, since then supported by taxpayers, and working diligently 40 hours a week, would now be completing a schedule of American wages and prices suited to 1937 conditions. Meanwhile, workers could not have left their jobs or groups, and factories could not have made new products; and only a Gestapo could try to enforce 1937 wages and prices in 1945.

So far as governmental interference now permits, American buyers and sellers from United States Steel to every girl buying hairpins still figure out these equations every day, while supporting themselves. Every customer in every shop does a share of the job, and for free. Capitalism has created an economy so productive and so complex that it can't work on any basis but individual decisions, and can't exist where individuals are not permitted to make the decisions.

I return to this typical textbook, *The Elements of Economics*. Our capitalist economy (p. 156) "frequently falls short of providing full employment, and at such times our standard of living is far below what it need be. The distribution of income is very uneven, and it is questionable whether the maximum social well-being is achieved with this unequal division. Finally, … the proportion in which certain commodities are found in the total output is far from ideal."

Why is distribution of income so uneven? The fact is that incomes in capitalism are much more nearly equal than in any other form of economy, and constantly become more nearly equal. The income-equalizing function of a free economy has operated here since 1840, as the U.S. Census figures would show Professor Tarshis. But on page 544 we learn: "When labor productivity is increased, less labor is needed ... to produce any given output. This fact is obvious – especially to the men who have lost their jobs as better methods have been introduced." (Oddly, this book elsewhere emphasizes the constant, enormous increase in the number of industrial jobs in our capitalist economy.) But the effect of the invention of rolling mills was to stimulate the production of rolling mills. (p. 545) "But once the rolling mills are in operation, labor is no longer needed to produce them. ... The effect of its [an invention's] introduction was to increase employment, while that of its use was to reduce it –assuming no change in the output." (p. 549) "The adoption of the invention is expected to lead to reduced labor costs per unit of output, and therefore to reduction in total wage payments. Since the outlay for wages is labor's total income, obviously a reduction in labor costs gives rise to a reduction in labor's income, if output remains constant. ... Labor's share in the total income of the economy will go down as the firm's profit goes up. Hence, there will be a shift of income from labor to employer."

But suppose an alert student asks, What happens when there is a demand for a larger output? He learns (p. 262) "... profit-seeking firms independently determine how much to produce and what price to charge. Each firm is free to produce as much or as little as it wants, and each firm is free to charge whatever price it wishes." (p. 264) "The most striking change in the American economy between 1939 and 1945 was the enormous increase in the demand for almost every kind of goods. Demand more than doubled for many items, ... What did firms do in response to this enormous increase in demand? They did two things. Almost all of them increased their output, and a large number of them raised their prices. ... Wholesale prices increased by approximately 35 percent ... Some firms were under even greater inducement to raise their prices, and the only reason they did not do so was government price control. There is no doubt, then, that an increase in demand will ordinarily lead a business firm to increase its output and to raise its price."

You and I may recall the increasing demand for radios which caused profit-seeking business firms to increase the output and raise the price from $600 in 1924 to $9.75 for a much better radio in 1935. But no freshman remembers 1924.

Why don't business firms produce the things we want? (p. 239) "Buyers do not mark ballots in our economy to indicate their preferences. If they did, we should know directly. As it is, the only indication is to be got from what they are willing to spend." (p. 240) "It is not a very accurate sign, for this reason: it weighs the importance of buyers by the amount of money each one has. ... When one man has $500,000 to spend, and another has $500, can we say that the output that corresponds most closely to total buying corresponds most closely to their preferences? No, for the combination [of goods] that attracts the largest sum of money is obviously the one that conforms almost entirely to the wants of the rich man, ..." (p. 273) "A person whose income is $500 a year is not able to indicate on the market any but his most pressing needs; one with $500,000 a year can indicate his very slightest want, and it is this indication that matters to business firms. The pattern of production, then, is biased. It responds much more strongly to the least pressing wants of those in the high-income brackets than it does to the relatively urgent wants of those in the lower-income group." (p. 243) "Our economy is unplanned. Each firm, as we have emphasized, determines its own output, and there is no central authority to see that total production conforms to buyers' preferences." (p. 249) "... our output is composed, in the absence of social control, of too many goods for the well-to-do. ..." (p. 248) "Can anything be done to achieve a better balance? Indeed yes. It is possible to give more buyers' votes – or more purchasing power – to the lower income groups by distributing income more equally." And Professor Tarshis reports truthfully the methods that governments use to do this, notably their ingenious schemes of forced loans and unequal taxation.

Unemployment, however, is the most horrible feature of all advanced capitalist economies, and the pivot of the Keynes theory. Chapter 26 describes unemployment with shattering emotional impact. Repetitions throughout the book deepen the horror. Here is a calmer passage (p. 345):

> Whatever the causes of World War II, they were certainly reinforced by the dreadful economic condition of Europe during the 1930s. And unfortunately for our self-esteem, a most important cause of Europe's depression was our own. Beginning in 1930, we exported unemployment to Europe on a lavish scale. For unemployment, like influenza, spreads without regard to customs barriers and national boundaries. It spread from this country to Germany and Italy, to France, Great Britain, Australia and Canada, and to most of the rest of the world. Nothing that these countries could do, or at least would do, was able to protect them from the effects of our severe depression. So economic misery grew in Europe. With that came the Hitlers and the Francos. ...

"Unemployment has been our most serious economic problem ... the most serious economic problem of all the advanced capitalist economies. ... With chronic depression in England and Germany in the nineteen twenties – " That will stop you. It is surprising that it did not stop Professor Tarshis. But how many adolescents, carried away by these harrowing emotions, will ask: Since depression was chronic in socialist Germany and socialized England after 1920, how did Americans begin to cause it in 1930? Some unbiased interest in economic history will easily discover that Bismarck and the German socialists began in the 1880s to cause the depression that ultimately produced Hitler.

Why do all advanced capitalist countries suffer unemployment, depression, poverty? In contrast to all other countries, obviously they don't. *It is always governmental economic action that produces and prolongs poverty.* But this is true: To the extent that governments do not prevent men from acting freely for their own interests, free men constantly invent new means of producing more wealth with less human energy; and since anything must be produced before it can be consumed, a free economy is always producing today more than it produced yesterday and is consuming today. And this fact, combined with a fallacy, is the nub of John Maynard Keynes' general theory.

It is true that at a given moment, a capitalist economy is producing more than it is consuming at that moment. Production is always increasing and consumption following it in Time. And a socialist mind stops the clock. To return to our capitalist bakers, they do in fact produce in this country every night far more bread than is eaten that night; uneaten bread is stacked high in the groceries every morning. And bakers, who used to work 12 to 16 hours every day, are now in fact unemployed a day or two every week, and for 16 to 17 hours every work-day; they don't work again until night, when that day's bread has been eaten. On this time-lag between production and consumption, plus a fallacy about saving, the Keynesians base their theory.

They argue that prosperity depends upon "full employment," and that "full employment" depends upon total consumption of total production when, and even before, the goods are produced.

In 1840, capitalism in the United States produced the unheard-of gross annual product of $2 billion. In 1946, under war-pressure, it produced $200 billion. Therefore, Professor Tarshis, a good Keynesian, reasons, (p. 521) "Out of a $200 billion gross national product, our consumption expenditures amount to about $135 billion. To reach full employment, therefore, we must sell $65 billion worth to non-consumer buyers – that is, to purchasers of investment goods. The difficulties of finding markets *year after year* [my italics] for $65 billion worth of investment goods ... are very serious. ... Since, as consumers, we are willing to purchase only five eighths of our full employment output, we have a low-consumption economy. ... If we had a high consumption economy, the attainment of full prosperity would be very much easier."

In other words, if Americans consumed all they produced and were always in danger of starving to death for lack of enough, as Chinese, Indians, and Russians frequently do, we would easily achieve full employment – indeed, a 12- to 16-hour day and 7-day week of it, as they do. But will college boys think of that?

They will learn from this textbook (p. 49), "In March, 1946, a total of 36.3 million men were employed in non-agricultural establishments. About 5.5 million of them were on government civilian payrolls – almost one man in every six. Only twice as many as that were employed by manufacturing concerns, though most of us think of the economy as being mainly engaged in manufacturing. ... In March, 1946, income payments to individuals were running at the rate of about $158 billion a year. Wages and salaries were being paid by the government alone at a rate of $19.2 billion a year ... about 8 percent of the total income received. Government is clearly ... an important source of our total income." (p. 349) "Our economy ... rose to new heights between 1940 and 1945, propelled upward by the Defense Program, Lend Lease, the war, and reconversion. By the spring of 1947 it was shuddering at the top. What about the future? Is our economy again headed for a terrifying dive into depression?"

If our national income falls to only $120 billion, we lose every year $80 billion, a sum "almost beyond imagination's power to grasp ... a reduction of about $2,300 for every family, to be deprived of the many goods that we could have enjoyed for $2,300 – the clothes, automobiles, better food, new furniture – is not a welcome experience. To have it all happen in one year, and then to have it repeated year after year, is almost more than one can bear. Worst of all –or, per- haps, best of all – it is avoidable."

How? How? We must learn how. (p. 354) "... the condition for a large output and high employment is that spending be high ... spending determines output and employment." (p. 355) "... total spending equals the sum of consumption, private investment, public investment, and foreign investment." (p. 565) "It is clear that an economy can lift itself by its own bootstraps ... depression can be remedied by increased spending. The greater the spending, the larger, within limits, is the output of goods and services. We can spend our way into prosperity."

That is to say that money must be spent before it is earned, that goods must be consumed to produce them. Should you be cast away naked on a desert island (as all persons are born on this planet, which itself provides no shelter but caves, no food but fruit and nuts, no clothes whatever) you must eat steaks, wear out clothes, houses, furniture, motor cars, in order to get them.

But this, says the Dean of the Graduate School of Yale, is "the best that the expert economist has to offer regarding the economic problems of our times." This is the theory that convinces Mr. Paul Hoffman; it is the theory of the Murray Full Employment Bill, which Congress approved in principles. This theory is now established in England; it is written into the new French Constitution; it is accepted in the Economic Committee of the United Nations and in the discus- sions of the International Conference on Commerce and Employment. And it is being taught in American schools and colleges.

The Elements of Economics plays upon fear, shame, pity, greed, idealism, hope, to urge young Americans to act upon this theory, as *citizens*. This is not an economics text at all; it is a pagan-religious and political tract. It inspires an irrational faith and spurs it to political action. From cover to cover there is not a single suggestion of any action that is not political – and Federal.

How can we spend our way into prosperity? We must increase consumption and investment; but first, we must understand that saving is not, and cannot be, investment, (p. 437) "The effort to increase saving only succeeds in driving the national income lower. ... It is of particular importance to remember that one person's spending is somebody else's income; ... If we spend less, ... we reduce the incomes of individuals who otherwise would have produced goods ... to zero, if they become unemployed. ..." Money saved may be (pp. 365–367) "... put into the bank, kept under the mattress, or used to purchase government bonds, corporation securities, a new machine, or a life insurance policy; it is still saving. ... Saving and investment are completely different. Investment is something active which helps determine income, while saving is merely a resultant, determined in part by the level of income. ... Saving is done – if a failure to act can be described as doing – by people ... as income recipients, while investment is carried on by business and government units and by foreign buyers." "... saving is in essence simply a failure to consume income."

This is a basic Keynesian fallacy. In his *General Theory* Lord Keynes says that a decision to save is, in effect, a decision NOT to eat dinner; it does not imply an intention to eat dinner at any future time. Saving is negative; saved money vanishes. This is obviously sheer idiocy.

In the real world, a free person works for no other reason than to get something that he wants to consume. A free man who doesn't get this, doesn't work. (This is the reason why socialist economies must enforce slavery, as Russians are doing again and British Members of Parliament are already urging.) Only a rare miser wants money itself; the sane reason for saving money is to spend it later. It is precisely because free persons work to produce in order to consume, and save to increase their means of consuming more in future, that a free economy maintains its own dynamic equilibrium, constantly producing more and consuming more. It is *because* capitalism is a "low-consumption economy," with a constant margin of *postponed* consumption or saving, that it is a dynamic economy, increasing and equalizing incomes and raising living standards.

The student now intent upon increasing immediate consumption learns, discouragingly, that we can do little to increase consumers' spending. It is remarkable static in our economy. Equalizing incomes will increase it, and we can equalize incomes, somewhat by manipulating interest rates, taxing only high incomes, and compelling corporations to distribute all profit, after allowance for depreciation. And we can use propaganda to discourage saving, but it is very hard to uproot old ideas and habits of thrift inherited from a past economy "as different from ours as it, in its turn, was from the Stone Age."

So we turn to investment. There are three kinds: private, public, and foreign. Private investment is the total business spending of business firms. We can increase it a little by changing interest rates and taxes, and perhaps by paying business firms to build unprofitable industrial plants, but to this there is the social objection (p. 511) that the business firms would own the plants. We cannot increase private investment enough, for (p. 509) "Social control over private investment is obviously imperfect, since it is undertaken by private firms when they believe expansion will pay, and no government body in a capitalist economy can tell a private firm to 'expand – or else'."

The student may wonder why business firms do not try to prevent unemployment since (p. 343) "In a depression, corporations earn less money. They actually earned about $30 billion between 1930 and 1940, whereas, with ... full employment, their profits would have been over $100 billion, ..." But a firm seeks profits; if it makes more profit by hiring fewer men, it hires fewer. And business firms permit private investment to fall because (p. 569) "our economy is relatively atomistic. No one business firm ... does enough investing to guarantee prosperity for the whole economy. ... The decision of one firm to reduce its investment from $200 million a year to $50 million cannot by itself cause depression." So it is not to the businessman's interest to maintain high investment "unless the objective factors were favorable."

Public and foreign investment remain. "Public investment of course is all the government spends for any purpose." And now the full, glorious opportunity bursts upon us, for (p. 513) "Because public investment, unlike private investment, is directly under social control, it is easy to turn on the tap and to turn it off again." "... public investment can be maintained at any rate we please – at $10 billion a year or at $100 billion. The money has to be appropriated by legislative action, and spent; and there is the investment. Thus, we can do as much public investment as we please."

Scrupulously, this text examines all objections, and all evaporate, (p. 529) "It is often alleged that we cannot afford to relieve unemployment because it costs too much to do so." "... it is hard to understand the sense in which the term *costs* is here used. But it is easy to understand that the costs of depression are immense and avoidable, and no economic sacrifice which incidentally makes us all better off is too great if it avoids these costs." Footnote: "There are, of course, very serious political difficulties involved. We may not be able to work out a scheme compatible with our political institutions by which government or private investment could be raised quickly enough. ..."

The public debt (p. 534) "is no problem, for the simple reason that the government controls the Federal Reserve Banks and can always compel them to buy government bonds. Anyone who controls a bank and is free to make the rules under which it operates will have no trouble in borrowing money." The government's credit cannot be exhausted, (p. 535) "Since as a last resource 'it can borrow from itself,' there need be no fear on this account." (p. 541) "There are no grounds for believing that a high public debt destroys the nation's credit or leads to a marked fall in the value of the dollar." When private investment is high, private debt is high; public debt rises when public investment rises, and (p. 519) "Why should it be better to increase the private than the public debt? Unless a clear answer can be given to this question, we may either have to choose between putting up with the problems of increasing debt or putting up with depressions."

Here is one clear answer, Professor Tarshis. There is a limit to debt, fixed by the debtor's ability to pay it. This limit operates on private debt, because private borrowers have no means of compelling lenders to lend them money. And, much more important, when governmental interference leads foolish lenders to lend more than private debtors can repay, they can all go broke – as they did throughout this country in 1793, 1820, 1837, 1857, 1872, 1892, and 1929 – without causing a quiver in the stability of this government. But when governments inflate currency, the governments collapse – as France did in the 1790s and as Russia, Germany, Greece, France have done within your memory, Professor Tarshis. When a government collapses, the result is depression and then some.

Lenin said that the surest way to overturn the basis of a society is to debauch the currency, because this action enlists all economic laws on the side of destruction and does this in a way that not one man in a million will see. Lenin not only said this; he demonstrated it. It seems unfortunate that Professor Tarshis's knowledge of the Russian economy does not include some knowledge of Lenin's economic theory and practice.

The Bolsheviks disintegrated the whole Russian economy and subdued the people to their tyranny by printing quantities of roubles without a "standard." And here is *The Elements of Economics* seriously insisting that we can finance unlimited government spending without taxing or borrowing; we can do it as we now finance our silly purchases of gold (p. 389) "simply by printing money."

You must read this book to see how plausibly and recurrently it presents this idea. We could adopt (p. 635) "a limburger cheese standard." If the government bought all limburger cheese that the world will produce, at a fixed price above costs of production, and paid for the cheese by printing money, "in the mind of this author there is no doubt that such a step would guarantee full employment in this country and indirectly in the world. The policy is obviously absurd, but not because it would fail to give us full employment. ..." Its absurdity is that "after all, our willingness to consume limburger cheese is about equal to our willingness to consume gold." We'd rather have houses, clothing, automobiles, highways, than limburger cheese. But printing money to pay for the 100-millionth ton of limburger cheese would be better than unemployment, for "if some of our workers are employed (no matter how uselessly), our total output of useful products will be higher than if they are out of work."

As to foreign investment, it is American dollars that foreigners spend for American products, (p. 391) "If we could only export one of the printing presses used for the manufacture of Federal Reserve Notes to, say, China, our foreign investment would be enormously higher." The cause of foreign investment is an increase in foreigners' desire to consume; and (p. 632) "naturally when the world propensity to consume increases, investment remaining constant, employment and income for the whole world will rise." An Italian woman wants a vacuum cleaner, but (p. 391) "since we do not empower Italian banks or the Italian government to print American dollars, she can get this currency only from us."

Our foreign loan (p. 632) "is not the initiating factor; it simply makes possible the transmission in our direction of favorable developments initiated in foreign countries." Aside from the familiar higher debt, a foreign loan costs us nothing unless it is repaid, for "since foreign countries ... are not allowed to print United States currency," if they repay a loan "they have fewer dollars left with which to buy our products."

The Elements of Economics was published in May. Columbia University adopted it immediately and is using it now in its Summer School, largely attended by teachers from all States. So far as I could learn, at the end of June this was the incomplete list of colleges that had then adopted it for use this winter:

> Yale University
> Stanford University
> Cornell University
> University of Texas
> Duke University
> Drake University
> Howard University
> University of Arkansas
> United States Coast Guard Academy
> Iowa State College
> Williams College
> Occidental College
> Manchester College
> Oregon State College
> Texas Technological College

The young Americans going to college this fall will be voters in 1950 and 1952. If they create the Central Planning Board presented so plausibly to their imaginations, if they try to solve all economic problems by adopting Lenin's method of overturning the basis of this society, have their parents no responsibility? Have the taxpayers and the rich patrons who support these universities no responsibility for their own property, their liberty, their country, and their children's lives?

Lord Keynes himself seemed troubled by the first results of his theory in practice when he wrote, in his last article before he died, "How much modernist stuff gone wrong and turned sourly and silly is circulating in our system, incongruously mixed, it seems, with age-old poisons."

There are sane economists who have been valiantly fighting these Keynesian fallacies, with little help from the men whose property and lives and countries they are trying to save, and less from politicians. Walter E. Spahr, Professor of Economics in New York University, is one of the few in the universities who openly and vigorously opposes the Keynesians. In his *The Management of Our Monetary System*, he writes:

> Wherever one finds a government dictatorship or an attempt at a governmentally-managed economy in modern times, he also finds a suspension of gold payments and a substitution of an irredeemable paper currency. ... A gold standard is perhaps the most important of the brakes which a people can exercise directly on their government in its management of the public purse. When there is mismanagement, the people present their paper money and government securities for payment in gold. Every individual can thus bring direct pressure to bear upon his government; it is not necessary for him to rely solely upon his representatives in Congress for protection. ...

Dr. Jacques Rueff, formerly Deputy Governor of the Bank of France and Directeur du Mouvement General des Fonds, now of the Institut d'Etudes Politiques, Paris, is equally outspoken. In an article entitled "The Fallacies of Lord Keynes' General Theory," in the May number of the *Quarterly Journal of Economics*, he says:

> "For all those concerned with the future of human society, there are no questions more important than those raised by Lord Keynes' theory, and no duty more pressing than that of passing judgment on the value of the explanations which it offers and the efficacy of the remedies which it suggests."
>
> "I am confident that this (Keynes) policy will not reduce unemployment but that it will have profound consequences upon the countries in which it is applied. Through the economic disasters to which it will give rise, it will re-establish in the world a regime based upon the suppression of all individual liberty."

Too many Americans are thoughtlessly optimistic and therefore easy-going and negligent; too many find an excuse in pessimism for their own laziness and timidity. I will say this: Every American who does not act to stop the teaching of these fallacies and lies in the schools and universities that he supports would be wiser to cut his own throat and thus quietly avoid the consequences that his idleness is bringing upon himself and his children.

The Elements of Economics: An Introduction to the Theory of Price and Employment, by Lorie Tarshis; Edited by Dr. Edgar S. Furniss. Houghton-Mifflin Company, Boston. 687 pp., index. $4.50.

The Fallacies of Lord Keynes' General Theory, by Jacques Rueff; an article in the *Quarterly Journal of Economics* for May. Harvard University Press, Quincy Street, Cambridge, Mass. May number of this magazine, $1.25.

The flyer made for the anti-Tarshis campaign singles out government spending for attack in the first place but closes with Lane's aversion to citizens engaging in political action.

SAVING vs. SPENDING

Which are You?

A NEW COLLEGE TEXTBOOK, *The Elements of Economics,* teaches that *saving* is bad; that *spending* is the secret of prosperity.   Do *you* think this makes sense?   Do you want it taught to your boys and girls?

Houghton Mifflin Co., of Boston, published this book in 1947. Already a score of colleges and universities have adopted it; some have listed it as required freshman reading.

The author, Prof. Lorie Tarshis of Stanford University, scorns saving in any form. "We can *spend* our way into prosperity," he says.

Of course everyone must spend as well as save. Spending is not bad in itself. A man who hoards all he gets, refusing to provide for his family, is not a good citizen. We all need to spend wisely and to save wisely.

But Prof. Tarshis will have none of this. His scorn for saving in any form is unconcealed: "Saving is in essence simply a failure to consume income." (p. 366) "While investment represents a positive activity, saving is a mere absence of activity." (p. 367) To him, "investment" cannot be done by individuals, but only "by business and government units and by foreign buyers." (p. 367) This alone is productive, and the only way individuals can get their money into productive channels is to *spend* it, not *save* it. If they save it, for example

by putting it in a savings bank, their money becomes economically useless. Money saved "can be put in the bank, kept under the mattress, or used to purchase government bonds, corporation securities, a new machine, or a life insurance policy; it is still saving." (p. 365).

If such teaching permeates a generation of American youth, the structure of our society will inevitably be shattered. To those who understand sound economics, Prof. Tarshis' teaching is both stupid and silly. But that does not make it less dangerous. If enough people can be persuaded to believe it and act upon it, the damage will be done. Unnecessary government expenditures will reach new, towering heights. Private savings will sink to an all time low.

Says Rose Wilder Lane: *"The Elements of Economics* plays upon fear, shame, pity, greed, idealism, hope, to urge young Americans to act upon this theory *as citizens.* This is not an economics text at all; it is a pagan-religious and political tract. It inspires an irrational faith and spurs it to political action." (*Economic Council Review of Books,* Aug., 1947).

SHOULD WE SIT IDLY BY, or should we oppose such teachings, NOW, before they have spread too far?

NATIONAL ECONOMIC COUNCIL, INC.

Suite 7501, Empire State Building,   New York 1, N. Y.

Two copies of this leaflet sent free to any address. 10 for 25c, 50 for $1, 1,000 for $10.

Flyer.

The campaign seems to have been most effective when it involved someone with influence in the community. Not surprisingly, the campaign encountered a good deal of opposition from universities who were in no mood to be told by those without visible credentials or even worse, featured in "Carlson's" *Plotters*, what texts they should or should not use. Here is perhaps the most interesting exchange in the Merwin Hart file of the Tarshis controversy. Frank Gannett as a newspaper publisher was enormously important in upstate New York. The provost of Cornell University wrote back to Gannett, a letter that drew a lengthy response from Lane.

The most surprising assertion is contained in the last full paragraph of the second page of Lane's response. When asked to justify her assertions, she replies this way:

> In so far as Provost Adams's letter is derogatory to me and to my review of this book, while I would not want to print this without Professor Schumpeter's express permission I think I may say that he read the review and expressed even enthusiastic concurrence with it as an accurate appraisal from a non-technical point of view. He said that he himself would not use its phraseology but he thought it even remarkably accurate as a fair and unbiased judgment of the book by one who is not a trained economist. Professor Joseph Schumpeter of Harvard has perhaps the highest standing among economists in this country and Europe.

We learn from correspondence with Arthur Diamond that the Harvard archive does have a letter from Schumpeter to Lane, but it is much later than the one she reports. Diamond tells us that he did not encounter the letter to which she is referring.

We begin with the letter from the provost to Gannett who passed on the Hart–Lane objections. This is followed by Lane's response to the provost by way of a memo to Gannett.

CORNELL UNIVERSITY
Ithaca, New York
Office of the Provost
October 22, 1947

Mr. Frank Gannett
Times-Union Building
Rochester 4, New York

Dear Mr. Gannett:

Upon receiving your inquiry, transmitted to us by Mr. Stutz, concerning the economics text by Tarshis currently in use at Cornell, we undertook to explore this entire situation. We now have reports from faculty members, summaries of discussions regarding the book and the methods of instruction in the elementary economics courses, and analyses of the several texts used concurrently. The facts of the case are summarized as follows:

Three textbooks are used in the elementary course in economics. They represent three different approaches to the subject.

Tarshis, ELEMENTS OF ECONOMICS, presents an analysis of employment and national income from the Keynesian point of view. The remainder of the book is in the main orthodox and no different in perspective and emphasis than any other general text.

Benham and Boddy, PRINCIPLES OF ECONOMICS, adheres to the orthodox tradition and is in direct contrast to the Keynesian viewpoint which colors part of the Tarshis text.

Hicks and Hart, THE SOCIAL FRAMEWORK OF THE AMERICAN ECONOMY, is strictly technical and does not mention any issues currently in controversy.

There are two underlying reasons why Tarshis was adopted as one of three texts. First, the book throughout is superior in readability and clarity, and as most of it is not concerned with controversial issues, this literary superiority weighed heavily in its favor. Second, the work of Keynes has introduced into the study of economics so many ideas and terms, which are used with increasing frequency even by those who disagree with his doctrine, that no modern course can omit them. Consequently, Tarshis' exposition of the Keynes doctrine was regarded as a merit, even though no permanent member of the Economics Department of Cornell shares that viewpoint. The young men and women who are now studying economics will someday be confronted with versions of this doctrine, in conversations, in editorials, and possibly even as political issues. It would be doing them a disservice to withhold ideas which are a part of current economic thought and to fail to train them in the ability to form and defend their own judgments. For this reason, classes

68   DAVID M. LEVY ET AL.

in elementary economics at Cornell are conducted as discussions with emphasis placed on enabling the student to weigh facts intelligently, to reason cogently, and to draw conclusions rationally on economic issues.

In another elementary course which is limited to one semester, the same approach is used. Because there is insufficient time to read more than one text and the others are too short, Tarshis is the only adopted text. That part of the book under question is dealt with briefly, for the students are asked to read only the summary chapters at the end of the sections which express the Keynesian viewpoint. Also, the restrictions of the book are carefully indicated, and the other side of the issue is presented in the classroom and through supplementary library readings.

The "service" course for engineers does not use Tarshis at all.

In certain respects, the Tarshis book represents a strictly Keynesian approach to current economic problems. This is clearly pointed out to the students and is offset by full exposition of the Classical doctrine. The review carried by the *Economic Council Review of Books* is written from a bias so extreme that few economists would agree with it. One of the several illustrations of this is its statement in italics: "It is always governmental action that produces and prolongs poverty." The review again and again quotes statements from the book divorced from their contexts with the result that the meaning of the author is distorted. While Tarshis states the advantages and disadvantages of free enterprise as he sees them, the review quotes him only on the disadvantages. Moreover, the review imputes statements to Tarshis which cannot be found in his book. No reputable economist would ever make such a statement as: "That is to say that the money must be spent before it is earned, that goods must be consumed to produce them." Nor does Tarshis say, as the review asserts, that corporations own patents to suppress them, that inventions eliminate jobs and starve workmen, or that advertising is economic waste. If the book were in any sense the kind of book that is portrayed in the review, it would never have been adopted as a text at Cornell or by any of the other distinguished institutions which are using it. A list of these is enclosed for your interest.

I hope the results of this inquiry will reassure you that the matter is fully in hand. I shall be glad to answer any further questions you may have in regard to it.

                                   Sincerely,

                                       s/

                                Arthur S. Adams
                                    Provost
a/m
Enclosure
Carbon copy to: Mr. Harry Stutz

[Memo of Rose Wilder Lane on Provost Adams' Letter of October 22, 1947, to Mr. Frank E. Gannett]

Danbury, Conn.

Provost Adams says that "the remainder of the Tarshis textbook – i.e., all except Part Four, which means all that part dealing with business firms, their determinations of output and profit-motive control of prices, and the comparisons between the American and Soviet economies –" is in the main orthodox and no different in perspective and emphasis than any other general text, and that most of this textbook "is not concerned with controversial issues." As regards textbooks at present, I think this statement is sufficiently accurate. Of course, the issue between free and collectivist economies, and classical and collectivism economic theory, is actually the one paramount issue today, but textbooks do generally present only the collectivist view. Doubtless, Provost Adams is sincerely ignorant that there is any other.

I agree wholly and emphatically with Provost Adams' view that no ideas should be withheld from students, that they should be made acquainted with all economic theories, including the Keynesian, and that the object of a university should be, as Provost Adams writes, "to train them in the ability to form and defend their own judgments."

This is precisely the ground for my primary objection to the use of such textbook as THE ELEMENTS OF ECONOMICS by Professor Tarshis. In order to train students in an ability to form and defend their own judgments, it is essential that their instructors and their textbooks distinguish between fact and opinion. It is not possible to have any opinion about a fact unless the fact itself is known. To judge between various and opposing opinions about a fact, it is absolutely necessary to know the fact that these opinions are about. Therefore, none of the many textbooks that make statements contrary to known and established facts should ever be adopted and used as reliable texts in universities.

Students of astronomy are not taught the pre-Copernican theory that the flat earth is the center of the universe and that sun, moon and stars revolve around it. Students of chemistry are not taught that the four elements are earth, air, fire and water. Students of economies should not be taught statements equally known to be false, about the American economy. To cite only one of many examples from the Elements of Economics by Professor Tarshis, "A century ago, our economy could not have severe depressions." This is not an expression of opinion, bat a false statement purporting to be a statement of fact. It is an unquestioned and unquestionable fact that the depression of 1854–1857 was the most severe depression in the history of the United States, a depression relatively worse, of course, than that of 1928–1932. And this is only one of many such false statements in this textbook.

Certainly, it is important that students hear every variety of opinion, and form their own. But when they are given false statements concerning facts, they have no means of judging the value of opinions, nor of forming any valid opinions of their own. Nobody alive in universities today was alive a century ago. Students must learn *the facts* about the American economy of a century ago either from textbooks or from instructors who have learned the facts from records, or the students can have no means of having any opinion about (for example) Professor Tarshis' view of the American economy.

It seems to me essential that responsible heads of departments in universities be able to distinguish between statements of fact, and expressions of opinion about fact, and that they do not adopt textbooks that contain obvious falsifications of facts about which there is no question. There are wide divergencies of opinion, all interesting and a number equally plausible, about the early discoveries of this continent, but I do not think there is any justification whatever for teaching students that Queen Elizabeth discovered it in 1862 [sic; i.e., 1526]. There is a wide variety of economic theories, and I think that students should be informed of all of them, but I do not think there is any justification for teaching them that there "could not be" severe depressions a century ago, or that increased demand causes business firms to reduce output and raise prices, or that the adoption of an invention increases employment but the use of the invention decreases employment. *Do the Cornell students who are studying Professor Tarshis's ELEMENTS OF ECONOMICS know the simple history of the American economy? do they have an outline of the unquestionable historical facts?* Will Provost Adams please give titles and authors of textbooks used in teaching these facts?

Two schools of basic economic theory, and practice, are opposed in the world; today the collectivist and the individualist. Nothing is more important than giving young Americans an understanding of "ideas which are a part of current, economic thought," as Provost Adams says. I heartily approve the unbiased exposition to them of both points of view.

Does Cornell use in its economics courses, on the one hand, the works of Proudhon, St. Simon, Ricardo, Marx, Lenin and, on the other, those of Bastiat, Say, Locke, Mill, Carey? For a statement of the two views, does Cornell use Haney's HISTORY OF ECONOMIC THOUGHT? or an equivalent text, if there is one (I am no economist) and if there is one, what is its title and who is the author? As an opposite to the Keynesian economics, does Cornell use the works of the Austrian school, such as Menger's and Boehm-Bawerk's or whose? Does Cornell require its economics students to be familiar with the works of the co-founder and first President of Cornell, Dr. Andrew Dickson White? In what economics courses is Dr. White's FIAT MONEY INFLATION IN FRANCE, for example, required reading? If clarity and readability are desirable, and

I think they are, this little book by Dr. White is unsurpassed in the field of economics.

THE ELEMENTS OF ECONOMICS by Professor Tarshis is collectivist throughout. Its whole treatment is a treatment of a non-existent entity, a collectivist concept, called "our economy." An unstated, taken-for-granted assumption has a much more powerful effect upon the mind then an overt statement subject to question and challenge and the assumption throughout this textbook is the Hegelian–Marxian assumption that State and Society are identical and that this entity is the economic entity of which business firms and individuals are merely components, the "pieces of the jigsaw puzzle." This book is not an economics text, it is a political treatise. Without exception, every action suggested or advocated in it is a Federal political action.

So far from its being "a full exposition of the classical doctrine," I do not find in it a single presentation of classical economic theory, and personally I shall be obliged if Provost Adams will point out one to me.

In so far as Provost Adams's letter is derogatory to me and to my review of this book, while I would not want to print this without Professor Schumpeter's express permission, I think I may say that he read the review and expressed even enthusiastic concurrence with it as an accurate appraisal from a non-technical point of view. He said that he himself would not use its phraseology but he thought it even remarkably accurate as a fair and unbiased judgment of the book by one who is not a trained economist. Professor Joseph Schumpeter of Harvard has perhaps the highest standing among economists in this country and Europe.

Provost Adams is quite correct, however, in saying that "few economists" will agree with my review of Professor Tarshis's book; few economists today are not Keynesians. Dr. Walter E. Spahr (quoted in the *Review*) and Dr. Anderson of the University of California in Los Angeles are among outstanding economists who aren't.

I haven't a copy of the Tarshis text here. Anyone can find in the places I marked, however, the passages supporting my statements that it says that corporations own patents to suppress them, that inventions eliminate jobs (the reference to starving workingmen is something to the effect that starving workmen whom the machines had thrown out of jobs did not see the value of machines) and that advertising is economic waste (advertising is a sign of the absence of competition where competition per se no longer exists, business firms compete in advertising.)

Evidently Provost Adams has not read the book. It might be interesting to ask him how carefully he has read it. Unless he has read it attentively, he can hardly say that quotations from it misrepresent it.

Speaking in general, nobody reads textbooks – except the hapless students and their direct instructors, who have nothing to do with adopting the books – the normal procedure is this. A college textbook must be written by an employed Professor able to insure the adoption of the book by his university (high school texts, ditto for high school textbooks by college Professors, are not used in high schools.) A more desirable book is a collaboration by two Professors in different colleges, insure adoption by both a still more desirable one is edited by still a third Professor in a third university. The editor does not read the book. I know of nobody who supposes that Dean Furniss even sees the textbook he "edits" and signs eulogistic prefaces for; I am told that his prefaces to anti-Keynesian texts are as enthusiastic as the one he signed for Professor Tarshis's. The editor gets a percentage of royalties in return for the use of his name, and influence in his university. The publisher does not read the book; he publishes it on the strength of its writers' academic support of it. The salesmen of course do not read it. The professors who adopt it do not read it; they adopt it because other universities have done so; every adoption enhances the book's prestige and weighs in favor of farther adoption – as Provost Adams shows by offering the list of adoptions as proof of the book's value. Such a list would have some worth as evidence if the men who adopt textbooks read them and approved their contents, but they don't. If you will investigate, you will find that this is true. Undoubtedly there are exceptions, though I know of none myself, but I have described the ordinary, general, accepted procedure in the book trade and the universities. Who adopted the Tarshis textbook for Cornell? and did he read it BEFORE he adopted it? It would be perhaps a good idea to hear direct from him, whoever he is.

LANE AND von MISES ON *HUMAN ACTION*

We return two years later to the second round of the Lane–von Mises discussion prompted by her review of *Human Action*. *Human Action*, as von Mises takes pains to emphasize, is an exercise in value-free economic science. When their old disagreement comes up, von Mises emphasizes that his support of democracy is "in my capacity as a private citizen and voter." That word "citizen," which features so centrally in Lane's review of Tarshis's book and in Hart's campaign against the text, must certainly have made her heart beat faster.

September 26, 1949

My dear Professor Mises,

Should you read my review of HUMAN ACTION, which the New York office of the National Economic Council doubtless will mail to you in its customary routine, would you please accept my apology for the incredible error in the spelling of "praxeology" as "praxiology"? Somebody somewhere in the intricacies of the printing trade, with all the kindness of superiority, is always correcting the style and the spelling of mere writers, as I'm sure you know. In this instance, the unknown authority has corrected both your spelling and mine. I shall correct it back again in the next NEC Review of Books,

Yours sincerely,

Rose Wilder Lane/ASL

[*Economic Council Review of Books,* Vol. VI, No. 10, October 1949]

One comparison probably will occur to every reader of *Human Action: A Treatise in [sic] Economics*, the new book by Ludwig von Mises. The comparison is with another book by a German refugee in a foreign country, published eighty years ago, another work of abstract thought beyond any popular comprehension, its publication known to only a few scholars and interesting few of them, a book that 200 persons bought during its first year and no more than a few thousand have read yet, the book that has wrecked the Old World and now threatens the safety of everyone alive. I mean of course the book that expressed, inspired and still animates the reactionary movement in modern world history: *Das Kapital,* by Karl Marx.

The comparison is between antagonists. *Human Action* is, at last, the intellectual annihilation of the Marxian fallacy. This book is intellectual leadership of the World Revolution. Its relation to Adam Smith and Jefferson is Marx's relation to Saint Simon and Fourier. I think that *Human Action* is unquestionably the most powerful product of the human mind in our time, and I believe it will change human life for the better during the coming centuries as profoundly as Marxism has changed all our lives for the worse in this century.

Human action makes the human world what it is, at any time. Every person's smallest act is shaped by his mind's view of truth, of reality. (When people thought that tomatoes were poison, they did not eat tomatoes; when they thought that men could not go underneath the flat earth, nobody went around the round earth. So long as men think that they are not endowed with liberty, they will obey orders, act as slaves, and create tyrants.) Our acts *originate* in needs and desires; we act *according* to our thought. Human acts make all relationships between persons, and these relationships of persons to each other make the conditions in which everyone lives, for the complex of these relationships is human society, the human world on this planet.

Nothing but a change in thinking can change the individual's acting, and nothing but a change in the individual's acting can change the conditions of human living.

Because thinking is a function of the human mind which, with human life, exists only in the individual person, every change in thinking begins in one person's mind. It is a rare mind that discovers a truth until then unknown, thus increasing human knowledge of reality and making it possible for others to live more reasonably; i.e., to make real "social gains" and truly to "improve social conditions." Most of us, at best, use second-hand thought; nearly always we act according to old, taken-for-granted views of reality that we don't think about at all. A century ago I never would have imagined eating a tomato.

So let us not underestimate the power of a great work of original thought, such as *Human Action*. This is the first major work in a new science: praxeology, the *science* of human action.

Readers of this Review have seen my feeble yipping that nobody knows the principles of human relationships. I have complained that as yet we have only the Bible's Eleven [*sic*] Commandments, orders which it is obviously expedient to obey; and, since obeying them is expedient, they must rest on principles which exist and operate in human action, as actually as the principles of physics operate in lifeless mechanical action. But (I protested) nobody has discovered those moral principles; nobody knows what they are.

Marxism's basic appeal to the hordes of pseudo-intellectuals and socialists called "economists" is the claim that the Marxian view of human affairs is scientific. Without questioning this manifest absurdity, its believers are acting according to Marxism and destroying humanity. The real scientists say nothing. The theologians say that suffering purifies the soul. And the suffering multitudes struggle blindly, with no notion of how to make this world what they want it to be.

In this intolerable situation, there is a cry for a "return to religion." I do not think that people have ever left religion. But the churches offer, at worst, magical formulas and Freudian theories; and at best they demand meek obedience to Divine Authority as stated by, or vested in, churchmen. It is not easy to believe that churchmen are infallible.

Unquestionably, all expedient, efficient, rewarding human action on this earth must conform to what men can only call the will of God. Human beings do not make the principles operating in this world; men must discover them. Men could not make a telephone until they began to discover the principles of electronics, or kerosene – much less gasoline – until they began to discover the principles of chemistry, nor a wheel until they discovered the simplest principle of mechanics. How then (I asked) can men make a human world that will work to the ends they desire, until they begin to discover the principles of human relationships? – those surely existing but not known principles of morality.

So far as I knew, nobody was trying to discover them. My ignorance was baffled by the first problem, that of method: How to begin a scientific study of human action, a subject that cannot be isolated and examined in rigidly defined conditions? It seemed that I couldn't even say to scientists what I meant. My utmost effort brought from America's greatest physicist the generous but wildly irrelevant reply that today most scientists believe in God. (Of course.) I had never heard of praxiology. Have you?

If you know more about this new science than I did, and if I have been boring you, I can promise that *Human Action* will be a dazzling and exciting revelation to you. For three months, I have been absorbed night and day in this book; I find it the strongest stimulant to thinking that I have got from print. It opens a whole new world to human thought.

Professor Mises, you know, is the founder and leader of the group of economists known as the "Austrian school." He and his pupils (Freidrich [*sic*] Hayek among them) are developing the science that Adam Smith, Cobden, Bastiat began a century ago and that the socialist reactionaries quickly embalmed, as Professor Bonn observed. The Austrian school revived scientific economics, and Professor Mises leads its development into praxiology, the new science of human action.

"Economics is the youngest of all sciences," he begins. "In the last two hundred years, it is true, many new sciences have emerged from the disciplines familiar to the ancient Greeks. However, what happened ... was merely that ... the field of study was more nicely subdivided and treated with new methods. ... The field itself was not expanded. But economics opened to human science a domain previously inaccessible and never thought of. The discovery of a regularity and interdependence of market phenomena went beyond the limits of the traditional system of learning. It conveyed knowledge which could be regarded neither as logic, mathematics, psychology, physics, nor biology. "Philosophers had long been eager to ascertain the ends which God or Nature was trying to realize in the course of human history. They searched for the law of mankind's destiny and evolution. But [they] failed utterly in these endeavors because they were committed to a faulty method. They dealt with humanity as a whole, or with other holistic concepts like nation, race, or church. They set up quite arbitrarily the ends to which the behavior of such wholes is bound to lead. But they could not satisfactorily [*sic*] answer the question regarding what factors compelled the various acting individuals to behave in such a way that the goal aimed at by the whole's inexorable evolution was attained. They had recourse to desperate shifts; miraculous intervention of the Deity either by revelation or by the delegation of God-sent prophets and consecrated leaders, pre-established harmony, predestination, or the operation of a mystic and fabulous 'world soul' or 'national soul'. Others spoke of a 'cunning of nature' which implanted in man impulses driving him unwittingly along precisely the path Nature wanted him to take."

"Other philosophers ... looked at things from the viewpoint of government ... [and] drew ambitious plans for a thorough reform and reconstruction of society. ... All were fully convinced that there was in the course of social events no such regularity and invariance of phenomena as had already been found in human reasoning and in the sequence of natural phenomena. They did not search for the laws of social cooperation because they thought that man could organize society as he pleased. ... If their utopias proved unrealizable, the fault was seen in the moral nature of man. ... What was needed to construct the ideal society, they thought, was good princes and virtuous citizens. With righteous men any utopia could be realized."

"The discovery of the inescapable interdependence of market phenomena overthrew this opinion. Bewildered, people had to face a new view of society. ... In the course of social events there prevails a regularity of phenomena to which man must adjust his action if he wishes to succeed. ... One must study the laws of human action and social cooperation as the physicist studies the laws of nature."

"Out of the political economy of the classical school emerges the general theory of human action, praxiology. The economic problems are embedded in a more general science ... Economics becomes a part, although the hitherto best elaborated part, of a more universal science, praxiology."

Surely anyone sees that here is a stupendous leap-forward in human thought. To imagine now what it means to the future is impossible. Everyone knows the transformation that increasing knowledge of the principles of the so-called "natural sciences" has made in the conditions of living. With such scientific knowledge of the principles operating in the relationships of persons to each other – think of it.

Human Action describes the method of this new science. This is the first appearance of scientific method in this field; that is, in the fields named economics, politics, morals, sociology, all the categories into which thinkers have divided the (in living experience, indivisible) complex of human activities. All the so-called "social sciences," all the sociologists, all the socialists called "economists" in all the universities and business and government jobs, thousands of college courses, tens of thousands of books in libraries and pouring from the presses, all are dealing with dreams and fantasies; the cold fact is that their so-called "science" has, literally, no scientific method. *Human Action* places them all with the medieval alchemists and Africa's Mumbo-Jumbo.

This book is a cataclysm. It would be folly to expect the academic world and its hangers-on to welcome this with salvos of applause.

After sketching the historical background and firmly establishing the philosophical and scientific bases of praxiology, after considering the problem of method and brilliantly solving it, *Human Action* applies the method chiefly to human economic action. Here are the praxiological analyses of production, exchange, the essential function of the promoter, speculator, entrepreneur (scientifically demonstrating the impossibility of socialist economy, so often demonstrated by history) prices, work and wages, money, credit, governmental economic action, war economy, and much more.

In all this I find only one brief passage that seems to me irrational. The whole work rests on individual action controlled by the acting individual; the market phenomena analyzed are those of the free market; indeed the analysis of economic calculation shows (again concurring with historical experience) that the only possible market is the free market. Yet, glancing at the political field of action, Professor Mises seems to say that action controlled by the acting individual is impossible. "The alternatives to the liberal and democratic principle of *majority rule* are the militarist principle of armed conflict and dictatorial oppression." Well, "rule" might mean the directing power of the free actions of a majority, as of consumers in the free market. But "He who uses his might to run the state, i.e., the social apparatus of coercion and compulsion, rules. Rule is the exercise of might in the political body. Rule is always based upon might, i.e. the power to *direct other people's actions* (My italics.)

If the alternative to a dictator's directing my action is its being directed by a majority of other persons, how can my own choice direct my action? How is a free market possible? And what becomes of the science of praxiology?

There is a third alternative: the American principle. The American political principle is not majority rule; it is the reduction and limitation of the *power to rule*, by means of the State's structure. Europeans have wrecked Europe by their inability to escape from the holistic concept of a ruled society. I hope that, for future editions of this certainly long-living book, Professor Mises may reconsider the praxiological view of human political action.

Human Action is the summation of a lifetime of great original thought held strictly to scientific discipline. I can give you no adequate impression of its scope, its brilliance, its values. The bits I have quoted will indicate the clarity of the writing. This is a book for thinkers; not difficult to read and not to be read without concentrated attention and ample time, it is for readers who delight in the precision and truth of abstract thought.

I rank *Human Action* with Rousseau's *Contrat Social*, Adam Smith's *Wealth of Nations*, Marx's *Das Kapital*, Darwin's *Origin of Species* as a force in human life. I think that this book begins and will stand for a new epoch in human thought, therefore in human action and world history.

R 4, Box 42
Danbury, Connecticut

October 4, 1949

My dear Professor Mises,

Would you and Mrs. Mises be guests of Mr. and Mrs. J. Howard Pew at the dinner welcoming Mr. and Mrs. Cecil Palmer, in the Sert Room of the Waldorf at 7:15 p.m., Wednesady [sic], October 26?

Mr. Pew has just returned from an extensive trip in South America and, overwhelmed with accumulated work, he has asked me to invite his guests for this evening. During his journey he read HUMAN ACTION and wrote me expressing his great enthusiasm. He is one of the few Americans who has realized for years the lack of intellectual opposition to collectivism and the increasingly urgent need for it; therefore, his understanding of HUMAN ACTION and his gratitude for it are unusual among Big Business men. I know that he will be more than delighted if you and Mrs. Mises will accept his hospitality at this dinner.

I hope that you may overlook the informal manner of this invitation and permit me to give Mr. Pew the pleasure of anticipating your company at his table. I should hardly have ventured to be so informal if Mr. Herbert Cornuelle had not encouraged me; he assures me that you will not mind these American ways. Until I hear from you I shall be hoping that he is right, and hoping that you and Mrs. Mises will accept this invitation. In that case, the New York office of the National Economic Council will send you the cards of admission and make the table reservations.

With all good wishes and again my applause and thanks for HUMAN ACTION,

Yours sincerely,

Rose Wilder Lane/ASL

October 7, 1949

Mrs. Rose Wilder Lane
R 4, Box 42
Danbury, Conn.

Dear Mrs. Lane;

I want to express to you my sincere thanks for your splendid review of *"Human Action."* I know that in some points there prevails a difference between your opinions and mine. The more do I appreciate the flattering observations you made in your article.

Mrs. Mises and I gladly accept Mr. Pew's and your invitation for the dinner welcoming Mr. and Mrs. Cecil Palmer.

Thanking you again for your fine article, your kind letter and the invitation.

Sincerely yours,

R 4, Box 42
Danbury, Connecticut

October 10, 1949

My dear Professor Mises,

Thank you for your note. I am glad, as I know Mr. Pew will be, that you and Mrs. Mises accept his invitation to the dinner for Mr. and Mrs. Cecil Palmer. Mr. Pew's office will send you the tickets.

The other guests at the table will be:

Mr. and Mrs. Herbert S. Chase. Mr. Chase is Vice-President and effective head of William Woods College, Fulton, Missouri. This is the college at which Churchill made his first open break with the Soviet regime, his "iron curtain" speech.

Mr. and Mrs. George Koether, whom you may know. Mr. Koether was with Leonard Read's Foundation for a time; is now an editor of *The Architectural Forum*.

Roger MacBride and his "best date," not known to me. Roger is a Princeton sophomore, son of Burt MacBride, senior editor of *Reader's Digest*. A youngster valiantly battling all Princeton odds in his effort to be intelligently (as well as emotionally) an anti-socialist liberal.

****

It pleases me very much, of course, to know that my review of HUMAN ACTION pleased you. But, again of course, there is no occasion for thanks. The opportunity to express my honest opinion of a book frankly in print is its own reward.

I wish that I might have an opportunity to make some slight claim upon you, for if that were possible I would exaggerate it and ask you to explain your advocacy of democracy for my own enlightenment and that of other American liberals. Your books endorse democracy without giving your basis for this position.

Perhaps you do not fully understand the perplexity that this causes. The effective intrusion of democracy into the American Federal structure has occurred so recently that it is within my own adult experience. The 20th-century amendments to the Federal Constitution, introducing democracy, appear to American liberals to be the essential basis of the present disastrous condition of interventionism, leading toward total socialization here. It is incomprehensible to us that the author of OMNIPOTENT GOVERNMENT and HUMAN ACTION opposes socialism while advocating democracy, which in our theory and in our experience is the basis and source of socialism. An analogy would be your having read, in Europe in 1930, comparable works by an American liberal demolishing Marxism but approving the National Socialist party. Such a self-contradiction in your thinking cannot actually exist; that is inconceivable to a reader of your work. But its apparent existence, our inability to explain it, and the absence of an explanation from you cause a confusion in our minds with which we are unable to cope at all.

In view of the great body of your work, it seems that there cannot be, in fact, such a fundamental and irreconcilable opposition between us in political philosophy as there seems to be. It will be a most useful service not only to me but to a number of your other [added by hand] American admirers and, may I say? disciples, if some day you will explain your position as an advocate of democracy.

With all good wishes,
                              Yours sincerely,

                         Rose Wilder Lane/ASL

October 15, 1949

Dear Mrs. Lane;

Thank you very much for your kind letter of October 10.

May I add a few observations concerning the difference in our respective opinions.

First of all I want to emphasise that my books do not "endorse democracy." In my capacity as an author of theoretical books, I abstain from the expression of any judgments of value. I merely try to point out why all those who "prefer life to death, health to sickness, nourishment to starvation, abundance to poverty" must endorse democracy if they want to attain their ends (p. 154, first and second paragraph). As I myself too belong to this group of people, I endorse democracy in my capacity as a private citizen and voter.

You say you miss in my book "the basis for this position." Please read: page 149, last paragraph, until the bottom of page 153.

Then please read the second and third paragraph of section 2 of the XXXVII Chapter (p. 859).

Whether there is a majority rule (democracy) or minority rule, in the long run the conduct of government affairs will always be guided by public opinion. What is needed to defeat socialism and interventionism is not to change the system of government, but to change public opinion by persuasion. The factor that ultimately determines the course of events is ideas, not constitutional provisions.

One of the arguments advanced against socialism is precisely that socialism and democracy are incompatible and that the realization of the socialist scheme must necessarily abolish democracy. As conditions are today, hardly any other antisocialist argument has such a convincing power with the voters in this country. In fighting democracy, supporters of freedom deprive themselves of a very powerful weapon and thus undermine their own positions.

In asserting that the effective intrusion of democracy into the American Federal structure occurred only recently in the twentieth century, you are, it seems to me, at variance with the terminology used by most authors. Think of Tocqueville. Or read the following words from the book of Ch. E. Merriam, *A History of American Political Theories*, first published *1903*;

"down to the present time ... the tendency of American political theory and practice must be regarded as essentially democratic." (page 343 of the 1924 edition.)

With all good wishes.

Yours sincerely

R 4, Box 42
Danbury, Connecticut
October 19, 1949

My dear Professor Mises,

It is generous of you to have replied to my protest, and I venture most diffidently to intrude again upon your time and attention, knowing that there are better uses for them than prolonging this correspondence. But I hope that I may try once more to state my view, since evidently I failed to express it to you.

(Of course, the factor that determines events is ideas. This is the reason why your work is vitally important and an error in it, if there be one, equally disastrous.)

HUMAN ACTION states categorically that there is no alternative to "rule." When "the power to direct other people's actions" by means of "the social apparatus of coercion and compulsion" exists, this power cannot be exercised by a majority. Madison, among others, explains this fact in No. 10 of *The Federalist Papers*, in the passage ending (I quote approximately, from memory) "History shows that ... democracies are as short in their lives as violent in their deaths."

It is, however, of no importance whether a few or many persons "rule." Numbers have no relation to or connection with this subject. It is the existence of "the power to direct other people's actions" by means of physical force used by persons upon persons, that is in question.

Where this power exists, it seems evident to me that a free market cannot exist. If I read your work correctly – as coinciding with my own view – a free market is directed by the uncoerced, not compelled, actions of individual persons, each of whom controls his own action according to his own choice, his choice being determined by his personal judgement of value. Praxeology, as I understand it, enlarges this narrow "economic" or catalytic view to cover all relationships between persons, that is, to include not only a free market but a free society.

The logical (and therefore practical) difficulty seems to be in reconciling a free society, including a free market, with the evident necessity existing among human beings for some use of force by persons upon other persons. A wholly free society is Stateless anarchy. A State is the "social apparatus of coercion and compulsion" which, if it is "rule, the power to direct other people's actions," controls a coerced, compelled, not free society.

A statement that the alternative to totalitarian State "rule" is majority "rule" is, 1, not a statement of an alternative, 2, not logically correct, 3, not historically correct.

Logically, the alternative to "rule" is absence of "rule," i.e., anarchy.

Historically, Americans devised a way out of this ancient dilemma. From their basic view of the nature of man (and from their practical experience), they formed a new concept of the State and therefore created a new form of the State, too clumsily expressed described [added in pencil, eds.], by "a government of Law, not of man."

The records are fragmentary and scattered, but in the historical source material you will find that the compelling reason for the work of the Constitutional Convention was the necessity of preventing democracy, on the one hand, and a relapse into monarchy, on the other hand. Democracy was the danger most feared. It was threatening in both Massachusetts and Virginia, in armed revolts of the illiterate and in Rousseau's influence among intellectuals. The incomparable political achievement of the Convention is the *structure* of the federation and the Federal government in a form (evident to any discerning reader) which makes both democracy and monarchy impossible by making a power to "rule" impossible.

The methods used to prevent and obstruct majority rule are notable here. In connection with the permitted direct election of members of the House, observe that qualification of voters is determined by State legislatures, remember that there was a property-qualification then in effect in the thirteen States, and note that taxation and spending of public funds is in the hands of members of the House who are elected bi-annually. The object is to keep control of taxation and of the use of public funds in the hands of property-owners; i.e., to protect the individual's natural right of ownership (a basic tenet of the Revolution) from encroachment by the State. This is not and was not intended to be majority rule. It is the nearest approach to majority rule that the political structure permitted.

Simply reading the Federal Constitution shows, even dramatically, that the idea of democracy has assailed this government only recently, and that democracy in practice has been made possible here only by so amending the Constitution as to destroy this political structure and defeat the purpose of its makers. The same fact is evident when, with much more labor, you read the State Constitutions, some 260 in number since the early 1800s.

Historical experience here is interesting, also, and apropos. Excepting the 13 colonies, each of these States has been made deliberately and peacefully, by agreement and co-operation, from a condition of anarchy. Local history varies enormously of course, but the essential pattern of action is the same in all. The State (as town, county, territorial "government") appeared as division of labor, as the specialization of function naturally arising from natural human co-operativeness. It was made for convenience and efficiency. The settlers live in anarchy. They co-operate in housebuilding, harvesting, hunting, defense against Indians. Criminals appear; the others co-operate against them, as Vigilance Committees. Population increases, work increases, criminals multiply, the Vigilantes are ineffective, themselves lawless and sometimes criminal. To settle the whole problem, to get rid of it, the settlers meet, "set up a government," elect a sheriff and a "justice of the peace." That is all; it is all they want and all they need. The sheriff's function is to protect them against the occasional Bad Man; the Justice's function is to keep the Sheriff from being Bad.

All the others go on about their business. They do not direct the sheriff's actions; nobody imagines his directing theirs. They do not even make laws; they assume that everyone knows that robbery, murder, assault, arson, are "bad." However dimly, they have a true concept of law, as natural principles existing in reality, not man-made. I myself have never found the word or the idea "democracy" in these early records.

Bastiat, in La Loi, expresses with some incoherence this same concept of the State, as being the individual's natural right to use force in his own self-defence, delegated by the individual to the public official; and therefore being a right to act *only* in defense of the individual's life, liberty and property against aggressors upon them.

I offer this view for your consideration: In relationships between persons (society), some actual or potential use of physical force by persons upon persons is essential, for the reason that a minority of persons use force to invade others' rights: life, liberty, ownership. The State is a group of persons having the legal (recognized; institutional) monopoly of the use of physical force by persons upon persons. It is essentially a division of labor, specialization, arising from natural human co-operation, and serving efficiency.

The individual being endowed with (naturally possessing) the powers or functions of life, liberty (self-control, responsibility) and ownership (possession, use and disposal, responsibility for use and disposal, of material things), he himself controls, directs, his own action; always, in all circumstances. He acts in accordance with his own choice, determined by his judgement of value in the given circumstances. (He is not responsible for circumstances which he cannot control; but in *any* circumstances he controls his own action, by his choice, determined by his value-judgement.) Therefore, a use of external physical force upon him *cannot* control, direct, his action. It can hinder, stop, or present his acting.

All State action, therefore, hinders, stops or prevents the actions of individuals in their relationships to each other (in society). Since the State is a use, actual or potential, of physical force by persons upon persons, its action inhibits or prevents the individual's acting according to his own choice determined by his value-judgement; since value-judgement and choice are the incentives to his action, such inhibition "discourages" his acting at all.

The State's attempt to "rule, to direct other people's actions," is *always* a prohibition and prevention of action. A State's permission to act is always a prevention of action, enforced by police power. ... To enter this country, a person must obtain a visa. This fact prevents the entry to this country of all persons to whom visas are not granted. An Englishman must have State permission to buy an egg; this prevents all other persons desiring eggs from buying them. Persons must have a licence to marry; this prevents marriages of various kinds in various places.

Since State action is always inhibiting – hindering, stopping, preventing – individual action, it seems to me obvious that the only correct State action is action to stop persons whose actions directly injure other persons. It seems obvious that the State should not act at all in regard to actions which are beneficial or are harmful to no one but the acting person.

This is essentially the American revolutionary view of the nature and function of the State. Madison explains its opposition to democracy; not that it matters whether one or a few or a majority "rule"; the opposition is to a "ruling" State. And experience (at that time, only Greek experience; Europe has had more, since Madison wrote) – experience shows that a majority, having political power, is swayed by "interests or passions" to trying to "direct other people's actions" by means of the State; and, since it is impossible that a majority directly control the State's action, the majority must and does set up a tyrant to act for it.

The alternative to a tyrant's tyranny is not the tyranny of a tyrant chosen by a majority. The alternative to "rule" is not "rule." The alternative to anti-social ("ruling") uses of the apparatus of coercion is a political structure so devised that it prevents any person or group of persons using its police force from using that force to infringe the rights of any other person.

The attempt here was to make such a political structur. It was the first attempt of the kind, and experimental; none of its makers thought it perfect at the time. They saw it as what it was – a first rough model, so to speak; a first foothold for their world revolution. One can see its flaws now. But the principle according to which they worked, the structure they made, its operation and the operation of American society during a century are historical facts; their political philosophy is a political philosophy, on record. It exists as an alternative to "rule" of other people by any *number* of persons.

****

I do not recall ever hearing the word, democracy, outside a classroom until during the early fighting in the World War. Its use by President Wilson was so unusual that it was generally believed that he was the first to use it in an official document. (I am told that research has discovered one prior instance.) John Adams wrote in his old age that he had lost his faith in God because he saw democracy in the west and was convinced that it would destroy the Republic.

In the free schools (before the importation of compulsory State schooling from Germany during the early 1900s), Fifth Reader classes (11–12 years old) learned the failure of democracy in Greece from "Ancient History."

The word and the idea has been used here, to my personal knowledge, since 1919 by Communists, with the intention of breaking down the Federal structure. I can't cite chapter and page, as I have lent the book, but in the second volume of THE CONQUEST OF POWER by Albert Weisbord (Phi Beta Kappa, LL.B., Harvard, member Executive Committee, Third International), the tactic is explained in detail, with its reasons.

I can't think of Alexis de Tocqueville too seriously. An acute and brilliant young man, an excellent writer, a hurried and harassed traveler through the wild American backwoods, he did a better job than most travelers have done in Soviet Russia. But it was essentially the same thing. He knew in France that America was a democracy, he came to see democracy; of course he saw it. Actually, there were traces of democracy in New England's Town Meetings and are yet in their few survivals. Many of Tocqueville's comments are highly amusing; his definition of individualism, for example. The first time I read it I laughed till I cried; I still laugh aloud when I think of it.

I have not read Merriam; in 1903 he was acute in seeing the *tendency* as "essentially democratic." It has been since the 1880s and began to form institutions on the State level during the second decade of this century; it appeared Federally also in the 16th and 17th amendments (1913).

I ask you to forgive this long letter, promising not to make again such a demand upon your courtesy. I hope only that I have expressed to you my own view; naturally I think it worth explaining and that it may interest you. Please don't feel an obligation to answer it in correspondence. Your books place any reader under great obligation to you, and I wouldn't subtract a moment from work that will, I hope, give us more of them.

With every good wish to you,

Yours sincerely,

Rose Wilder Lane/ASL

We now come to the reviews of the new economic textbooks in the August 1950 issue of the *Economic Council Review of Books* (Vol. 7, No. 8). Watts takes credit for what he reprints in his *Away from Freedom*, but as we noted above, not all of the material is included in the reprint. He does not offer an explanation.

War news makes headlines; the conflict of ideas does not. Yet, back of the war-makers are always the ideas which determine what men fight for and what they do with defeat or victory. Wrong ideas are destroying angels which sap people's strength or misdirect their energies.

That is why the radical change which recently took place in the teaching of economics in American colleges and universities is as important as the outbreak of war in Korea.

Until three years ago, the most widely used textbooks were still in the classical tradition. They left the impression that, despite its faults, free enterprise could at least bring about full production and full employment – if people wanted to try it.

Today, the most popular textbooks present a very different view. They note all the shortcomings which the classicists attributed to capitalism, but they go much further. They present an elaborate new system of economics designed to prove that free enterprise is a system "without a steering wheel or governor." Because of this, they say, a "mature" economy, like that of the United States, must suffer an intolerable degree of unemployment and low output unless government comes to its rescue with controls far beyond anything advocated or accepted by the classicists.

Typical of this "new economics," as its devotees call it, is the book which now holds first place in college adoptions: *Economics: An Introductory Analysis*, by Paul A. Samuelson, professor of economics at the Massachusetts Institute of Technology. Other writers of the same school of thought are Seymour Harris, Theodore Morgan, Richard Ruggles, Lawrence R. Klein, and Lorie Tarshis. (Titles of their works are listed at the end of this REVIEW.)

These authors and teachers, along with hundreds or thousands of their associates and converts, are deliberately and systematically undertaking to effect what they themselves call a revolution in the thought of American college students. This revolution means an overturning in such basic ideas as those relating to thrift, individual responsibility and the right of private property. If successful, therefore, it will affect the welfare of the American people as directly and as vitally as the advance of Soviet arms abroad.

Until recently, these men did not hesitate to call themselves "Keynesians." Lately, some of them have been calling their view "the national-income approach." The more outspoken of them, however, still acknowledge Lord Keynes as their Great Liberator. This is because he revived and popularized an old pattern of thought which is the core of their system. If you want to understand the meaning and importance of "the new economics," therefore, you should know something about its patron saint, John Maynard Keynes.

During the 1920s the problem which caused most debate among economists in England was unemployment. For every year after 1920 up to World War II, unemployment in that country remained above 10 percent of the labor force, a level equalled only twice before in the preceding 60 years.

Classical economists said that the causes of this chronic unemployment were interferences with free enterprise: heavy taxes and government restrictions; unemployment doles, which acted as subsidies to idleness; and trade union wage-kiting and restriction of output. The remedy, these economists argued, was to remove or reduce these burdens and restrictions.

British trade union leaders, of course, vehemently declaimed against this line of reasoning. So did the Fabian socialists, who held many academic positions. However, the attack on the free-market theory of prosperity lacked academic prestige until Keynes, a professor at the University of Cambridge, joined in.

At first Keynes (pronounced Kanes) argued that cutting wages was the wrong remedy for unemployment because of the strength of the unions. He said it would take years of mass unemployment to break down current wage rates, and that was too high a price to pay for free markets. England had seen the end of laissez faire, he argued, so economists might as well stop preaching it. The only feasible remedy for the unemployment problem was currency inflation to raise the price level so that employers could afford to pay the money wage rates demanded by the unions. He proposed also to devalue the British pound to enable British exporters to sell their goods in foreign markets.

The classicists replied that this would be dishonest and dangerous. It would mean cutting the purchasing power of wages, and it would work only if the workers could be kept in ignorance of what was going on. If or when they learned the truth, they would demand wage increases to match the rise in living costs. This would nullify any possible benefits of inflation in raising the demand for labor. Furthermore, the devaluation of the pound would mean partial repudiation of England's foreign obligations. This would violate a trust and endanger the business of England's bankers who were financing most of the world's international trade.

In short, Keynes' critics accused him of using the argument of political expediency to justify a bad economic policy.

From this point, Keynes seemed to find it necessary to work out a line of argument to show that wage-maintenance and currency inflation are not only good politics but good economics, as long as there is less than "full employment." In order to do this, he had to find some cause for chronic, large-scale unemployment other than high wage rates, high taxes, and the dole. He found it in hoarded (uninvested) savings.

Classical economists had taught that people save mainly in order to invest or to accumulate funds to be spent later. The savings are mainly left in the banks, which lend them to businessmen. These business borrowers, in turn, spend ("invest") the savings for goods and services, thus maintaining the circulation of money and the demand for labor.

The reply of Keynes and his disciples is that saving and investment "are largely done by different people and for different reasons." Consequently, "Whatever the individual's motivation to save, it has practically nothing to do with investment or investment opportunities." (Samuelson, p. 254) It is only an accident if investments equal the sums which individuals are attempting to save. The propensity to save is relatively stable, except that it rises as incomes rise because it takes time to change people's spending habits. But investment opportunities are highly variable because they depend "on the dynamic and relatively unpredictable elements of growth ...." Therefore, "So far as total investment or purchasing power is concerned, ours is a system without a steering wheel," "the system is in the lap of the gods." (Samuelson, pp. 255, 256)

In an economy with an open frontier, a high rate of invention, and a growing population, say the Keynesians, the opportunities may be sufficient to cause entrepreneurs to bid for and borrow all of the funds which consumers want to save. In a more "mature" economy, however, like England in the 1920s and the United States since 1929, this equality between investment and savings is less apt to occur, especially since an increasing share of the income is paid to the rich who have a high propensity to save. Eventually a time comes when the opportunities for profitable investment fail to keep pace with the amounts individuals try to save. Total spending then declines. Goods remain unsold, or are sold at lower prices, so that entrepreneurs suffer losses equal to the amount by which attempted savings exceed investments. Some wage earners lose their jobs and dividends are cut. Consequently, national income and savings fall until attempted savings once more are equal to investment.

This new point of equilibrium, however, may find a large part of the labor force unemployed. This unemployment will persist until something occurs to make spending for consumption and investment run ahead of incomes.

How then do the Keynesians propose to abolish this chronic, mass unemployment? They reply: Increase the nation's total spending by government intervention, which they call *compensatory fiscal and monetary policy*. Says Morgan, "To set the responsibility for attaining and maintaining full employment on the shoulders of individual consumers or individual businessmen is absurd." (p. 169) According to Samuelson, author of the leading college text book in economics,

"The private economy is not unlike a machine without a steering wheel or governor. Compensatory fiscal policy tries to introduce such a governor or thermostatic device." (p. 412)

This compensatory policy involves: (1) "reducing incentives to thrift" by taxing the thrifty and subsidizing consumers, and (2) "the manufacture of money" to finance an increase in government "investment."

In order to reduce thrift ("the propensity to save"), the Keynesians propose that "we" increase "social-consumption expenditures." By this they mean that government should extend social security to everyone, raise the level of payments, and add items like low-cost medical care, says Lawrence Klein:

"We need a non-profit institution like the government, which can provide a comprehensive, minimum program of social security in order to reduce the propensity to save. This program must cover the entire population, and it must cover all those contingencies which cause people to save on a large scale for the future." (pp. 176, 177)

Another way to reduce thrift is by heavy taxes on upper-bracket incomes and on estates and inheritances. (Morgan, pp. 187, 198)

Some Keynesians suggest that government might do a few things to stimulate private investment: provide aid to small business, give subsidies for the building of low-cost homes, compel licensing of patents, and reduce interest rates.

However, they do not hope for much success along this line. Tarshis, for example, says that a wealthy economy like the United States "cannot long maintain full employment through high private investment, because its stock of capital equipment will rise rapidly toward the danger point even if it is low enough at first to provide sufficient profitable outlets for investment." (p. 512)

Keynesians look to government for the new "investment" necessary to raise the national income to the full-employment level. "If we take enough of this public investment medicine, it appears that we can cure any depression, so long as we are willing to keep on taking it." (Tarshis, p. 518) And by government "investment" Keynesians mean all government purchases of goods and services, including the hiring of tax collectors, purchase of battleships, or building of monuments. (Tarshis, pp. 388, 389)

Of course, these authors prefer that government spend for useful rather than useless objects, but "as far as present total purchasing power and employment are concerned, wise domestic investment is no more powerful than ultimately foolish investment ...." Boondoggling is better than nothing "because of the favorable respending effects of those who receive government expenditures." (Samuelson, pp. 371, 434) Morgan says that "even from the point of view of output, it is better to employ men in digging holes and filling them up than not to employ them at all; it is better to employ men to make products which we thereupon dump in the middle of the ocean than to leave them idle." (p. 182) He thereupon quotes from Keynes: "Pyramid-building, earthquakes, even wars may serve to increase wealth. ..." Giving money to foreigners to buy our goods is also a form of "investment," even though we get nothing in return.

"If we could only export one of the printing presses used for the manufacture of Federal Reserve Notes to, let us say, China, our foreign investment would be enormously higher."
(Tarshis, p. 391; cf. Samuelson, pp. 271, 272; Morgan, p. 206)

This Keynesian tolerance for boondoggling is easier to understand if one keeps in mind that the theory makes spending and consumption the key to prosperity in a mature economy, not production or thrift.

Among useful government "investments," Keynesians propose more TVAs, airfield construction, public housing, rural electrification, and Federal aid to education.

These government "investments" may be financed by taxes, borrowing private savings, and manufacture of money. To be fully effective in giving employment, however, they must be financed in some way that does not simply take money that would otherwise have been spent. Therefore, Keynesians prefer that government compensatory spending be financed by manufacturing money. Says Morgan, "The manufacture of money by banks is a cheap and simple process ...." (pp. 243, 244, 254)

All Keynesians recognize, of course, that their program calls for a "managed currency" and inconvertible paper money. If the banks are to create deposits with regard only to the government's need for funds, they must ignore the question of their gold reserves. Keynes and all his disciples, therefore, belittle and berate the gold standard. Samuelson says "it made each country a slave rather than a master of its own destiny." (p. 380) Tarshis ridicules it by comparing it unfavorably with a limburger cheese standard. (pp. 331, 635)

They realize that their "loan-expenditure" policy might lead to a dangerous degree of price inflation, but they think some inflation is a good thing and they agree with Klein that "There is no reason why intelligent economic planning cannot be of just the correct amount, that amount which gives permanent full employment and stable prices." Klein continues:

"There are several administrative methods of gaining full employment without inducing inflation. If the economic planners are given complete control over the government fiscal policy so that they can spend when and where spending is needed to stimulate employment and tax when and where taxation is needed to halt upward price movements, there will be no problem of associated inflationary dangers." (p. 180)

Since such powers do not rest with the Congress, he says, the alternative is price control. "The OPA served us beyond all best hopes and wishes during the war, and it did not infringe upon any fundamental liberties, only upon the liberty of greedy profiteering. This organization can serve us also in peace." Samuelson points out that effective price controls would involve a degree of planning "perhaps" incompatible with "present" philosophical beliefs of most Americans, but he offers no other objection as long as it is coupled with rationing. (pp. 435, 465, 466)

The chief roadblock which Keynesians find in their loan-expenditure route to prosperity is the businessman's unenlightened fear of mounting government debts. This fear, they assure us, is quite unfounded. Rapidly increasing debt is merely a price we pay for prosperity. "If we do not want high debt, high interest rates, high wages, and high prices, then in effect we do not want high employment and prosperity." (Tarshis, pp. 504–506) The only question is whether the government can always find a buyer for its bonds. "In the final analysis this is no problem for the simple reason that the government controls the Federal Reserve Banks and can always compel them to buy government bonds." "There is no sign that a high debt exhausts the credit of the government. ... And since as a last resource 'it can borrow from itself,' there need be no fear on this account." (Tarshis, pp. 534, 535) Anyway, as Klein says, "An internally held public debt can never be a burden, because we owe it to ourselves." (p. 182) Samuelson concludes that the national debt might double during the next 25 years, permitting an annual deficit of 10 billion dollars, without reason for concern. (pp. 428–433) Morgan says that the burden of the debt may be reduced by permitting price inflation, and he suggests that a rise of 1 to 2 percent in the general price level each year would be beneficially stimulating to the economy. (pp. 242, 243)

Since Keynesians advocate so many forms of government intervention to secure "full employment," no one should be surprised to find them favoring it for many other purposes. If the government should take a man's earnings merely because he is trying to save too much, why should it not take them on the ground that someone else needs or wants them more. If government should own power plants, why not also railways and steel mills?

Samuelson, the leading text book author of this school of thought, says that the question of political freedom and civil liberty has little or nothing to do with the matter of government control of the economy. He goes on to analyze the workings of a socialist society to show, he says, how an ideal capitalistic system would work and to "discover a possible method of attacking the almost unbelievably complex problem of socialist planning." (p. 590) "In a moment," he continues, "we shall see that there is nothing sacred about the results achieved by a free market system ...." (p. 591) He concludes that his study of socialism reveals the faults of private enterprise: inequality, monopoly, wasteful advertising, needless differentiation of products, distortion of consumers' tastes and beliefs, and the wastes of unemployment and the business cycle.

Morgan says that "Probably, majority opinion agrees with our own national policy that the right of a man to engage in business for himself is not a basic freedom." (p. 175) He adds that the meaning of "capitalism," "freedom," and "right" are matters of opinion.

You may not like the Keynesian program. But can you show the error of the reasoning back of it? Do the facts of history and business experience support it? Many honest college professors can't see what's wrong with it. Will college sophomores? Or seniors?

The theory is supported by charts and diagrams that make it look scientific and exact. Its technical terms delight the pedant – "propensity to consume," "liquidity preference," "multiplier," and so on. It proposes to make use of statistics which the United States government publishes often – statistics on national income, savings, investment, consumer spending, and the like. Many people regard these figures as exact and highly significant, and the plan for using them as guides for "compensatory fiscal and monetary policy" seems simple and practicable. Finally, it supports the argument of everyone who wants government to do something for him or to his neighbor. Is it any wonder that students eat it up?

If you know Marxian dogma, you can see numerous similarities between it and Keynesian doctrines: the theory of a declining rate of return from investments and increasing unemployment; emphasis on the depressing influence of savings in a "mature" economy; theories of an irresistible tendency to monopoly, increasing concentration of wealth and income, and the inevitable doom of free markets; advocacy of social security, progressive income and inheritance taxes, a managed currency, government control of banking, government ownership of certain industries, liquidation ("euthanasia") of the rentier class, and so on. (Harris, pp. 406, 544)

Like Marxism, too, Keynesianism is collectivistic and mechanistic. It deals with people in classes and masses, in averages and aggregates. It proposes to relieve the individual of responsibility in a variety of ways. It represents property rights as mere privileges from the state to be given or taken away according to the will of the ruler. It makes persons appear to be slot machines which operate in predictable ways when the right coins are inserted.

Most Keynesian economists, however, claim that they come not to destroy capitalism, but to save it. Consequently, they get a hearing in places which would be closed to a professed socialist. The important question is what are likely to be the results of the program they advocate, not what are their motives.

For readers interested in further study of the "new economics," I should comment in more detail on the books mentioned above, as well as on others of a similar nature.

Economics: An Introductory Analysis, by Paul A. Samuelson, is breezy in style, and the author often plays peek-a-boo with the reader, using innuendo and insinuation, even double-talk, to create an impression where he is reluctant to take a forthright stand. This makes the book appeal to educators who believe they teach a student to think by puzzling and confusing him. However, Harris classes Samuelson with himself as a "staunch Keynesian," and no one will question this classification after perusal of Part II of this Number One on the hit parade of elementary textbooks.

Income and Employment, by T. Morgan, is easy reading; one of the best statements of Keynesianism by a Keynesian.

The Keynesian Revolution, by L. R. Klein, contains more of the technical jargon of Keynesianism. However, it also contains useful background information about Keynes, and the chapter on "Keynes and Social Reform" shows how far the theory leads toward complete government "planning."

The Elements of Economics, by Lorie Tarshis, is probably the most frankly Keynesian of all full-length elementary textbooks. Reviewed here August 1947.

Modern Economics, by A. E. Burns, A. C. Neal, and D. S. Watson, is more matter-of-fact in tone than the Tarshis book, and its authors do not so often show the full implications of their ideas in the realm of government policy. For that reason the book appears less extreme and is not so likely to draw fire from the opposition. However, it is thoroughly Keynesian in point of view.

Elementary Economics, by J. A. Nordin and V. Salera, is much like the text by Burns, Neal and Watson.

In the next issue of the *Review,* I shall deal with certain anti-Keynesian works, in particular, *The Economics of Illusion,* by L. A. Hahn. I shall then state my belief as to the basic errors of the Keynesian "model."

Economics: An Introductory Analysis, by Paul A. Samuelson; McGraw-Hill Book Company, Inc., 1948. $4.50. 622 pp.

Income and Employment, by T. Morgan; Prentice-Hall, Inc., 1947. $4.35. 304 pp.

The Elements of Economics, by Lorie Tarshis; Houghton Mifflin Company, 1947. $4.90. 699 pp.

The Keynesian Revolution, by Lawrence R. Klein; The Macmillan Company, 1947. $3.50. 218 pp.

Modern Economics, Arthur E. Burns, [by] Alfred C. Neal, D. S. Watson; Harcourt, Brace and Company, 1948. $5.00. 954 pp.

Elementary Economics, by J. A. Nordin and Virgil Salera; Prentice-Hall, Inc., 1950. $6.00. 420 pp.

The New Economics: 'Keynes' Influence on Theory and Public Policy. Edited with introductions by Seymour E. Harris; 661 pp., bibliography, index. Alfred A. Knopf, 1947. $6.00.

An Introduction to National Income & Income Analysis, by Richard Ruggles; McGraw-Hill Book Company, Inc. 333 pp., index. $3.75.

A detailed, clear statement of Keynesianism for students who have had some of the elements of accounting. The author mentions some of the difficulties that may be met in using the Keynesian "model" to forecast all control business fluctuations; but he treats these as problems to be solved, not as invalidations of Keynesian theory or practice.

Watts's September 1950 contribution to the *Economic Council Review of Books* (Vol. 7, No. 9) considers some important writings in opposition to Keynesian analysis. Watts's listing of Arthur Burn's National Bureau of Economic Research (NBER) report as part of the opposition to Keynesianism prefigures the great NBER work of G. Warren Nutter as well as that of Milton Friedman and Anna Schwartz. What surprised us most in our conversation with Richard Ware was a central role Burns played in the post–World War II revival of market liberalism (Levy & Peart, 2011). Watts takes the occasion to make public his criticism of von Mises's democratic political views.

Why did the outbreak of war in Korea precipitate a sharp drop in the stock market? And a wave of panicky stock piling by consumers? Don't people know what's good for them? For years Socialists have been telling us that capitalists want war to make them prosperous. Now the apostles of the "new economics," disciples of the late Lord Keynes, preach much the same doctrine. According to this theory, which is well-entrenched in our colleges and universities, a cozy little war like that in Korea, costing a mere $10 billion or so a year, should guarantee full employment and prosperity as long as it lasts.

For example, the popular and respected Stanford professor, Dr. Lorie Tarshis, says this:

> ... there are two obstacles to prosperity in a wealthy economy (like that of the United States): such an economy needs an *enormous* volume of investment ... and because its stock of capital goods is already great, it does not always provide a large number of favorable investment opportunities. We must now add a third difficulty: it cannot long maintain full employment through high *private* investment, because its stock of capital equipment will rise rapidly toward the danger point. ... It seems to be an *almost impossible* task to raise *private* investment to the *astronomical* figure that is now needed; and an even harder problem to keep it there." (*The Elements of Economics*, p. 512, reviewed here, August 1947.) (italics mine)

So, says Tarshis, in order to avoid economic collapse or stagnation, "we" must find some outlet other than private investment for the "enormously high" savings that Americans – victims of old Ben Franklin's outmoded maxims – foolishly keep trying to accumulate. That other outlet, of course, is government spending. And what surer way of overcoming the protests of the benighted advocates of balanced budgets than a war?

True, says Keynes and his disciples, it would be much better for government to spend on useful things like power plants, roads and schools, than on wars. Nevertheless, said Keynes, "if the education of our statesmen in the principles of classical economics stands in the way of anything better" even a war or an earthquake may serve to enrich a nation.

The doctrines back of this conclusion make up the "Keynesian Revolution" which I described in last month's *Review*. It is the brand of economics set forth in the most popular textbooks now in use in American colleges and universities. It is accepted by certain widely read business commentators as a sound basis for business forecasting. It is the theory of many leading politicians and the dogma of most trade-unionists.

In its essentials, this brand of economics is as old as the use of money. In one form or another it has been used again and again to justify government extravagance and to defend schemes for inflating currency or credit. It was the theory John Law persuaded the government of France to let him try out in the early 18th century. The result was the Mississippi Bubble, the best known boom and bust of recorded history up to 1929. A century later, Lauderdale, Malthus, and Sismondi advanced much the same views.

Now, in the 20th century, this gospel of inflation is as popular as ever, and it seems to have even more academic prestige than in any of its previous visitations.

In its present reincarceration, the theory is attributed to the late John Maynard Keynes, English economist and for many years adviser to the British government. However, another world-famed economist, Dr. L. A. Hahn, has all along claimed the doubtful honor of refurbishing and reissuing what he now regards as the fool's gold of economic theories. In a book of essays entitled, *The Economics of Illusion*, Dr. Hahn confesses that "Keynesianism is a sin of my youth," which he committed several years before Keynes got credit (or discredit) for it.

As a young economist and banker in Germany in 1920, Hahn ardently espoused the idea that easy credit policies are necessary to keep a modern economy fully stimulated and working at top speed. Without this stimulus, he thought, it would get clogged with unused purchasing power, or savings. The result would be unemployment and idle factories. A few years later, as he saw the results of these easy-money policies, he came to regard inflation as a worse evil than deflation. Therefore, he re-examined his theories and concluded he had been mostly wrong in his original explanation for depressions.

The causes of business depression he now finds, not in oversaving, but in a necessary readjustment after a preceding credit inflation. In addition, he says, depressions may be aggravated and prolonged by "deflationary policies" (which he does not describe), and by conditions which prevent reduction of costs and restoration of profit margins after the excesses of the boom are liquidated. The conditions preventing or delaying adjustment are mainly (1) wage rigidities protected by unions and wage-hour laws; (2) burdensome taxes on job-making enterprise; and (3) government restrictions on trade and production, such as tariffs, crop controls, exchange restrictions, and price controls.

At first, says Hahn, currency-and-credit inflation speeds up spending and increases employment because certain costs (e.g., wage rates, rents, and interest charges) lag behind selling prices of the products. This stimulating effect, however, lasts only until the lagging costs catch up to the rise in prices – as they soon do. After that, further inflation can only raise the general price level and reduce confidence in the currency. The growing mistrust leads to a flight of capital, which in turn sets off a degenerative spiral of growing unemployment, increasing currency inflation, rising prices, and further export of capital.

Therefore, Hahn says, the Keynesian theory that currency inflation and increased spending can increase employment is valid only if one assumes a lag in wages, and this lag will continue only as long as wage earners can be kept in ignorance of what is going on.

> "For it [the Keynesian view] presupposes an economy whose members do not see through the changes brought about by monetary or fiscal manipulation – or, as some might say, the swindle. Above all, it presupposes that people are blinded by the idea that the value of money is stable – by the 'money illusion' ..." (pp. 166, 167)

Hence, he calls Keynesianism "the economics of illusion."

Most people will agree with Hahn that a policy which depends on such an illusion has little chance of success in a nation of free discussion and collective bargaining. In fact, union wage demands now generally run ahead of any increase in overall spending, at least in the United States.

Keynesians are coming to recognize this fact. Samuelson, for example, says that the possibility that wages and prices may begin to soar as spending increases, even though there is still unemployment and excess capacity, is "America's greatest problem and challenge." "If businessmen and trade-unions react perversely to an increased demand, fiscal policy cannot be relied upon to achieve and maintain full employment." The alternatives he offers, if "business, labor and agriculture" do not learn to curb their demands, are: (1) a reserve army of 10 million jobless; (2) some degree of inflation most of the time; or (3) government price and wage controls. Elsewhere he shows that the first is intolerable. He does not choose between the other two alternatives, but he does not represent either as necessarily disastrous. (pp. 435, 436, 594f) One looks in vain in this leading textbook for any suggestion that the problem of "excess savings" and "underinvestment" can or should be solved by restoring a free labor market to encourage private investment. Nor does he propose a return to a free labor market to prevent wage-kiting by trade unions.

It is in these matters that Hahn takes issue with the Keynesian view. He contends that (1) there cannot be an excess of savings or chronic underinvestment in free markets; and (2) the remedy for chronic unemployment is the reestablishment of a free Jabor market and removal of trade barriers. An easy money policy, he says, can stimulate employment only for a short time. If it is used to overcome the depressing effect of too-high wage rates or monopolistic price-maintenance, it aggravates the very evils that are at the root of the trouble. Eventually it sets in motion the degenerative cycle of runaway inflation.

In *The Economics of Illusion*, Hahn does a fairly good job of following the Keynesians in the twists and turns of their dialectics to ferret out some of their inconsistencies and fallacies. He is one of the best-known critics of Keynesian doctrine. He undermines his own case, however, by recommending the use of the deficit-financing stimulant in recovery periods and by condemning the "hyper-classicism of those who opposed attempts at reflation" in the early 1930s.

What Hahn objects to, therefore, is excessive use of the policy or to bad timing, rather than to the policy itself.

> "In order to restore confidence in the price structure, the government is justified in compensating, and even obliged to compensate, the lacking private demand by proper expenditures for which it acquires the means by loans, not by taxes." (p. 104, cf. pp. 60, 169, 175, 237, and elsewhere)

But who is to decide when the producers have completed their adjustments and thus merited a helping hand from government? If government recognizes that the time for recovery has arrived, why don't investors? Does government get a sudden access of wisdom in the trough of a depression?

And where is the government to get the money for its compensatory spending? Here Hahn accepts the Keynesian view that the gold standard must be abandoned. In place of it he favors a "money-free" economy, in which bank deposits will be as good as cash and there will always be plenty of money to meet bank runs. He agrees that discount rates should be determined by domestic credit needs rather than by the need for protecting gold reserves. This, he says, makes Keynes' "liquidity preference" concept an anachronism. A demand for liquidity in the form of bank deposits is no longer deflationary because the banks can keep their funds invested and the government can provide paper money to keep these funds always liquid. (p. 157f)

Hahn fails to see or point out that it was this "money-free" policy which caused the inflationary boom of the 1920s. He fails also to do more than hint at the various interventionist policies, dating far back into the 19th century, which made the depression of the 1930s the worst in modern times.

This story – the record of government's role in the boom-and-bust of 1929–1939 – has so far been told best by the late Benjamin M. Anderson, Jr. in his *Economics and the Public Welfare*, published just after his death last year.

The title which the author originally gave the book was, "When Government Plays God." The publishers vetoed this title on the ground that it would shock some people and would hurt the sales of the book in academic circles where it is usually necessary to appear disinterested, or "moderate." Doubtless the publishers were right, but Dr. Anderson, I think, believed that people need to be shocked about the results of government currency management, and I doubt that he cared whether or not he sold any books to those who are disinterested about wrongdoing.

At any rate, "When Government Plays God" describes the theme of the book. Seldom have facts been so marshalled to show the progress of a plausible theory in wreaking havoc with the economic life, not merely of one nation but of every nation.

The first phase of the New Deal in the United States Dr. Anderson dates back to 1924 when the Federal Administration of this country dictated an easy-money policy – "an immense artificial manipulation of the money market" for political purposes. However, according to the author's own account, he should have dated it from 1914, for it was then that the politically created and controlled Federal Reserve Banking System began operating.

As Dr. Anderson himself shows, the United States Government used this system, its own creature, to finance the inflation of World War I and the postwar boom of 1919–1920. True, the Federal Reserve Banks regained some independence of action in 1920, but their tardy and moderate increases in rediscount rates in 1920 were blamed for the depression which followed, and thereafter they were never again free of political direction and interference.

Dr. Anderson tells vividly and in detail how this political domination of bank policies brought about the runaway stock market boom of the late 1920s, and how the subsequent crash and depression were intensified and prolonged by "frantic governmental economic planning" which began even while the stock market crash was going on. For the most part the account seems to me as clear and readable as a newspaper account of a bank holdup.

And a bank holdup is about what the United States Government staged in 1933 when it seized the people's gold and induced a subservient Congress to give the President authority to issue inconvertible paper money and reduce the gold value of the dollar. After quoting Senator Carter Glass concerning the dishonor and fraud of this action, Dr. Anderson says:

"To the grand old Senator, morality was something written in the Heavens, eternal and unchangeable. But the pragmatic philosopher ... was no less shocked than the Senator. There is no need in human life so great as that men should trust one another and should trust their government, should believe in promises, and should keep promises in order that future promises may be believed in and in order that confident cooperation may be possible. Good faith – personal, national, and international – is the first prerequisite of decent living, of the steady going on of industry, of government financial strength, and of international peace."

"The President's course in connection with the gold standard and in connection with the Thomas Amendment represented an act of absolute bad faith. ... The Government was bound by its solemn promises, and the President was personally bound by his campaign utterances and by the platform of his party. It was dishonor." (pp. 317, 318)

So the moral indignation of an economist who saw that trust and good faith are the foundations of all human cooperation broke forth in bitter condemnation of those who sought to promote prosperity by deceit and spoliation.

Indignation, however, must be governed by understanding. It is Anderson's microscopic and expert examination of the financial record that gives his *Economics and the Public Welfare* its authoritative weight and penetration.

In this clear and detailed moving picture of events, however, you may find something of which even its producer was scarcely aware. As he describes the inflation of 1924–1929, Anderson attributes it to the "weakness" and "bad judgment" of certain Federal Reserve officials in yielding to political influences. He suggests that different men might have acted differently if given the same opportunities.

But was it mere accident that the control over the Federal Reserve System was in the hands of "weak" men? Will government long tolerate officials (e.g., members of the Federal Reserve Board) who show good financial judgment instead of good political judgment?

Many persons, like Senator Carter Glass and Dr. Anderson, who strongly favor private enterprise in banking as a general rule, make an exception in favor of government control of "central bank policy." They see the many advantages of close cooperation among individual banks. One obvious way of getting this cooperation is to set up a banker's bank, like the Bank of England and the Bank of France (which used to be privately owned). Such a central bank, however, is a sort of monopoly, and it has a tremendous responsibility for the soundness and safety of the entire banking system, with a corresponding opportunity for private profit and public harm. This monopoly and responsibility, it is argued, cannot be entrusted to private control. Therefore, most advocates of central banking propose that the central bank must be like a public utility, "regulated," though not "managed."

The founders of the Federal Reserve System in 1913 were warned of the danger of political control of such a bank, but they hoped to prevent political "abuses" by such devices as that of permitting the private banks to elect most of the directors of the 12 Federal Reserve Banks, and by giving long-term appointments to the members of the Federal Reserve Board. Most classical economists, even among those most devoted to free enterprise, still cling to the belief that somehow the monetary system can be managed by a government-appointed board which will not be subject to political influence – "like the Supreme Court."

Careful reading of Dr. Anderson's book should shake that belief, especially if one keeps in mind also the outcome of the Reconstruction Finance Corporation to which Anderson gave grudging approval. As *Economics and the Public Welfare* makes clear, the Federal Reserve officials, as a rule, have been among the most honest and intelligent persons that could be found. They acted politically because they were political officials appointed to do a political job, not primarily an economic or financial job. In fact, the entire Federal Reserve System was and is a political creature. Furthermore, as in the case of so many other forms of government intervention, the excuse for it had been provided by government restriction of private enterprise in this field from the beginning of the Republic. But that's another story.

What Anderson does realize and make clear as few economists do is the fallacy of the quantitative theory of credit control, the fallacy which is at the root of all demands for currency inflation by government.

In order to get at the meaning of this, let us consider what credit is. Credit arises when one person transfers to another his services and goods, or valid claims on services and goods, in return for a promise-to-pay-later. For example, the employee gives credit to the employer when he works for a week before payday. A customer gives credit to a merchant when he sends money to pay for something before the merchant ships it. A seller advances credit when he sends goods before he receives the money. Credit is not, therefore, a matter of bank checks, bank notes, or figures on the banks' books. Instead, it is an uncompleted exchange of goods and services. The pieces of paper, like bank checks and bank records, are merely memoranda of credit transactions, not credit itself.

Banks serve as credit brokers, not credit manufacturers, except as government interferes. They record credit transactions and act as clearing houses for the credit developed and used by individuals and business firms. They keep books for the real manufacturers of credit, who are the exchangers of goods and services.

A great deal of credit, in fact, may be created and used with little or no use of the banks. In certain parts of the United States in the first part of the 19th century, banks were forbidden by state laws. In those places business developed with comparatively little bank credit, and even with comparatively little money. Not that the rate of turnover of money was so high, but that the volume of credit developed along with trade and industry as businessmen became their own bankers. A trusted merchant, for example, would buy the products of farmers and artisans, giving them in return purchase orders good at his store. In that case, the producers sold the goods on credit to the merchant. The credit was liquidated when these producers came back to the storekeeper and exchanged his IOUs for his goods. Or, if the merchant owned a stock of goods to begin with, he could sell on credit to producers, and they could discharge their debts later by delivering their products to the merchant.

In such a society, the volume of credit obviously depended on the amount of goods produced and exchanged. This amount, in turn, depended on the efficiency of producers and merchants – their ambition, inventiveness, ability to cooperate, richness of soil – and on ONE OTHER THING. That ONE OTHER THING was *trust*.

This trust had to include trust in the fairness of the terms of trade as well as trust in one another's productive efficiency. It included the "meekness" which is necessary for those who are to prosper until they "inherit the earth." Self-interest in seeking a gain could not become greed which tries to make all the gain in an exchange.

When these conditions are present – a fund or flow of goods, good faith, and trust – there is credit. The supply of credit rises and falls with the amount of exchangeable goods produced, and this amount depends on the efficiency of producers, including merchants and others who help arrange exchanges. It does not matter whether the goods are commodities or services, durable goods or perishable, consumers' goods or producers' goods (tools and machinery), the quantity of credit in free markets depends on its quality as measured by its command over goods. This quality, in turn, depends on the faithfulness with which producers and traders meet one another's expectations in production, trade, and finance.

The banker is not needed, then, to create credit. He keeps records and acts as agent for producers and traders in ascertaining the creditworthiness of individuals in particular transactions when the owners want such service. As his customers gain confidence in his work, many of them let the banker record all of their credit transactions, except perhaps those that involve only a short period of time. Then people mistakenly come to think that the bank is the originator of the credit.

On the other hand, if the goods are sold on credit to people who don't keep their promises (perhaps because their plans go awry), there is trouble. The bases for credit, both goods and trust, are destroyed. Credit shrinks, and people complain of a shortage of money and credit. Then government may come in to "coin bad debts" by printing paper money to pay them. This permits and encourages the mistakes or bad investments which caused the first losses. In other words, the government's attempt to make up in quantity of credit instruments (paper money or bank deposits arising out of issues of paper) for a failure in credit quality causes further decline in both quality and quantity of credit.

Mistakes and losses are bound to occur in use of credit. To provide for them, a wise producer strives to accumulate reserves of valuable (exchangeable) goods, or valid claims on such goods. Such reserves, or "savings" (gold, raw materials, stocks of finished goods), improve a man's credit rating and increase the quantity of his credit. A nation whose citizens have abundant wealth has an abundance of credit and buying power if the people want to trade with one another and with other nations. It is not the efficiency of its banking system which makes the

United States the world's greatest reservoir of credit, but the people's vast output and stock of exchangeable goods, including gold.

This should make clear what the "hyper-classicists," whom Hahn scorns, regard as the basic economic fallacy of Keynesianism. Keynesians regard stocks of goods as a demand for credit – a drug on the market until buyers turn over money or pieces of paper (banknotes or bank checks) for the goods and take them off the market. Anderson and other "hyper-classicists" regard goods (including services) as the origin and basis for a supply of credit, or buying power. This credit is put to work as terms of trade (including wage rates) are arranged and goods (including services) are exchanged.

According to Anderson, therefore, the practical remedy for an apparent shortage of credit is not to print money to give to possible buyers. Instead, the remedy is to take away the barriers to the production and exchange of goods. Currency inflation merely dilutes credit and redistributes it. Credit that is advanced for non-productive purposes, such as military expenditures, causes an accumulation of incompleted exchanges, debts for dead horses, disequilibrium, and loss of confidence, with both reduced ability and reduced willingness to extend credit or to get it. Then there must be a writing down of debts, or else the debtors must accept a lower level of living while they repay their creditors. In other words, the terms of trade and finance must be revised or stagnation ensues.

From the beginning of World War I, as Anderson shows, inflation caused more and more distortion, unbalance, and waste of resources. During the 1920s, governments throughout the world tried to protect one class of producers after another against the effects of this unbalance by printing money to pay their debts or to maintain prices and wage rates. In other words, governments tried to cure the unbalance by increasing the quantity of money and credit through ... *coining debts*. This only served to perpetuate and increase the unbalance and to cause continued deterioration in the quality of credit, exhaustion of reserves, and finally repudiation of obligations. It was not a surplus of savings, a lack of investment, or overproduction that brought to an end the boom of 1928–1929, Anderson contends, but a shortage of new savings and depletion of liquid reserves due to losses on bad quality loans and investments.

A study by Professor F. A. Lutz, *Corporate Cash Balances, 1914–43*, bears out Anderson's thesis that hoarding of funds was not a cause of the 1929 crash. As far as Lutz's figures show, corporations usually spend their money as fast as they get it, and 1928–1929 was no exception. Contrary to the assertions of Keynesian economists, these figures indicate that business savings are very closely related to investments.

Corporate "surpluses," therefore, are not mainly cash. They are not hoarded or surplus funds. They are the value of all that the corporation owns, including buildings and machinery, after deducting the amount of liabilities and a certain rather arbitrary figure to represent the stockholders' investment. Business saves to invest, not to hoard cash or because it does not know what to do with the money, and it spends the money it invests as quickly as any other money it pays out.

One other point, however, should be made clear. The depression of 1930–1939 was no ordinary one. As Anderson shows, it was not merely a "natural reaction," or "period of correction" resulting from previous excesses. It was characterized by more government "planning" than any other in modern times. This "planning," so the politicians and their supporters said, was intended to stop the depression and prevent its recurrence. Much of it, however, consisted of new restrictions on trade, aimed at raising or maintaining certain prices. These restraints reduced the credit and buying power of other producers. In Anderson's view, it was these "dynamic," "positive" policies of government which made the depression so long and so severe.

This suggests the basic political fallacy in Keynesian thinking. This fallacy is the belief that government, which is legalized coercion, can manage the economic affairs of its citizens, as it tries to do in managing the banking and currency system. For, in managing the amount and use of money and credit, the government is indirectly managing the daily work and lives of the citizens – from determining what persons get new houses to deciding what persons get a chance to play golf.

Anderson suggests the fallacy of this government "planning" by the title he originally chose for his book: "When Government Plays God." Professor Ludwig von Mises's latest work, *Human Action*, reviewed here October 1949, and his booklet, *Planned Chaos*, explain how and why each step in government interference with the free market aggravates the unbalance which was the excuse for the preceding step. He describes also how it causes government to move toward totalitarianism.

Unfortunately, Mises fails to understand the nature of the American form of government as it was originally set up – a government of limited powers. He speaks of it as a "democracy" and implies that democracy is the road to individual freedom. Of course, the two things are quite different. Otherwise, *Planned Chaos* is one of the best available brief criticisms of the managed-economy idea. Most of the time the author writes in terms of individual freedom, or the free market, leaving no doubt that it, rather than democracy, is the essential condition for economic progress. Mises views Keynesianism as merely one of the more insidiously effective ways of bringing about "planned chaos." As Keynes himself said before he became a "Keynesian":

"There is no subtler, no surer means of overturning the existing bases of society than to debauch the currency. The process engages all the hidden forces of economic law on the side

of destruction, and does it in a manner which not one man in a million is able to diagnose."
(*The Economic Consequences of the Peace,* p. 236.)

The basic moral fallacy of Keynesianism, however, is not brought out by any
of the writers mentioned above. This fallacy is the mistaken belief that human
rights are created by government (or "Society"), and that what government (or
"Society") created, it can take away.

The fact is that the rights of self-defense and private property are necessary
to human life and to society. Man can exist only as he asserts and defends these
rights against invasion whether by government or by private persons. Therefore,
he cannot cooperate with his fellows except as they respect these rights. As these
rights are violated, people fight or flee from one another, and to that extent society
disintegrates and people perish.

Human rights, therefore, are prior to society. Protection of them is the only justification for law and government. When government fulfills this function, society
develops and prospers. When government infringes on human rights, including
property rights, it destroys the cooperation, or society, which supports it.

The essential condition for human rights and freedom is non-interference.
This idea is expressed in the prohibitions of all great moral codes: "Thou shalt
NOT kill!" "Thou shalt NOT steal!" "Thou shalt NOT bear false witness!"
"Thou shalt NOT covet!" Within the family there is a positive injunction: "Thou
shalt honor thy father and thy mother!" But this means thou shalt NOT palm
them off on someone else to care for when they are old. Furthermore, it enjoins
a duty of the children to parents. It does not give parents a right to enslave their
children.

Again, in the Constitution of the United States, especially in the Bill of Rights,
we find that freedom means non-interference. The little word NOT is repeated
over and over again.

It is this word NOT which Keynesians ignore in human relations. They put no
limit on government authority over the individual and his property except that of
political expediency. This is what makes their doctrine essentially collectivist, or
socialist. They take a dim view of the doctrine of natural rights. For example, they
consider it quite proper for government to seize a citizen's gold, fixing its own
price for it, if any, and refusing to pay it out again except at its own pleasure and
on its own terms. They consider it not in the least reprehensible for a government
to announce a change in its paper price for gold, thereby arbitrarily redistribut-
ing property between millions of persons doing business in international trade
and finance. Could any actions be more arbitrary or show greater indifference to
individual rights? Yet, in the Keynesian view, such actions are matters merely of
political and financial expediency, no more to be judged moral or immoral than a
decision to paint the courthouse grey instead of green.

Similarly, Keynesians propose that government seize (by taxation) the earnings of the well-to-do and give them to the poor in order to reduce the "natural propensity to save." They consider this "progressive" or "liberal." Instead it is a return to the collectivist immorality in which our cave dwelling ancestors so sluggishly existed.

Keynesians show the same indifference to property rights in their proposal for manipulating price levels. Dr. Morgan, for example, mentioned in last month's *Review*, suggests that it might be a good thing to have sufficient inflation to raise the general price level by 1 or 2 percent a year in order to reduce the burden of interest on the national debt and to stimulate business and employment. This would be equivalent to a capital levy of that amount each year on all savings accounts, bonds, and insurance policies, besides an increase of 1 or 2 percent each year in the tax rate on fixed incomes.

Likewise, the Keynesians propose to redistribute property and income between debtors and creditors by reducing interest rates. Keynes suggested it might be possible and desirable in this way to liquidate the *rentier* class, that is, bondholders and other holders of fixed-income obligations.

In view of this indifference to property rights, one should not be surprised to find a Keynesian economist supporting almost any proposal for increased government authority if he thinks it may help to reduce savings, raise or fix prices and wage rates, reduce interest rates, or "socialize" investment.

Conversely, you will find that the Keynesian economist has a low regard for the intelligence, responsibility, and integrity of individuals – unless they are in government employ! Since he regards savings for one's old age or other future needs as a dangerous practice, he has little respect (in theory, at least) for what most people regard as essential elements in character, namely, the desire and ability to be responsible for one's own welfare. Saving, according to the Keynesian, is not the result of foresight, planning, and self-control. It varies with income, he says, and is the result of inertia in habits of spending, outmoded Puritanism, or neurotic fears.

The fact of the matter is that saving is the cause of higher income far more often than higher income is the cause of saving. No matter what the income level, saving takes thought, planning, self-denial, and careful discrimination in such forms of self-indulgence as patronizing the arts and endowing universities. If wisely invested, savings may help raise one's income. Furthermore, thrifty people are ones who take thought of the morrow and therefore learn to produce and earn more than their less foresighted neighbors. That makes their incomes higher.

The Keynesian cannot admit this. It would make his impressive charts, tables, formulas, and graphs worthless. Once it is granted that his figures deal, not with automatons, but with self-determining individuals who can and do decide for themselves what they will do, his theories lose all value for purposes of prediction and control.

When the Keynesian is brought up against the fact of individual self-determination and variability, therefore, he proposes that government abolish these conditions which upset his calculations! That is, he proposes that government abolish individual freedom and responsibility by means of a social-security program. This program he advocates, not alone on the ground that "we can't let them starve," but on the theory that government can stabilize business by taking over the function of saving. Of course, he is likely to use all of the other social-security arguments to reinforce his own. Consequently, we find Keynesian economists arguing for the social-security program on the ground that people can't save, won't save, and shouldn't try to save. They are hardly likely, therefore, to impress upon their students that thrift and self-reliance are important virtues in the modern scheme.

The Keynesian also displays something between contempt and hostility for the qualities of successful business men. He represents profits as resulting from either or both of (1) a difference between the rate of interest and the "marginal efficiency of capital," and (2) monopoly and high-pressure salesmanship. In either case, the recipient of profits is given little or no credit for earning them by useful service.

This Keynesian antipathy or indifference to the qualities developed in free market arises from the belief that free markets are economically undesirable (e.g., the capital markets) and politically impracticable (e.g., the labor market). Moreover, as difficulties arise in carrying out their proposals for "socializing" saving and investment, economists of this persuasion are prone to advocate more restriction of markets rather than less.

Some persons defend the Keynesian approach on the ground that it is useful in business forecasting in a managed-currency world, even though it may be taking us all to perdition. According to Hahn, however, events follow Keynesian predictions only under special circumstances and for short periods. According to Anderson, the Keynesian analysis always leads to precisely wrong conclusions. Dr. Rufus Tucker, in an essay entitled, "Mr. Keynes' Theories Considered in the Light of Experience," gives numerous illustrations supporting Anderson's view. Dr. Arthur Bums, President of the National Bureau of Economic Research, in his Twenty-sixth and Thirtieth Annual Reports, points to certain facts about business cycles that appear inconsistent with the Keynesian theories.

Certainly, a business forecaster is leaning on a broken reed if he relies on the following notions to be found in the most popular economic textbooks now in use in American colleges and universities, *Economics,* by Paul Samuelson:

"... we must not forget that the real national product of the United States is an ever-growing thing." (p. 433)

"A fairly *optimistic* assumption is made that at 164 billion dollars of disposable income, there will be *as much as* 148 billion dollars of *consumption* ... (p. 442; italics mine)

"The credit of the Federal government actually improves in bad times . . . (p. 416) ... and deteriorates in good." (p. 426)

Is Keynesianism the sort of economic education parents want for their sons and daughters? Keynesian economists are trying to effect a revolution in people's ideas about money and credit, saving, and investment. They say in effect: "Spending makes wealth." "The wealth of the rich is the cause of the poverty of the poor." "What makes law makes right?" How does this brand of thinking affect the student's daily life and conduct?

The question is not merely one of money. It is one of character and conduct. A man's understanding of human relations determines his attitude and conduct toward his fellows. The way a man uses money reveals and determines the man himself. Some of us think there is a profound truth in the advice Micawber gave to David Copperfield. Thriftlessness means irresponsibility, disregard for one's obligations to others, and indifference to the rights of others. That way lies trouble for anyone and everyone.

Keynesian economists may not deliberately teach students to be spendthrift and irresponsible, or greedy and covetous. But they certainly do not stress the value of thrift and self-reliance, or a zealous regard for property rights.

Are these qualities no longer important? Can man and society function without them?

*****

The Economics of Illusion, by L. Albert Hahn; Squier Publishing Co., Distributor: New York Institute of Finance, New York, N. Y., 1949. $4.00. 273 pp.

Economics and the Public Welfare: Financial and Economics History of the United States, 1914–1946, by Benjamin M. Anderson; D. Van Nostrand Co., Inc., N. Y., 1949. $6.00. 602 pp., index.

Corporate Cash Balances, 1914–1943, by Friedrich A. Lutz; National Bureau of Economic Research, N. Y., 1945. $2.00. 132 pp., appendix, index.

Planned Chaos, by Ludwig von Mises; The Foundation for Economic Education, Irvington-on-Hudson, N. Y., 1947. $0.65.

The Economic Doctrines of John Maynard Keynes, pp. 28–52: "Mr. Keynes' Theories Considered in the Light of Experience," by Dr. Rufus S. Tucker; National Industrial Conference Board, Inc., New York, 1938. $0.50.

New Facts on Business Cycles, by Arthur F. Bums; Thirtieth Annual Report, National Bureau of Economic Research, Inc., N. Y., 1950. Available on request.

Lane's final letter to von Mises makes a comparison with Stalin, which perhaps explains why the archive contains no evidence of a response.

Route 4, Box 42
Danbury, Connecticut

September 11, 1950
My dear Professor Mises;

Undoubtedly you know Wilhelm Röpke. I have read some of his work in French translation. Now the university of Chicago Press is publishing, later this month, an English edition of his THE SOCIAL CRISIS OF OUR TIMES. On page 86 are these words, part of a paragraph:

"Benjamin Constant, Toqueville [sic], John Stuart Mill, Alexander Hamilton, Madison, Calhoun, Lecky, and many others who cannot be charged with reactionary views, have pointed out that democracy – and democracy more than any other political system – can lead to the worst forms of despotism and intolerance if bounds are not set to it by other principles and institutions, and it is this limitation in all its aspects that we must call the liberal content of a political structure. There is hardly any need to draw attention to the germs of modern totalitarianism latent in Rousseau or even more in the radical theorists and practitioners of Jacobinism, in order to furnish convincing proof that the collectivist state has its roots in the soil of unlimited democracy. ... Its (the collectivist state's) antithesis is not democracy ... but rather the liberal principle which erects a bar against the power of the state. ... This is usually what we have in mind when we picture democracy as the antithesis of the collectivist state, but we know now of what dangerous obfuscation we are guilty in doing so. There is no denying it: the collectivist state is rooted in the masses (to which professors can belong as well as workers) and it can only exist under conditions of society for which precisely the extreme democratic development is an excellent preparation but which is the direct opposite of the liberal ideal."

Since I – and, I am told, all other liberal Americans who have tried to show you that you are aiding the destruction of your own refuge by advocating democracy in the United States –have been unable even to engage your serious attention, I make a last attempt to get you to listen to some of your fellow-Europeans.

It is the predicament of the world revolution that, having reduced and restricted the use of force (the State) on a small area of the earth, it creates a little area of freedom into which rush refugees from the whole globe, escaping from the power of their own States, and bringing with them their reactionary, counter-revolutionary beliefs and influence. To deny them sanctuary is to abandon the basic principle of the Revolution (as Congress did, partially, in usurping power to restrict immigration, during the 1920s.) To admit them is to be in the fantastic situation of an army engaged in battle and enlisting the enemy's soldiers in its own ranks. If it might be possible really to enlist you, Professor Mises – your knowledge, your intelligence, your genuinely revolutionary power of thought – in the cause of human freedom, what a gain that would be. But when the undeniable value and weight of your work is politically destructive here, really Stalin should add Leonard Read to the Politburo to maintain a balance.

Yours sincerely,

Rose Wilder Lane/ASL

We close with a letter to Lane from Read suggesting that von Mises's democratic views were to be handled with the greatest delicacy, which might speak to the fate of Watts at FEE.

[Foundation for Economic Education Letterhead]

September 13, 1950

Mrs. Rose Wilder Lane
Route 4, Box 42
Danbury, Connecticut

Dear Rose:

Your letter to Mises sounds pretty rough to me, particularly after returning from the Mt. Pelerin Conference and observing both Roepke and Mises in action.

While I will concede the brilliance and rightness of Roepke's statement as quoted, and admit once again my own utter dislike for the use of the word "democracy" as description of the kind of society we have in mind, I must insist that Roepke is an awful double-talker and doesn't even belong in the same company as Mises. Roepke hit this particular note right and glory be for that.

My journal of the trip and my comments on the Conference, now being typed, will shed some light on this. A copy is reserved for you and will go forward perhaps Monday.

I do hope to see you soon.

Cordially,

bc: Dr. Mises

Leonard E. Read/ASL

PROPERTY AS A FUNCTION OF POLITICS: A WORK ON PROPERTY AND POLITICS, APPARENTLY AUTHORED BY HEINRICH VON TREITSCHKE

Warren J. Samuels

I. INTRODUCTION

Politics and judicial decisions have in some fashion been conducted in the United States (and elsewhere) as a contest between adversaries. The legal representatives of the two parties articulate the competing sets of claims generally in a manner that represents the legal or jurisprudential version of their clients' respective attitudes. The judge(s) who hear the case and the justices who consider the appeals also tend to do likewise. A "final" decision by the United States Supreme Court (or any State appellate court) and any dissenters to a majority decision will very likely be composed of similar language.

At the heart of the adversarial process is a juxtaposition that is frequently ignored or skirted, even obfuscated. Yet it is at the core of the dispute and its resolution. The juxtaposition is between law treated as an extension of the parties' respective personal positions and physical self, on the one hand, and law treated as a social phenomenon, on the other. The latter is seen by the devotees of the former to comprise "socialism" precisely because it posits *public* purpose.

Documents on Government and the Economy
Research in the History of Economic Thought and Methodology, Volume 30-B, 117–138
Copyright © 2012 by Emerald Group Publishing Limited
All rights of reproduction in any form reserved
ISSN: 0743-4154/doi:10.1108/S0743-4154(2012)000030B005

This chapter reports on a set of notes that bears on the impasse that seems to have grown over the decades between the seemingly inevitable two sides in such confrontations. The juxtaposition that the notes summarize was and to this day remains central to the conventional practices of adversarial law. The notes include a proposal to treat a court case (e.g.) as a means of promoting economic welfare. The proposal, reasonable and manageable, although, to my knowledge, nowhere adopted, is to switch in whole or in part from treating the conflict underlying the case as between two parties each preoccupied with the potential losses or gains coming to them depending upon the decision. Decisions which are framed, argued, and written in terms of individuals, their identities, and so on are more apt, I hypothesize, to develop more serious grudges against the Court system, against law, and, yes, against individuals, by the losing party, than would decisions articulated in terms of public purpose. However, that is not necessarily the case.

II. SOME PRELIMINARIES

The typical case is one in which each side concentrates on making a sustainable presentation articulating its position. The person who has no (official) position in the case may nonetheless participate through the submission of an *amicus curiae* brief. The documentation is likely to echo or anticipate the parties' respective treatment of law as an extension of the parties' personal position and interests. *Black's Law Dictionary* first notes that such a brief likely includes material pertinent to the case of which the court appears likely to be ignorant, miscomprehend, and/or unduly narrowly apply, and is in danger of being committing an error. *Black's* then notes that in such a brief a person "is allowed to introduce argument, authority, or evidence to protect his interests" (Black, 1968, p. 107).

Cognizance should also be taken of the *Code of Professional Responsibility*. The Preamble to the Code commences with paeans to several concepts or phrases, e.g., that the continued existence of a free and democratic society depends upon recognition of the concept that justice is based upon the rule of law grounded in respect for the dignity of the individual and his capacity through reason for enlightened self-government. Law so grounded makes justice possible, for only through such law does the dignity of the individual attain respect and protection (Black, 1968, p. xvii).

The key words are primitive terms for which an audience of auditors or readers must inevitably supply its own definitions – definitions that likely will differ materially from one person to another. From different perspectives, the terms seem to be either ends or means, or both. "Justice," e.g., can be seen as both.

Other passages tend to place the position of lawyer on the side of continuity of legal arrangements. Yet the Code also includes the statement that:

> Within the framework of these principles, a lawyer must with courage and foresight be able and ready to shape the body of the law to the ever-changing relationships of society. (Black, 1968, p. xvii)

Thus, does the *Code of Professional Responsibility* of the American Bar Association handle the problem of dealing with the perennial concept and associated issues encountered in working out what Joseph Spengler (1948, 1968) called the problem of order, namely, in addition to the conflict between continuity and change, between freedom (or autonomy) and control, and between hierarchy and equality? I suspect that "balancing" relative hardship in working out solutions to conflicts between continuity and change of law by law is possibly the most contentious of all – and I have intentionally not even mentioned the conflict between legislature and court, between Common and Constitutional Law, on the one hand, and Statutory and Administrative Law, on the other.

Lawyers remain en masse in charge of the economic, social, and, especially, political system for a number of reasons: (1) the growth of statute and administrative law, (2) the growth of legal practice, (3) the diffusion of private legal practice to encompass and requirement of some minimal knowledge of all of the forms that law may take, (4) the teaching of the several forms of law, (5) the jealousy, fear, and loathing once conspicuous if not dominant and still apparent to open-minded observers in local bar association circles, however muted, (6) the enormous decline in opportunities to learn law by doing law in law firms, (7) the enormous growth of a variety of legal publications, (8) the more or less slow passing and/or eclipse of those traditional Common Law lawyers who insisted upon a set of rules of judicial interpretation of statutes to minimize the impact of statutes on Common Law, (9) the good sense of the academic leaders of law not to denigrate or exclude earlier generation of lawyers, (10) the older lawyers' continued opportunity to acquire work, income, and status, and (11) the government's continued reliance on lawyers. For a time after World War II, the possibility of serious, if gentlemanly, low-key conflict between economists and lawyers (at least among the academicians in both groups) seemed real but did not materialize.

The lawyers have done, I think, a better job than have economists of managing the relations between orthodox and heterodox members of their profession. I am relatively short on the knowledge required to reach accurate conclusions in these matters. The disciplines of economics and law have a number of characteristics in common. The one most relevant here is the tension evident in each field between methodological individualism and methodological collectivism. The former arises when the judge and scholar take, as they usually do, the view that the case is between individual interests. The latter arises when the social functions of litigation, e.g., are center stage, because the approach recommended by the ultimate author of the notes underscores that the decision applies to all persons in the relevant jurisdiction, and not only the particular parties to the case. The basic difference is the tendency that in the former only arguments pertaining to the individual parties are given status, whereas in the latter considerations relevant to the society as a whole are mandated.

Another way of considering the two different approaches is to think in terms of welfare. The use of the term "welfare" does not refer to programs of varying sorts to enhance the living conditions, lives, and opportunities of the poor. Its focus is on the development of increases and decreases in well-being by the society as a whole. The problem is that whatever the focus there is no coherent way to determine whether, e.g., the development of medical technology, all things considered, contributes a net increase or decrease in welfare.

III. HEINRICH von TREITSCHKE

The document consists of notes from a work apparently attributed to "Treitschke," presumably Heinrich von Treitschke (1834–1896). (I can think of no other reason for the use and placement of his name and the pages.) Treitschke was a German professor, politician, and publicist. His father was an officer in the Saxon army, rising to serve as governor of Königstein and military governor of Dresden. The son was prevented by deafness (apparently the result of an accident while a youth) from entering either the army or electoral politics. He taught at Freiburg, Kiel, Heidelberg, and Berlin (Humboldt), and succeeded Leopold von Ranke as historian of Prussia. He strongly supported the Hohenzollern dynasty; advocated colonial expansion; and is widely thought responsible, at the least, for anti-British feeling in Germany. He was an extraordinarily prolific writer of his own (historical and other) books and essays. He also edited the monthly *Preussische Jahrbücher* for 23 years (1866–1889).

As a historian, he took a very strong pro-Prussian position, so much so that he changed his citizenship from Saxony to Prussia. He argued in favor of assimilation, and therefore the disappearance of Jewry from German (if not European) society. He was a very influential teacher of civil servants. The anonymous author of the entry on Treitschke in *The Columbia Encyclopedia* (Columbia Encyclopedia) wrote that "he exerted tremendous influence, particularly on the younger generation."

Treitschke applauded the periodic expulsion of Jews from European countries, at least the exorbitant taxation of their income and property and the expropriation or confiscation of their property. Princes, he urged, can treat Jewish property as their own. The Jewish people might even be penned up in patrolled reservations, with their synagogues, prayer books, and schools destroyed, rabbis forbidden to preach, and their homes and other property either destroyed or confiscated. Attention should be given to who really is a Gentile.

Treitschke started his professorial and intellectual career as both a nationalist and a liberal; for some reason, however, he became increasingly conservative. His ultranationalism praised national strength and its promotion through what is now seen as colonialism and imperialism as well as general aggression against ones neighbors. The Hobbesian picture of European society described (and, in effect, promoted) by Treitschke helped extend the longevity of traditional rivalries among nations, including the two world wars of the twentieth century. Treitschke wrote a great deal, mostly on German history and politics. For many people, mention of Treitschke and of his view of politics readily elicits the thought of his having been a precursor to Adolph Hitler and two world wars.

IV. THE NOTES

The manuscript published below was given to me by Edwin E. Witte in May or June 1957. Witte was a long-time professor of economics at the University of Wisconsin. He was completing his year term as president of the American Economic Association and also retiring at Wisconsin.

The 6″ × 9″ paper is, as it was then, brittle. Unfortunately, a small amount of original material has been lost along the sides of the sheets. It appears to this editor that no significant loss of text material has taken place because of the passage of time and varying conditions of office, home, and weather.

No indication of the original work's title or date of publication or of the date or purpose of the notes is to be found in the materials given to me by Witte.

Notwithstanding the gracious assistance of several other scholars,[1] I have been unable to identify the specific book (and/or edition) by Treitschke that Commons summarized in the notes (it is possible that such book indicates another author). The original publication that the notes appear to summarize may have been published in German, with Commons translating the material into English; or the material may have appeared in one of the translations of his work into English. Treitschke's principal and apparently best-known works, each of which went through numerous editions in German, were *Politics* (complete English translation of the two German-language volumes, London, 1916, and an abridged translation, Hans Kohn, ed., 1963).***

V. THE CONTENT OF THE NOTES

Should a reader correctly identifies the author – Treitschke or someone else – and the title of the source of the notes, I will be delighted to acknowledge same in *Research in the History of Economic Thought and Methodology*. Fortunately, I have been able to use book and electronic sources to prepare these introductory and interpretive comments. I have used the search services of Norton, Google, SpringerLink, and Ask.com in part by specifying the search topic as Heinrich von Treitschke or Treitschke or Treitschke + Commons + property.

The analysis and argument is, however, clearly Treitschke's whoever else may deploy, or deplore, them. The themes that seem to have interested Commons echo throughout Treitschke's writings, namely, that property is a product of the political process, that politics (and not the ideological legitimization of either politics or property) is the source of that property, and that therefore property is a social and not an individualist phenomenon. The working out of the law of property is, to Treitschke, what government and law is fundamentally about.

The reader must be wary. These ideas of Treitschke should not be equated with the utterances of those who consider Adam Smith to be the founder or at least the forerunner of present-day notions of laissez-faire (Robbins, 1953; Samuels, 1966; Samuels & Medema, 2005, 2009; Samuels, 2009; Samuels & Johnson, 2011). The fact is, so far from considering the revision and indeed the expansion of legal social control to ipso facto constitute a socialist threat to freedom. Smith considered property and government important and inevitable. Smith is recorded by a student in his class on Jurisprudence as arguing that:

> In the age of commerce, as the subjects of property are greatly increased the laws must be proportionally multiplied. The more improved any society is and the greater length the several means of supporting the inhabitants are carried, the greater will be the number of their laws and regulations necessary to maintain justice, and prevent infringements of the right of property. (Smith, 1978, p. i.38 16, contrast Leoni, 1961).

Treitschke was one of the, if not the, most important and most controversial nineteenth-century German historians. Sigmund Neumann (1937, p. 101) wrote in his biographical entry on Treitschke in the first *Encyclopedia of the Social Sciences (Neumann)* that Treitschke pursued history with the pragmatic purpose of "furthering the political ideas current in his time" – more specifically, with "the avowed purpose of advancing the cause of German national unification under the militant and aggressive leadership of Protestant Prussia." Treitschke "sought to expound a political system of historical and ethical laws in opposition to the prevailing theory of fixed natural laws and above all to the unique importance of the State whose essence is power *(Machtpolitik)*."

The understandings, or beliefs, that no natural laws are operative, that both ordinary and constitutional judicial decisions have no absolutist basis, and so on are seemingly accepted by most, although by no means all, adults. They stand independent of claims such as Treitschke's. He was, after all, attempting to market his version of nationalist and racist policies.

Many of Treitschke's ideas are anathema to present-day Western scholars and others, including this author. That history was the result of the activities of strong, charismatic leaders, what political liberty meant, as Neumann puts it, is "a liberty politically limited by the State," are empirically correct.

Some, perhaps most, scholars will accept the idea that empirical/positivist approaches to law need not, ought not, and will not likely be grounded in or tend to State repression. One can accept social control, e.g., law, and morals, without assuming that social peace requires the premise that all men are malevolent. The modern – although not always satisfactory – assumption is that the institutions and activities of social control are needed because of the growth of population, density, and interaction, as well as to control the malevolent.

Treitschke, however, went beyond the latter assumption. He supported and justified ethnic and racial cleansing (as it later came to be called), violence, and murder, and lauded war and aggression both within political units and between them, i.e., imperialism. Some people having Treitschke-type beliefs have tried to sugarcoat the policies; for whatever it is worth, I do not know how much Treitschke might have done so. Some ideas are intolerable in themselves and/or in their results.

He did not equivocate: going to (especially an aggressive) war for your country was honorable; scholarship was inferior to propaganda (perhaps not at various times and in various ways); historiography inevitably is and should be a political activity. Treitschke was very much in the tradition of German romanticism, a form of conservatism, such as constructed by Joseph de Maistre, Immanuel Kant, and George Wilhelm Friedrich Hegel, along with British versions developed by Edmund Burke and Thomas Carlyle, among others.

Not surprisingly, many scholars have concluded that Treitschke's ideas and writings helped prepare the German mind for the ascendance of Adolph Hitler, the Nazi Party, the Holocaust, and World War II – that Hitler's rise to power would have been unthinkable without Treitschke and others with comparable ideas. Needless to say, many other scholars, pointing to other phenomena, disagree.

Treitschke, however, arguably went further in a different direction from his evident version of nationalism. How much is material and how much is a matter of seeking to appeal to different groups (to people with different beliefs, feelings, and policy views), even though the arguments may conflict or not hang together well, are hard to say. For example, Treitschke and others rejected socialism (whatever the term may have meant to them or whatever purpose the use of the term may have served). He rejected, however, the view that the State's first (i.e., primary) function is to secure life and property to individuals. If that were the case, he asks, how is it that the individual will also sacrifice life and property to the State? For individualists know and/or are sensitive to individualist arguments, and it was a principal objective of Treitschke to establish that notwithstanding the conventional claims made by the parties to a case and those who agree with them, including judges who should know better, disputes are settled by reference and weights assigned to the elements of the important conflict, *social purpose*. The first essential function of the State to Treitschke is to define and assign rights, not merely to protect them. The next essential function of the State for Treitschke is the *conduct* of war.

Just as there are varieties of psychological theory, religion, economics, and pretty much every other topic, so too are there varieties of conservatism, the State, liberalism, rights, and so on. Within every group of thinkers there are topics on which several authors agree and other topics on which they disagree.

Most commentators, it seemed to Treitschke, focus on the elements of property in a defensive manner. This is brought about by the concentration of litigation and the interests of many judges, legislators, and specialists on superficial (although not necessarily unimportant) individualist grounds. Some are able to weave together using both types of materials. This includes those who consider politics to be a function of ethics and those who regard ethics to be a function of politics. Politics is thus stripped of all traditional ideals and conceived as a function of the sheer power of the State. In this manner, twentieth-century ideologies and mythologies determine which elements of German history should be placed in the foreground (e.g., high politics, culture, and social structures) and which should be consigned to the background (here one can find the liberal dimensions of rationalism and anti-Semitism). But the specification of examples is selective even in this regard. (Here, if this exercise were a play, it might enter conflicting examples from one side of the stage.)

The text is in Commons' longhand. Editing has been kept to a minimum. Only slight effort has been exerted to tease out the words completely or largely missing due to loss of brittle paper. A set of three asterisks (***) is used to indicate missing word(s). In instances such as the word "cultures" in the first sentence after the initial listing of the three types of theory, only "cult" remains after flaking; either "culture" or "cultures" seems useful. Some alterations have been made to provide stylistic consistency, being careful to not thereby introduce substantive change of meaning.

The document consists of 10 sheets. At first glance, the relation of the 10 sheets to each other is confusing. The only sheets with page numbers run from 3 to 9. These, however, are on the fourth through the tenth sheets. The first sheet in the group, which surely is a first, or title page, is unnumbered, as are the next two sheets. The numbering commences on the fourth sheet, with the number 3, and concludes with the number 8 on the ninth sheet. The document as a whole concludes two-thirds down the unnumbered tenth sheet.

A possible but as yet inconclusive means of solving the problems of (1) confirming the author of the original document and (2) identifying the source may have been either wittingly or unwittingly provided by Commons himself. The notes include what apparently are the page number(s) in Treitschke's work from which the argument and points of interest to Commons were taken. If the sequence of cited pages was in arithmetical order, it would suggest a means of determining the sequence of sheets. The sequence and location of cited pages within the 10 sheets of cited pages is as follows:

Unnumbered sheet 1: pp. 55, 61
Unnumbered sheet 2: pp. 18–19, 20–23, 24
Unnumbered sheet 3: pp. 8–9, 10, 14ff.
Sheet numbered 3: pp. 25, 28, 29–30
Sheet numbered 4: pp. 31, 32
Sheet numbered 5: pp. 35
Sheet numbered 6: pp. 35–36, 37–38
Sheet numbered 7: no page citations fully discernible
Sheet numbered 8: pp. 40–41, 47ff, 48–49
Unnumbered sheet 4: no page citations

The sequence is broken by the first three sheets. It also seems to be the case that, by subjective judgment reached through considering the elements of the argument alone, the sequence as such is not important.

If the sequence of elements comprising the argument is of little significance by itself, the substance of the argument is, however, very deep and potentially very important. The text of the notes on the 10 pages runs as follows.

[First unnumbered sheet]

P. 5   PROPERTY AND THE PRINCIPLE OF DISTRIBUTIVE JUSTICE

John R. Commons

Three theories of property, or groups of theories:

1. Hugo Grotius – social contract
2. Hobbes, Montesquieu – legal
3. Locke – labor

The latter had more bases in primitive culture, because it lay at the bottom.[2] But in our comp[etitive] production "property is based on the existence of [the] individual as such it is the necessary physical and moral extension of the individual. But this idea of property is only justifiable insofar as it takes into account the fact whether (1) each individual is an industrious member of the community, (2) that the idea can be realized only by the State through legal duties and restrictions upon property, and these must be imposed in the interests of the whole community. The new Political Economy pays attention to the ethical and legal *duties* of *Property* and *property-owners*, the old Political Economy to duties of the *propertyless* and to the *rights of property* (p. 5).[3]

The rights of property are not independent of law, and law has justice and equality (i.e., ethical ideas) for its aim.

Even those who deny ethical ideals never[theless] indirectly assume them – they do not aim at [equa]ity but at aristocracy of wealth or birth (p. 61).

[Second unnumbered sheet]
Treitschke, while advocating critical methods in science and religion, opposes them in ethics and economics – such questions as fair price, labor's share in distribution (pp. 18–19). He bases his arguments in economics on certain fundamental dogmas:

1. Natural inequality of mankind. Answer: while there may be inequalities in the endowments of children of the same family due to natural causes, yet differences in *social classes* are due to historical-social causes, e.g., (1) deterioration of negroes in U.S. owing to methods of breeding; (2) deterioration of working classes in Germany and England who, for three centuries, have been oppressed and consigned to stunting kinds of work (pp. 20–23).

If these results are due to nature then there can be no human progress, and men are like brutes. But in human society there is a progressive conquest of nature by means of civilization and moral principles (p. 24). Men resist the powers of nature through (1) the reforming spirit, (2) intelligent contrivances, (3) labor unions, (4) adherence to a standard of life (p. 24).

2. Treitschke holds that in the everlasting *** things there are constant unchanging *** of marriage, property and social org[anization]. The autocratic structure of society and *** has been the framework *** (p. 25).

[Third unnumbered sheet]
   1. Treitschke accuses them of holding that all men are created by nature equ[ally]. On the contrary Sch[moller] holds that differences are due both to nature and to civilization (pp. 8–9).[4]

2. Treitschke accuses them of demanding the enjoyment of all products of civilization for all men, i.e., communism. On the contrary they set up an ideal towards which they wish society gradually to develop, although recognizing that the ideal may be unattainable (p. 10).
3. Treitschke accuses [Gustav von] Schmoller (1) of communism, i.e., *** [and] (2) of the *** of a distribution according to merit. These are inconsistent, and come from misrepresentation of Schmoller's actual position.
4. Treitschke accuses them of pessimism (p. 14ff.). But they hold that there has been an immense bettering of social conditions extending even to the lowest classes. This however does not make them blind to the injustice and inequalities that actually exist.

[Sheet numbered 3]
*** all history has moved and in which future history will move (p. 25) – that a democratic organization is only an exception, wherever it can be proved to have existed – that the present democratizing process will never reach its ideal.

Answer: He gives an extreme interpretation to the idea of equality—It is only held that this idea can be reached in gross and in general. The State can do something to bring about such ideals, contrary to the dictum of Treitschke.

3. Treitschke holds the dogma of freedom of exchange to be inviolable. This dogma is as utopian as the hope of abolishing the State, or of healing social evils by doing away with ***, or by extending rights of electi[ve] franchise (p. 28).
4. The ethical element of monogamy, property and right of succession does not lie in the fact that they been common in other times, i.e., in their abstract idea, but in the fact that the laws respecting these institutions are adequate, in a definite time and a definite people, to maintain a just and ethical order, and an ethical education of society (pp. 29–30).

[Sheet numbered 4]
It is usually asserted that the difference between the old and new schools of Political Economy is in the importance given by the latter to the functions of the State. But the difference is deeper. The new school might be consistent with their principles and advocate even a lessening of State interference. The difference lies in the new conception of the relations of ethics and law to Political Economy (p. 31).[5]

The older economists held that there was no national economy, national capital, or national income, but only a sum of individual economies. But the economies of individuals of the same nation stand in different relations to each other than they do to the economies of individuals of other nations. The economic life of a people is influenced not merely by being under the same government, but by a community of *speech*, of *history*, or *remembrances*, of *morals*, of *ideas* (p. 32).[6]

[Sheet numbered 5]
It is held that economic activities do not fall under the ethical standpoint, but a technical, [three-quarters of an inch or so of blank space on this line, suggestive of an intention to add something]. But the simplest technical operation is undertaken with an end in view, and as part of a system, not with superfluous means. Pure force of nature and want necessitates only a passing exertion, undertaken on the spur on account of lawyer, etc. But our idea of labor contains a moral element. "Labor is that rational self-activity which strives by continuous exertion to bring about something in the system of human objects which is recognized as right; it has become in a certain sense an object in itself, so that it stands for us as the school of all virtues, as the preserver of all possessions, as the basis of our social organization." In Political Economy we investigate the relations of individual economies to one another and to the whole, and so with operations in which the technical side receives a coloring, a form or direction from ethics and law. Economic life begins as the mere natural instinct urging [individuals] to the supply of natural needs. But ethical feelings, aesthetic needs and the intellect gradually shape a frame in which they operate, and this frame, by transmission, comes to be a sacred religious order into which the individual is born (p. 35).[7]

[Sheet numbered 6]
Not only do the larger economic institutions depend upon custom, being sustained by law, such as slavery, serfdom, feudalism, guild system, freedom of industry, [and] organization of agriculture, but all minor questions, such as markets,[8] the flourishing of a trade, the subordinate questions of cash or credit payments which influences the prosperity of different classes, the question of home or factory industry – [that] supply and demand do not affect price and consumption directly but through the customs of the particular people. In one place, with established customs of trade, an oversupply will lead to increased speculation, in another, with different customs, to a long depression of prices, e.g., a fall in sugar leads to increased consumption in England but not so in Germany. The whole question is a matter of the moral history of a given time and people (pp. 35–[3]6).

Individualism as a starting point in economic affairs is an unlimited superfluity. It is the essential basis for all economic systems, that out of which they are made. But it explains the phenomena no more than the statement that a machine is made of iron explains the nature of the machine.[9] There must be, besides, a knowledge of the psychological evolution and character of the given people (pp. 37–[3]8).

[Sheet numbered 7]
Connected with the idea of individualism are two false ideas.

1. That through all social history there is a constant normal form of organization towards which society is progressing, and that the State can interfere with this advance only to the detriment of society.[10] This is opposed by [Friedrich] List, [Johann Gottlieb] Fichte, [Wilhelm] Roscher, [Karl] Knies, [Bruno] Hildebrand.
2. That every form of natural environment, every climate, every period of capital formation, and of population, every period of technical progress determine an absolutely necessary order of economic life. These are important, but not the only elements. There are also the ideas of civilization of the period, moral and aesthetic ideas. Every economic organization is not merely for the production of material goods, but for the production of moral factors; e.g., the education of the coming generations of laborers, the securing of such industry, leisure, responsibility, honor and family life, for individuals, that the progress on which future well-being depends, may be secured.[11] These are not questions of natural order, but of spiritual, ethical, psychological causes.The object of economic organization should be to obtain the highest technical excellence, always subordinated, however, to morals and law, so as to lessen evil results.[12]

[Sheet numbered 8]
The present technical operations and great machinery are indispensable. But they do not impose women and child labor, the distribution of product, the distribution of losses – these depend on morals and law, the civilized ideas of the time. Great undertakings are imposed by the present State of industry, but whether these should be undertaken by individuals, companies, corporations, communities or the State is a question of the psychological factors, i.e., of ethics and custom, of ideas of civilization and law (pp. 40–41).[13]

The distribution of product, depending upon inheritance, is regulated by custom and law, not by natural law, which is only the war of all against all, or robbery and murder (p. 41).

Development of Custom into Law (p. 44ff). In earliest times there [was] no distinction between Law, Religion and Custom. But as individuals break away

from Custom, the people put at least a part of their custom into the stricter form
of law. There are then the two ~~fields~~ divisions of social structure, (1) Custom,
with public opinion and esteem as its executive organ, and (2) Law with civil and
compulsory State processes. Beyond this are the regions of free individual morality. Those who argue for freedom do not want absolute unregulated freedom, but
[continued on next sheet]

[Sheet numbered 9]
they think custom *** than law *** the better regulator. The question is not,
therefore, one between regulation ["Rule" is written above regulation], between
rule of law and rule of custom (p. 47ff.).[14]

The demand for freedom of the older economists has aided the development of
trade for the middle classes, but not for the welfare of the lower classes.[15] When
freedom is advocated, there must be taken into consideration with it the forces
that rise to power with the removal of restrictions. If these work more evil than
good they must be restricted. Freedom is an empty room – what grows up in it
depends upon the natural and moral-intellectual forces which find a place ~~spring
up~~ in it (pp. 48–49).

It arose in a time of transition and similar transitions have occurred: (1) in
[the] time of [the] first Roman emperor, (2) in [the] time of [the] 15th century in
Germany, (3) in [the] 15th and 16th centuries.

VI. INTERPRETATION AND DISCUSSION

Commons' argument

Our conception of property projects property to be the necessary physical and moral extension
of the individual.

It is justifiable insofar as it takes into account whether each individual is an industrious
member of the community and that the idea can be realized only by the State through legal
duties and restrictions in the interests of the whole community.

The old Political *** economy pays attention to the duties of the propertyless and to the rights
of property, the new Political Economy to the ethical and legal duties of property and property
owners.

May be said to constitute that treatment of any individual, in respect of right or restriction,
must accord with the interests of the whole community; insofar as the State, in identifying
rights and duties, must choose between conflicting claims of interest and right, must base its

decisions not on the identity of the respective individuals but on the interests of the whole community.

This is in principle no different from a certain important (but poorly understood and frequently recklessly and ideologically applied) part of Adam Smith's argument in which he invokes the "invisible hand" without it adding anything to his argument, "As every individual, therefore, endeavors as much as he can both to employ his capital in the support of domestic industry, and so to direct that industry that its produce may be of the greatest value[,] every individual necessarily labours to render the annual revenue of the society as great as he can. By preferring the support of domestic to that of foreign industry, he intends only his own security[,] and his own gain ..., and he is in this, as in many other cases, led by an invisible hand to [frequently] promote an end of the society the public good" (Smith, 1976, p. IV.ii.9).

Commons affirms the role of considering the whole community in working out the system of rights and restrictions, e.g., in choosing between conflicting claims of interest and right. Smith does likewise by assuming that "render[ing] the annual revenue of the society as great as" can be the criterion constituting, as Commons puts it, "the interests of the whole community," or as Smith does, "the public interest," or "the public good."

Both Smith and Commons, at this point of their respective arguments and language, contemplate that there is in "the interests of the whole community" a "public interest" or "public good" that must, or should, be applied in law making. In the case of Smith, this is evident in his reasoning in both the *Wealth of Nations* (1976) and his *Lectures on Jurisprudence* (1978).

There is a difference between the ordinary conception of property and that of Smith and of Commons. It is expressed by Commons' statement of the ordinary conception, in which he notes that *** "productive property is based on the existence of [the] individual as such," "it is the necessary physical and moral extension of the individual," whereas to both Smith and to Commons the necessary conception is that of *public purpose*. That is to say that the deciding body – the legislature and/or the courts – is not choosing between the concepts of property advanced by parties to the conflict but choosing the public good, public interest, social welfare, etc., which the decision should promote. That this is the situation is obfuscated by the fact that each party to the conflict thinks largely only in terms of what they think will enhance their position. The privateness of property thus postulates that the law of property should promote private and not public purpose. The irony is, however, that Treitschke's position is applauded by those who desire to extirpate all social characteristics of property yet seem compelled to rely upon social purpose as the basis of property.

Treitschke's argument

Treitschke's approach to property, based on reliance on considerations of social values and not private values, is significant in several ways. No hard and fast line exists between putatively social and putatively private values. The introduction of social considerations serves to remind people that, after all absolutist legitimiza-tion is given voice, property is a social construction; indeed, such legitimizations are, intentionally or not, contributions to a social process. This is true of all nominally private properties created by monarchs in order to reward their supporters. The distinction enables the identification and conflict between two types of arguments each advocated as conservative. One position proposes that existing claims of property rights must be resolved on the basis of maintaining traditional values, i.e., that the process of working out the respective relative rights of property is a social process. The other position is that the introduction of allegedly social considerations is a not-so-subtle means of advocating "socialism." For one position, therefore, the use of "social values" functions to promote the values deemed to be social, whereas the denigration of "social values" accomplishes the opposite. The juxtaposition of these two views suggests several twists which may, or may not, advance serious discussion. One twist occurs when the rival claimants of rights each has an elaborate and seemingly impregnable battery of arguments because until some change in context changes their relative positions, as William Blackstone put it, as absolute and despotic decision makers over their respective propertied domains, they are essentially equally situated. A second twist occurs when the contest over change of law devolves into a contest over whether present-day government has the same power as earlier governments to make law. A further twist is that each such contest over continuity versus change has reciprocal elements, such as is embodied in Ronald Coase's theory of externalities. The final twist is that in each contest a choice must be made that ultimately rests on pure choice. All efforts to more or less permanently ground some basis of property are a will-o'-the-wisp, deceptive, illusory, and lack serious intelligent intellectual substance. Some people learn that they have been targets for psychological mobilization, manipulation, and sacrifice. They may also learn that laws that they were led to believe ostensibly controlled and limited certain aspects of manipulation of substantial importance to the related political process were themselves merely contributions to the political process from which policies emerge. One example is the rules of campaign finance in the light of the First Amendment's prohibition of abridging the freedom of speech. Statutes that help finance elections in exchange for the candidate limiting their spending financed by private contributions from donors in the State have a flaw unless they are attended to and prevented by the relevant legislature. Candidates can get around, evade, or finesse a limitation in various ways. Assume, e.g., two States, Sa and Sb; two candidates (from a larger number in each State), Ca and Cb; and one or both of the States having a statute limiting the amount of money that a citizen of the State can contribute to any one candidate in a given election. A devious candidate (or a representative of the candidate) can approach someone, perhaps known to be sympathetic to the election of that candidate, and propose that each candidate arrange for their respective proxy donations be made in the donor's name as a citizen of "another" State. Now we have the two donors, Da and Db. Da contributes as an outsider to the campaign of Cb, and Db contributes to the campaign of Ca. The candidates have pretty much the freedom of action in spending that they had before the passage of the one or two statutes limiting intrastate contributions to campaigns in exchange for limiting campaigns to a certain level. This situation is a complete negation of campaign finance control and is reinforced by legislation either not providing for or banning the publication of the names of either all donors to all campaigns or only the out-of-state donors to the campaign of the candidate(s).

A further matter relevant to and illustrative of the social aspect of property: Is the regulation of property to be considered indicative of a legal right to devote some of one's property = assets = wealth to a candidacy under and within the toothless statutes? Or is it an example not of politics as the extension of oneself, but of asking questions about the public purpose which the statute is intended to achieve? Does an effective control statute constitute "socialism"? Is it "social-ism' for a government to control spending on an electoral campaign? Is it enough to control your property and your money as you like? Is it enough, for present purposes, to convince you that the deepest question is what type of society will permit such comparatively easy evasion of its laws? Also, are people equal in their ability to arrange such reciprocal out-of-state, even out-of-country, dona-tions? The U.S. Supreme Court has overturned certain restrictions on campaign financing. For most if not all purposes, does that decision have any influence on the issue of individual versus social nature of law and legal decision making? Should it?

The same problem arises in connection with individualism. Most Western economic thought postulates given individuals in ways that beg the question of the origins of the individual. The individual is *not* given: the individual is a func-tion of the social belief system, the social control system, and the market process itself. Neoclassicists such as Frank Knight and substantially all institutionalists acknowledge and even stress that individuals, markets, and government are made by the economic process itself. Frank Knight urged that the chief product of the economy is man. It is good training and solid educational value to provide models of alternative modes of decision making.

The principal fundamental lesson deriving from the Treitschke–Commons position was and remains hardly original with them. Property is a function of politics – such is an empirically accurate proposition. Politics is the process of people working out the content of property. This constitutes the inexorably social nature of politics and policy. Accordingly, it makes sense to understand property, policy, and politics in *both* individualist and social terms, and not one to the exclusion of the other.

What constitutes public purpose, therefore, is also not given. Politics, including the politics of property, is the process of working out, of making and not merely finding, public purpose.

As analytically attractive as legal, or legal-economic, theory emphasizing not individual interests but public purpose may be the discussion of issues in the context of Common and Constitutional Law decisions is not a purely social solution to the problems raised by Treitschke and Commons. This is so because the replacement of individual interests with social interests is likely to consist of the language of social purpose, but the construction of that language would strongly amount to the transformation of claims of individual interests into the language of claims of social purpose. The situation under the rubric of "public purpose" law would be largely the same as that under the rubric of "private interest" law. The difference is substantively linguistic: the language of public purpose law would replace the language of individual interests. There is no likelihood that decisions of courts' legislative committees will be based on public purpose any more than it is at present. The language of public purpose may replace the language of individual interests, but the content of law and legislation will be driven by individual interests – more or less socialized (societized) and more or less different, depending on the ideology or mind-set of public officials. The results of decision making will continue along historical paths. The language of individual interest will continue to produce social purpose *indirectly*. That is the reason, I think, that Commons could stress institutions of collective decision making but did not settle on public purpose as a fundamental concept in his formulation of institutional economics.

Property, even intellectual property, such as incorporeal property, as well as other types, is empirically superior in that, first, the ability exists to observe it being created and used and, second, any naturalist or supernaturalist interpretation, ceteris paribus, will have one additional premise, pertaining to the existence of God and to divine reasoning. By the principle of Ockham's razor, the non-metaphysical explanation is preferable: it is the ability to see property created, as in the drawing up of enabling statutes and of contracts, and to see it used in practice. A further aspect is the substantial, if not enormous, diversity of property systems, rights, means of ownership registration, and, *inter alia*, legal protection and other aspects of the characteristics of property systems. It is infinitely more difficult to imagine and explain divine motives in, first, creating and distributing multiple property systems and, second, have them undergo different evolutionary paths with no reasonable evidence of their convergence. (The foregoing applies to both national systems of property and, as in the United States, 50 different

State systems, with occasional ambitious attempts to give effect to a sense of one coherent system.) It should come as no surprise that property is a primitive term. I wonder if any writer, theologian or otherwise, has attempted to attribute to God an interest in experimenting with such minute issues in formulating and changing the law of property at the level of nitty-gritty details.

The following includes partial summaries, revisions, extensions, and so on:

Private property is chosen, and conflicts between claimants over whose interests count are settled in part on the basis of judgments as to public welfare or purpose, and not individual claims alone.

Private property is a function of politics. The State is the political process which works out solutions to conflicts over private interests and different definitions of reality and of public purpose.

Interested parties often resort to assertions of ostensible absolutes, e.g., grounded in Nature or Deity, and associated with a suitable author or book, with the intent of selectively or idiosyncratically rendering property immune to legal change.

The results of the political process are a function of the structure of the political process. Accordingly, interested parties seek to so structure and so use the political process that the basis of property is that which is believed to be most conducive to the parties' own welfare, including their personal versions of public purpose.

Those who seek to establish (selectively, of course) private property as transcendent to government are doomed, therefore, to be necessarily sensitive to ideological, theological, and other beliefs, especially the change of those beliefs. Both the actuality and the prospect of unwelcome ideational change impose an ongoing but, ironically, changing need for the rearmament and modernization of the intellectual bastions and other fortifications of the system. Thus, the period of the cold war evidenced, on both sides, enormous efforts to maintain, shore up, and add to the more-or-less ill-fated beliefs left by history, as it were, to the corrosive impact of the efforts of the disaffected and the alienated, the growing status of positivist knowledge, and so on. Every seriously threatening military weapon enjoyed by one side elicits comparable demands and efforts on the other side. New theories of international trade, imperialism, labor markets, politics, capital, and, yes, of property itself were formulated. If one side investigated paranormal means of action, the other side hurried to start and/or to catch up. The same is true of the technology of space exploration. It is exquisitely symmetrical.

VII. THE PRESENT IMPASSE

The difficulty can be stated quite simply: No conclusive test exists with which to approach, explain, and/or solve any decision-making situation, the individualist or the social. That is why solutions must be worked out.

NOTES

1. I am indebted to Y. S. Brenner, Daniel W. Bromley, Lucia Kolesarova, Steven G. Medema, Ingo Pies, Bruce Pietykowski, and Keith Tribe, for assistance.

2. An important point is made here, it seems to me, namely, that at any point of time there exists more than one theory of property. There may well be a tendency to represent the entirety of a period's theories of property by giving premier status to the newest-formulated or most recently adopted theory. Doing so likely would misrepresent the array of theories for the period in question. Two centuries later it *may* be accurate to emphasize that earlier newest-formulated theory, if in fact its increasingly enhanced ranking is shown to be true. But even in that case, it is likely that for a substantial period of time after its initial formulation that theory co-existed and competed with other, older theories. New theories must confront already-formulated theories, and the latter may well be more comfortable to then-contemporary thinkers, and continue to have a sizeable following for some time.

3. These lines establish that for Commons, first, law is neither natural nor somehow given but is a human construct and, second, law can create, enforce, change, and/or give effect to different groups differently. Similarly, Political Economy can assume either the rights of the propertied and the concomitant duties of those without property, or the rights and duties of both groups. The following lines reiterate that law is not independent of the State and that law gives effect to one or another concept of justice and equality; hence, law is inevitably a normative, or an ethical, phenomenon. Here and throughout the notes, Commons distinguishes law as a general category from the actual law and the choices institutionalized in law that identify and protect or leave exposed different interests differently, similarly with ethical ideas. Those who prefer to avoid the conflictual nature of society, law and economy can readily assume institutions out of analytical bounds or outside the scope of economics. One important facet of these ideas is a distinction between sentiment (say, which affirms or denies the effectiveness of ethics or law), i.e., wishful thinking, and fact (say, which recognizes the operative significance of law and ethics).

4. Commons, in effect, is agreeing with Frank Knight's dictum that the principal product of the economy is man.

5. Commons, for most if not all practical and theoretical purposes, adopts, albeit with relatively less attention to the market (exemplifying Smith's principle of the division of labor, the market plus framework approach to the economic role of government, political economy, and the scope of economics put forth by Lionel Robbins (1953), and subsequently by the present editor (Samuels 1966), in exposition of the theory of economic policy of Adam Smith and English classical political economy as a whole. The market plus framework approach posits a framework of both legal and non-legal social control, the latter consisting of custom, morals, religion and education. The approach stresses the continuing social construction of reality and the inevitability of tensions over the substantive content of legal and moral rules, the relations between law and morals, the relative scope of legal and moral rules, and so on, as well as tension between public recognition and discussion of the foregoing topics and the need felt by some people for quiet on such topics lest the effectiveness of absolutist

legitimization be compromised (for example, it is difficult to otherwise reconcile human construction of law and morals with, for example, the judicial finding rather than making of law. Such tensions account for much of the difference and much of the conflict between analytical jurisprudence and legal realism and between neoclassical and institutional economics. That is to say, one does not know from the text of Commons' notes what either he or Treitschke precisely have in mind by using such terms as "old school", "new school", "natural needs", and so on. Steven Medema is correct when he notes that "Given all of the approaches that were in the air at the time of JRC's writing, it would be helpful for the reader to know exactly to what he is referring here" (Medema to Samuels, email of July 21, 2010). My inclination is to consider that such terms are used here as primitive, i.e., undefined, terms and that whatever meaning Commons might have preferred, he is here either only or principally endeavoring to establish Treitschke's meaning. The term "natural needs" is used by a number of economists in the late nineteenth century. Some authors reflect one or another version of naturalism; some seem to intend to distinguish basic needs from contrived wants.

6. Commons, in seemingly adopting the position outlined here, anticipates the present-day view which identifies the scope of economic studies to include not only morals, law, custom, religion and education, but linguistics, historicity and historiography, and so on.

7. The language, "this frame, by transmission, comes to be a sacred religious order into which the individual is born," combines the sacred as a form of absolutist formulation and Frank Knight's argument that man is made through these social processes. The "sacred religious order" need not involve a formal religion; the common characteristic is sacerdotal treatment. There were numerous commonalities between Commons and Knight; each man was able to reach fundamental social processes, each in his own way stressing the limits of "individualism" and "individual" as a starting point (Medema to Samuels, email of July 21, 2010).

8. Designating markets to be a "minor question" can illustrate a strategic linguistic emphasis on legal and moral (and other) institutions in order to compensate for their neglect by mainstream economists focused on the market *or* an antithesis per se to markets or to their use both in fact and ideologically to finesse the claims of non-business, e.g., labor and consumer, interests. Otherwise, the preceding lines further attest to Commons' emphasis on a broad scope of economic inquiry, the legal foundations of the economy in general and of capitalism in particular, and the importance of institutions. Later in this and in the succeeding paragraphs one reads of questions being "a matter of the moral history of a given time and place" (the use of "moral" here is not to acclaim a particular set of moral rules but moral rules or morality as a category, in sync with Adam Smith) and of the necessity of "a knowledge of the psychological evolution and character of the given people." Needless to say, much thereof in practice is undertaken for social control, rather than scientific, purposes.

9. This statement exemplifies Commons' attention to, even emphasis on, deep (thick?) explanations.

10. The emphasis on "only" makes the point the logical equivalent of the frequent invisible-hand use of Frederick Hayek's principle of unintended and unforeseen consequences to identify such consequences of government action as negative and of private economic activity as beneficial (positive). Adam Smith, in his principal discussion of the matter, has several different linguistic formulations, including "than would otherwise," "might not otherwise," "necessarily," "naturally," "as in many other cases," and "frequently." In externality theory, the problem is whether an externality is to be reckoned positive or negative, a reckoning made infinitely complicated and amenable to ideological formulation by the reciprocal character of externalities.

11. Here again is language synonymous with the idea considering the making of man to be the product of the economy.

12. Although the language illustrates the problem, "The object of economic organization should be to obtain the highest technical excellence, always subordinated, however, to morals and law, so

as to lessen evil results" takes the problem to a common but questionable level; "highest technical results," "morals," and "law" remain essentially primitive (undefined) terms.

13. Here is further evidence of Commons extending the scope of institutions.

14. This is an example of the inevitable tension between law and morals in the market plus framework approach to Robbins' theory of economic policy. Steven Medema wrote that "this emphasis on customs, etc. is also very consistent with Smith – and also harkens forward to recent work: minimally in the recent work on social norms, etc. through the rational choice lens, but more strongly to the work of Elinor Ostrom" (Medema to Samuels, July 21, 2010). Of course I agree. But what does that say about the neglect by economists of these and other topics, especially law, for two hundred-plus years?

15. Commons felt that such was the result of business control and use of government, evident in his *Legal Foundations of Capitalism* (1924) and elsewhere.

REFERENCES

Black, H. C. (1968). *Black's law dictionary*, rev. (4th ed.). St. Paul, MN: West Publishing.

Columbia Encyclopedia. *The Columbia encyclopedia*. Retrieved from http://www.encyclopedia.com/topic/Heinrich_von_Treitschke.aspx.

Leoni, B. (1961). *Freedom and the Law*. Princeton, NJ: Van Nostrand.

Neumann, S. (1937). Treitschke, Heinrich von. *Encyclopedia of the social sciences* (Vol. 15). New York, NY: Macmillan.

Robbins, L. (1953). *The theory of economic policy in English classical political economy*. London, UK: Macmillan.

Samuels, W. J. (1966). *The classical theory of political economy*. Cleveland, OH: World Press.

Samuels, W. J. (2009). The Invisible Hand. In J. T. Young (Ed.), *Elgar companion to Adam Smith* (pp. 195–210). Northampton, MA: Edward Elgar.

Samuels, W. J., & Johnson, M. (2011). *The invisible hand*. New York, NY: Cambridge University Press.

Samuels, W. J., & Medema, S. G. (2005). Freeing Smith from the 'free market': On the misperception of Adam Smith on the economic role of government. *History of Political Economy, 37*(2), 219–226.

Samuels, W. J., & Medema, S. G. (2009). 'Only three duties': Adam Smith on the economic role of government. In J. T. Young (Ed.), *Elgar companion to Adam Smith* (pp. 300—314). Northampton, MA: Edward Elgar.

Smith, A. (1976). *An inquiry into the nature and causes of the wealth of nations*, Oxford, UK: Oxford University Press.

Smith, A. (1978). *Lectures on jurisprudence*. Oxford, UK: Oxford University Press.

Spengler, J. (1948). The problem of order in economic affairs. *Southern Economic Journal, 15*(July), 1–29.

Spengler, J. (1968). Economics: Its history, themes, approaches. *Journal of Economic Issues, 2*(1), 5–31.

INTRODUCTION TO NOTES FROM WARREN J. SAMUELS'S COURSE ON THE ECONOMIC ROLE OF GOVERNMENT

Marianne Johnson, Martin E. Meder and
David Schweikhardt

In May of 2011, the possibility of publishing course notes from his graduate-level course on the Economic Role of Government was discussed with Warren Samuels. This course was offered as a seminar, as a part of the field of public finance, or as a self-standing course. For more than the last decade before his retirement, and for some years after his retirement, the course was taught at Michigan State University as Economics 819, The Economic Role of Government; it was developed and taught exclusively by Samuels (Samuels, 2003). In response to an inquiry about the publication of his class notes, Samuels responded:

> I have a great deal of material from the course: my lecture notes, with changes each time, or most of the time I gave the course; I also have, I think, material from the committee which was given the task of responding to interested people's personal interest in having a major under the title "organization and control of the political economy." The people were Al Schmid, Bob Solo, and me. (By email to Marianne Johnson, May 18, 2011)

The publication of this brief discussion of Samuels' career and teaching philosophy, along with notes from his graduate class on the Economic Role of Government, is intended to share a small portion of the materials used in his class.

Documents on Government and the Economy
Research in the History of Economic Thought and Methodology, Volume 30-B, 139–149
Copyright © 2012 by Emerald Group Publishing Limited
All rights of reproduction in any form reserved
ISSN: 0743-4154/doi:10.1108/S0743-4154(2012)000030B006

Like many scholars, Warren Samuels' teaching philosophy was a reflection of his experiences as a student. Consequently, students enrolled in Samuels' classes would recognize elements of his thinking and his teaching in his experiences as a student that occurred decades before. Three episodes recalled by Samuels in his biographical writing provide evidence of his development from a student into a teacher. As Samuels recalled:

> Several of my motivations and orientations can be traced to these early periods [in high school and as an undergraduate]. These include the desire to do my own thing in my own way and to pursue an intellectual life and a repugnance for the mythological and often disingenuous absolutist formulations that characterize social control and much conventional and even otherwise sophisticated thought. They also include the relativism and social constructivism – perhaps the very essence of postmodernism – that has marked my work. Although I find it exceedingly difficult to determine the precise origins of my ideas, several specific lessons and insights were learned in high school and undergraduate school. These lessons ultimately have to do with the philosophical foundations of my approach to the world in general and to institutional economics in particular. (Samuels, 1995)

The first of these lessons occurred when Samuels attended Miami Beach Senior High School. Among his many significant experiences, a history teacher assigned to him a book by the historian James Harvey Robinson. Robinson, a historian at Columbia University and The New School for Social Research, was a leader of the movement in historiography known as "New History." Samuels recalled the impact of this book on his scholarly work:

> This [Robinson's book] had a profound impression on me, as it introduced me to the conceptual difference between "official" and "actual" or "hidden" history, or between conventional and unconventional accounts; that is, it acquainted me with the possibility of multiple accounts and interpretations. The same events could be given different meanings, especially in the context of providing education as a means of socialization, which, of course, is what history teaching in K-12 is largely about. History is a discipline of multiple stories. (Samuels, 1995)

And:

> I also learned, because of a teacher I had who gave me a book by James Harvey Robinson, that you could tell different stories of American history, particularly constitutional history. That opened my mind, and I'm sure that was her intention, to ... be careful about buying into anything ... whole hog without knowing what you were doing. And if you did that, you probably weren't buying into it whole hog. (Buchanan & Samuels, 2008)

Though the title of the book given to Samuels is unknown, an indication of the nature of Robinson's thought that must have affected Samuels is evident in Robinson's book, *The Mind in the Making* (1921), which emphasized the creation of a general frame of mind and an open-minded attitude over a particular method of studying human affairs.

A second example of Samuels' student experiences that shaped his role as a teacher is shown in his experience as an undergraduate student at the University of Miami (Florida). In a course on Government and Business, the assigned text was Robert Dahl and Charles Lindblom's (1953) classic *Politics, Economics and Welfare*. Samuels later claimed "the book demonstrated to me that one could discuss the economic role of government in a meaningful and useful abstract, theoretical way that was not necessarily and inextricably overwhelmed by either ideological preconceptions and manipulations or the issues of the day" (Samuels, 1995). In particular, Dahl and Lindblom examined politics through the lens of "partisan mutual adjustment" in which conflicting interests must negotiate agreements that must make trade-offs in those conflicting interests. Samuels would later see this as part of the John R. Commons process of "working out" the rules of the legal-economic nexus. Indeed, the subtitle of Dahl and Lindblom's book, *Planning and Politico-Economic Systems Resolved into Basic Social Processes*, provides a hint of Samuels' future scholarly interests in (a) the identification and explication of the legal-economic nexus and (b) the examination of the legal-economic nexus at its most fundamental (basic) levels.

The final example of the student experiences that shaped Samuels' scholarly worldview came in graduate school at the University of Wisconsin:

In September 1954, I began my graduate studies at the University of Wisconsin. I had taken a course on institutional economics at the University of Miami, and I went to Wisconsin because of its John R. Commons institutionalist tradition. At that time, the only book written by an institutionalist that I had wholly read and carefully outlined was Thorstein Veblen's *The Theory of the Leisure Class*. I have never regretted the decision to attend Wisconsin, which then was at the tail end of the reign of Commons's students. I received deep insights into the economic role of government and both wide and deep training in the history of economic thought, my two principal fields of interest. At the University of Wisconsin, I was very much influenced by ... Harold Groves's philosophical approach to questions of public finance; Selig Perlman's perceptive and personal approach to questions of capitalism, socialism, and social reform; Walter A. Morton's direct, non-ideological, and even somewhat cynical approach to questions of theory and policy; and Martin Glaeser's and Kenneth Parsons's diverse approaches to Commons. Robert Lampman, for whom I was a teaching assistant during a semester when he replaced Edwin Witte in the undergraduate Government and Business course, reinforced the Commons-Witte approach to the subject and also indicated that there were truly fundamental issues involved in the subject. As a graduate student, I had major fields in economic theory, including monetary economics; history of economic thought; the economic role of government; and labor economics; with an outside field in sociology, largely in the tradition of Max Weber under Hans Gerth. Perhaps the most subtle influence on me was the encouragement and reinforcement, as an individual and as a scholar, that I received from my professors. Edwin Witte could not have been more encouraging, nor could the others. The graduate program at Wisconsin at that time – 1954–1957 – both permitted and encouraged students to be their own person and to do their own thing. (Samuels, 1995)

Particularly important was the influence of his major professor, Edwin E. Witte, and Witte's "down-to-earth but deep approach to the economic role of government" (Samuels, 1995). In Witte's view, the term "political economy" was preferable to the word "economics" because political economy "directs attention to the important role of government in the economy" (Samuels quoting Witte in Samuels, 1967). In particular, Samuels wrote, Witte "objected to the consideration of government as simply the regulator of business with government considered as an exogenous force, for the economic involvement of government in his view went much further and deeper" (Samuels, 1967). What was needed in examining the economic role of government, Witte insisted, was a nonideological analytical approach that identified "the basic relationship between legal and economic (private market) and non-legal forces [that defined] viable interaction [such that] changing details and change in the pattern of interests supported through law was coupled with continuity in the basic relationship[s]" (Samuels, 1967). By adopting such an approach, Witte believed, the normative elements of policy analysis – either hidden, unintentional normative assumptions or intentional ideological and propaganda assumptions – would be revealed and subjected to examination and analysis.

These three experiences are emblematic of the many experiences that shaped the career of Warren Samuels as a scholar and a teacher.[1] Most especially, these three examples influenced Samuels' work in two specific ways. First, the common element in these three experiences is that a scholar must approach a problem with an open mind, that is, willing to question all dimensions of the problem at hand. If doing so leads a scholar to question accepted disciplinary wisdom or to explore beyond traditional disciplinary boundaries, so be it. Thus, dealing with issues of political economy would, inevitably, lead one to explore not just the discipline of economics but also law, philosophy, political science, history, psychology, sociology, religion, and more. This explains the prodigious knowledge in areas beyond the boundary of "economics" but within the realm of "political economy" that Samuels possessed and that he challenged students to develop.

Second, Samuels believed that analysis of political economy problems must begin at their most fundamental, or basic, level. Indeed, Samuels wrote that "When I was a student, I acquired the habit of asking myself, whenever I read or heard something, what are the most fundamental questions (or ideas) with respect to which this has meaning or takes a position?" (Samuels, 1995). This question goes to the heart of Samuels' scholarship and his teaching philosophy. For example, in his edited volume, *Fundamentals of the Economic Role of Government*, Samuels posed to authors the question, "What are the most fundamental things you can say concerning the economic role of government?"

In a later volume, *The Fundamental Interrelationships Between Government and Property*, Mercuro and Samuels posed to authors the question, "What are the most fundamental things you can say concerning the interrelationships between the institutions of government and property?" (Mercuro & Samuels, 1999). As recorded in the class notes published here, Samuels would also pose this question to his students. In posing such a question to himself and to his students, Samuels was seeking to (a) develop a "positive approach to government as an economic variable" (Samuels, 1972) and (b) "put the [inevitably] political back into political economy" (Boettke, 2001). This question that defined Samuels' scholarly career and teaching philosophy was the product of his early experiences with Robinson (the adoption of "a critical open-minded attitude"), Dahl and Lindblom (toward the working out of conflicting interests through the "politico-economic systems resolved into basic social processes"), and Witte (to examine "a down-to-earth but deep approach to the economic role of government"). This was the legacy that Warren Samuels passed on to his students.

The title of Samuels' course is itself telling. While other graduate programs offer courses titled "Law and Economics" or something similar, Samuels's title clearly and definitively sets the tone – the Economic Role of Government, which he defined as the "analysis of the fundamentals of the economic role of government with focus on social control and social change; legal basis of economic institutions; applications to specialized problems and institutions" (first lecture page of the 1996 course notes). His approach was "heavily Institutionalist, with a focus on systemic issues ... [but which would] not attempt to reach conclusions about policy of government or what government should do" (1996 course notes). Samuels emphasized that the "polity and economy are two aspects of the same thing" (1996 course notes) and that "In a market economy = lots of government. So it is not about how much government, *but what interests government protects*" (1996 course notes).

The notes reproduced here were taken by Marianne Johnson in the fall of 1996. The second set is a compilation taken by Patricia Aust Sterns, Brady Deaton, David Schweikhardt, and James Sterns in the fall of 1999. The two sets of notes, despite being close in time, provide an interesting comparison; they serve as a cautionary tale for researchers relying on such archival documents. It is clear that the style of note-taking can lead to different emphases, as does the interests of the particular student. In this sense, notes should not be taken as a verbatim recording of an instructor's thoughts, but rather as his/her ideas telescoped through a specific point of view.

Minimal stylistic changes or other corrections have been made to the notes. Articles and verbs have been added for easier reading and abbreviated words

are now spelled out. All graphs are reproduced as drawn. Occasional explanations, more detailed identifying information, or comments by the editors are also
included in square brackets or in accompanying footnotes. All underlined phrases
or words and all words written entirely in capital letters are reproduced as they
are written in the notes. These are original emphases, though whether they can
be attributed to the recorders or Samuels is not remembered. In discussing the
project, Samuels claimed that:

> Not surprisingly, your main problem is going to be – no, not my handwriting, which was more
> legible then than now – but which set of notes to use. Inasmuch as I have not compared any
> two of them [I do not even know how many I have], I have no prejudgment. Several designs
> are possible: student A's notes; supplementing A's notes with B's notes – which itself has
> several variants; combining them on a more or less ad hoc basis. (Email from Warren Samuels
> to Marianne Johnson, May 18, 2011)

We have chosen to follow Samuels's suggestion and publish here course notes
taken in the Fall 1996 and the Fall 1999 semesters. We compare these two sets
of notes to examine the differences in the content of the two courses, with notes
from the Fall 1999 semester, which was the last time Samuels taught the course.

COMPARISON OF TWO SETS OF NOTES

The two sets of notes, taken only three years apart are substantially similar in
organization and content. We document differences identified in a line-by-line
comparison in Table 1. Generally, the 1996 course notes reproduced here more
prominently feature the work of legal scholars, from Oliver Wendell Holmes to
St. George Tucker. Curiously, many of these references were removed from the
later version, as well as nearly all discussion on legal precedent established by
Supreme Court cases. The overall effect of these changes is a marked shift away
from a critical legal studies approach to the economic role of government and
toward a more focused neoclassical lens.

A second difference is a shift toward modernity. The 1996 course notes contain
numerous references to classical elements in the familiar forms of Plato, Aristotle,
and Xenophon, as well as outdated examples of "current events" in the vein of
Nixon and Freud. By 1999, these were replaced with more topical examples on
people and topics such as Monsanto, the national basketball association (NBA),
and Deborah Stone, a government scholar at Dartmouth. Related, the notes from
1999 include 10 new readings, 9 of which are by Samuels. Most are materials
written and published between 1996 and 1999.

One final, though key, difference is related to redundancy. These notes reflect
an ultimately less polished version of the class than the later iteration. The bulk of

Table 1. Comparison of Economic Role of Government Course Notes, 1996 and 1999.

	General Comments	
Additions	**Deletions**	**Alterations**
Lindblom on topics "partisan mutual adjustment" and "social welfare function."	All references to Plato, Aristotle, Richard Nixon, and Oliver Wendell Holmes.	1999 is significantly less repetitive. Examples: 1. In 1996, the topic "common law" appears in each part of the lectures, whereas in 1999 it is only discussed in Part III. 2. Similarly, in 1996, the topic "law as language" was discussed in Parts I, II, and III. In 1999, it was only covered in Part III. 3. "Laissez-faire" was covered in Parts I, III, and IV in 1996, but only in Part I in 1999.
		John R. Commons is referenced many times throughout 1996 notes on property, value, courts, the market, and collective action. In 1999, only his views on collective action are mentioned.
Part I: Introduction to the Economic Role of Government		
Emphasis placed on three key dichotomies: freedom vs. control, abstract markets vs. actual markets, laissez-fair vs. activism.[1]	Discussion of problems associated with the Pigouvian version of the neoclassical approach removed.	Critical Legal Studies: the 1996 course notes state the critical legal studies approach is a logical, deductive process. The 1999 course notes state that it is experiential and inductive, and specifically denies it being logical and deductive.
Clear enumeration of the differences between the neoclassical approach and other approaches.	Terms "cognitive dissonance" and "intellectual schizophrenia" removed from discussion of Critical Legal Studies.	Individualism and Collectivism: 1996 emphasizes the dichotomy between normative individualism and normative collectivism. The 1999 course notes state that the key difference is not between normative approaches, but between methodological individualism/ collectivism and normative individual vs. collectivism.
Normative collectivism.		

Table 1 *(Continued)*

	General Comments	
Additions	**Deletions**	**Alterations**
Part II: Law as Social Control		
	St. George Tucker example and references to Freud.	Many of the approaches to understanding the role of government were removed from this section, but appear in other locations. Example: The market-plus-framework approach discussed here in 1996 is found in 1999's Part III under the market as a concept section where Samuels discusses how laws and businesses create a structure for markets.
Part III: Law and Economics of Property		
One main point under "What is Government?"	Keith Tribe and the history of economics in law schools.	
"Government is politics, and politics is government. The alternative is dictatorship."	Introductory section discussing approaches to Law and Economics of Property. Ex: Marxist, Critical Legal Studies, Neoclassical, or Institutionalist views.[2]	
Monsanto and Microsoft examples, New York Stock Exchange and NBA claims to ownership of information.	Green vs. Frasier, Section on Theories of Law removed, as well as references to Xenophon on government.	
Principle of unintended consequences.	Section on Historical Elites that Control Government removed.	
Deborah Stone on the flaws in the rational model.		
Discussion on the evolution of economics as a science modeled on physics.		

Part IV: Applications and Contrasts

Rule of Law added to equal protection section.	Rawls *Theory of Justice*.	*Miller v. Schoene* removed from compensation principle section and discussed in the appendix under legal-economic nexus.
	Removal of legal precedent from discussion of compensation principle: *Smyth v. Ames*, *Shelley v. Kramer*, *Munn v. Illinois*; as well as discussion of Fifth Amendment in takings clause.	Section on equal protection is much larger in 1996 than in 1999. Some things removed: externalities, fines vs. jail time, *Theory of Justice*, historical cases, human rights.
	Section dedicated to the Coase Theorem.	In 1996, regulation and deregulation was discussed here, in 1999 it fell under the discussion on markets in Part III.

Appendix on the Growth of Government

Ballard Campbell *The Growth of American Government*	
Increased expectation of rights as a factor in the growth of government	

[1] These are all discussed elsewhere in 1996, but clearly compiled at the top of the introduction in 1999.

[2] These lenses are still discussed more broadly in Part I of 1999.

the material from these notes that is seemingly absent from the later course was perhaps removed for the sake of brevity, as it overlapped with material covered elsewhere, rather than being indicative of any real absence. However, the extent that this can be contributed to Samuels' organization of the course versus the note-taking style of the different students is difficult to ascertain.

As noted, Table 1 provides a complete list of the differences between the respective courses. This has been compiled for the sake of convenience into three categories: additions (material present in the 1999 notes that was absent from the 1996 notes), deletions (material included in the 1996 notes but absent from 1999), and alterations (materials that have undergone noteworthy changes).

Being Samuels' student was a memorable experience, partly for the thousands of pages of reading he would assign in a single semester, but mostly due to the care and effort he invested in every student. As Ross Emmett remembered,

> Many of us experienced his generosity to students, young scholars and anyone else who wanted to join the great conversation. His goal and passion was to broaden and enrich that conversation, and he was as happy to engage in conversation with a young scholar as he was with a Nobel laureate. (Emmett, 2011, online)

See also Davis (2012). Samuels was a compelling lecturer, who wrote little on the board, but seemed to have an encyclopedic grasp of his material, referring only in a limited way to his lecture notes. He was perfectly happy to abandon the day's topic for a compelling question or discussion, challenging students to critically think through ideas. On more than one occasion, the class ran a 30–45 minutes long because Warren was so absorbed in his topic and, as students, we didn't want to interrupt. It is hoped that the notes published here impart some flavor of the experience.

NOTE

1. These three examples are a small fraction of the experiences that influenced Samuels' work. For a full discussion of his experiences, see Samuels (1995) and Buchanan and Samuels (2008).

REFERENCES

Boettke, P. J. (2001). Putting the 'political' back into political economy. In *Economics broadly considered: Essays in honor of Warren J. Samuels* (pp. 203–216). London, UK: Routledge.

Buchanan, J. M., & Samuels, W. J. (2008). Politics as exchange or politics as power: Two views of government. In S. J. Peart & D. M. Levy (Eds.), *The street porter and the philosopher: Conversations on analytical egalitarianism* (pp. 15–41). Ann Arbor, MI: University of Michigan Press.

Dahl, R. A., & Lindblom, C. E. (1953). *Politics, economics, and welfare: Planning and politico-economic systems resolved into basic social processes.* New York, NY: Harper and Row.

Davis, J. (2012). Obituary: Warren Samuels (1933–2011). *European Journal of the History of Economic Thought, 19*(1).

Emmett, R. (2011). RIP: Warren J. Samuels, 1933–2011. Blog *Political Economist and Historian of Economics,* (August 18). Retrieved from http://pl842.pairlitesite.com/2011/08/18/rip-warren-j-samuels-1933-2011/. Accessed on April 12, 2012.

Mercuro, N., & Samuels, W. J. (1999). *The fundamental interrelationships between government and property.* Stamford, CT: JAI Press.

Robinson, J. H. (1921). *The mind in the making: The relation of intelligence to social reform.* New York, NY: Harper and Brothers.

Samuels, W. J. (1967). Edwin E. Witte's concept of the role of government in the economy. *Land Economics, 43*(2), 131–147.

Samuels, W. J. (1972). In defense of a positive approach to government as an economic variable. *Journal of Law and Economics, 15*(2), 357–394.

Samuels, W. J. (1995). The making of a relativist and social constructivist: Remarks upon receiving the veblen-commons award. *Journal of Economic Issues, 29*(2), 343–358.

Samuels, W. J. (2003). *A companion to the history of economic thought.* Oxford: Blackwell.

Samuels, W. J. (2005). How I taught law and economics. *Australasian Journal of Economic Education, 2*(1 & 2), 1–54.

NOTES FROM WARREN J. SAMUELS'S 1996 COURSE ON THE ECONOMIC ROLE OF GOVERNMENT

Edited by Marianne Johnson and Martin E. Meder

Economics 819   Warren J. Samuels
Economic Role of Government   Fall 1996

Course Objective: Analysis of the fundamentals of the economic role of government with focus on social control and social change; legal basis of economic institutions; applications to specialized problems and institutions. Attention to fundamental problems and alternative approaches and their application to practical questions of government policy regarding property, contract, tort, and regulation.

Class Procedure: Mixture of lectures and discussion.

Examinations: (1) There can be an *optional* take-home midterm examination, encompassing the material covered to that point in the course. This can enable the student to check his or her progress but will not count in the determination of the final grade. This exam must be arranged by interested students. (2) There will be a written final examination during the regular final exam period, which will be comprehensive with regard to all materials covered in the course. It will be *open book*: the student may bring any written materials whatsoever to the exam but no other assistance may be used. (3) There can be a research paper; see below.

Documents on Government and the Economy
Research in the History of Economic Thought and Methodology, Volume 30-B, 151–265
Copyright © 2012 by Emerald Group Publishing Limited
All rights of reproduction in any form reserved
ISSN: 0743-4154/doi:10.1108/S0743-4154(2012)000030B007

Course Grade: The final grade will be based on either (1) final exam 100% or (2) research paper 50%, and final exam 50%.

Paper: Each student can prepare a research paper from among the following topics:

Topic 1: *Inequality and the Equal Protection Clause: School Finance*

Discussion: The Fourteenth Amendment to the US Constitution says in part that no state shall "deny to any person within its jurisdiction the equal protection of the laws." A series of court cases has considered whether the equal protection clause can be applied to the phenomena of different school districts within a state each spending significantly different sums per student on education, at least in part because of their differential wealth. Somewhat independent of those cases, a number of states (including Michigan) have attempted to either equalize per student district spending or establish, through state funds, floors to that spending. Consideration of the idea of equal protection in a world of inequality raises serious and subtle analytical and policy questions, questions that pertain as well to other nations and to other problems.

Project: The paper will (1) summarize the findings and reasonings of the various court cases (federal and state) and (2) analyze the analytical and policy questions raised by the theory of equal protection in a world of inequality.

Principle Sources: *Index of Legal Periodicals*, case reporting systems (documents library)

Topic 2: *The Nature, Foundations, and Significance of Contracts of Adhesion (Standardized Contracts)*

Discussion: The typical conceptualization of private contract, especially in the market economies, and in economics in general, is that of an agreement whose content is reached by consent between willing buyers and willing sellers. The reality may well be different: The typical contracts into which we enter, to the extent that they are formalized, are drawn up by one of the contracting parties, perhaps in regard to relevant law, and the other party either accepts or rejects the terms and conditions thereof. These are called contracts of adhesion (adhesion contracts) or standardized contracts.

Project: Investigate the nature, substance, origins, and modes of change of contracts actually used in the real world. Select six (6) industries or economic areas and personally contact two firms in each industry (setting up appointments in advance). The student will inquire as to the nature of the contracts into which the firm more or less regularly enters; the source or origin of those contracts; the mode(s) by which those contracts change over time; the degree to which the other prospective contracting parties can affect the content (terms and conditions) of the final contract; and so on. Remember we are principally, if not solely, consumers, and that many firms are both "consumers" of the products of other firms and sellers of their products to either other firms or households. Industries or economic areas can be identified by looking at the categories found in the Yellow Pages of the telephone directory. Examples: automobile parts supply firms; machine fabrication public utility services (water, electricity, telephone, gas); legal services; medical services; metalwork fabrication; construction; wholesale food; transportation; and so on. Use your imagination. Choose six different areas and two firms within each. Think in advance of the information you want to acquire, and what questions are necessary to elicit that information. Revise your questions upon experience. Be prepared to direct the interviews with your own questions but also to follow a nondirect interview procedure (interspersing your own questions to make sure that all desired topics are covered), the latter being a sensible way of acquiring unexpected information. Try to secure sample copies of written contracts.

Part I of the paper will summarize the general theory of and literature dealing with contracts of adhesion. Part II will summarize your field research and present conclusions based thereon. Part III will evaluate (a) the general theory of and literature on contracts of adhesion and (b) the treatment of contract in economies, in the light of your field research and its conclusions.

Principal Sources: A list of relevant materials, to c. 19–65, can be found in Warren J. Samuels, "Legal-Economic Policy: A Bibliographical Survey," *Law Library Journal*, vol. 58 (August 1965), pp. 230–252, esp. p. 248. Subsequent materials can be found in *Index of Legal Periodicals*. See also Warren J. Samuels, "Law and Economics: A Bibliographical Survey, 1965-1972 [*sic*]," *Law Library Journal*, vol. 66 (February 1973), pp. 96–110.

Topic 3. *"Property" as a Discursive Concept*

Discussion: All discussion uses language. *Among* the key questions pertaining to language are (1) Do words, and the concepts ensconced in words, represent anything in reality independent of mankind? (2) If words relate to something in reality independent of mankind, then how do we know that they relate correctly or accurately? (3) What is the role(s) of words in social control in the social construction of reality?

Project: The concept of "property" ("private property") is fundamentally important in both law and economy in the Western economic system. Inquire into how the theory of property relates to the foregoing (and perhaps other) questions. Inquire into how the theory of language can be applied to those questions.

Principal Sources: A list of relevant materials, to c. 19–65, can be found in Warren J. Samuels, "Legal-Economic Policy: A Bibliographical Survey," *Law Library Journal*, vol. 58 (August 1965), pp. 230–252, esp. pp. 245–246. See also *Index of Legal Periodicals*; Warren J. Samuels, "Law and Economics: A Bibliographical Survey, 1965-1972 [*sic*]," *Law Library Journal*, vol. 66 (February 1973), pp. 96–110; and contemporary studies on the social nature and role of language (usually listed as literary criticism, hermeneutics, deconstruction, social linguistics, (modern) rhetoric, and so on.

Topic 4. *The Economic Role of Government as a Problem, Ultimately, of Legal Change*

Discussion: One of the themes of the course is that contrary to the claims of laissez-faire or noninterventionism, government is fundamentally present and operative in the economic system and that the question is not whether or not there will be government, or minimum government, but whose interests will the governed be used to support [*sic*]. A corollary is that given the fundamental presence of government even in an essentially market economy, questions of economic policy (broadly understood or defined) are typically not questions of the presence of government but of legal change of law, that is, legal change of the interests to which government gives its support.

Project: Identify, analyze, and critique the theories of law and social change which are involved in the idea that the economic role of government, in practice, is a problem, ultimately, of legal change of law.

Principal Sources: A list of relevant materials, to c. 19–65, can be found in Warren J. Samuels, "Legal-Economic Policy: A Bibliographical Survey," *Law Library Journal*, vol. 58 (August 1965), pp. 230–252, esp. 243–244. See also *Index of Legal Periodicals* and Warren J. Samuels, "Law and Economics: A Bibliographical Survey, 1965-1972 [*sic*]," *Law Library Journal*, vol. 66 (February 1973), pp. 96–110.

Topic 5. *The Social Context of Takings Law*

The Fifth Amendment takings clause has become a critical focal point for several important issues: continuity vs. change, the conditions of the social reconstruction of reality, the role of government as an initiator and/or ratifier [*sic*] of change and as a mode of conflict resolution, the nature and source of rights, the conflict between eminent domain and police power principles, the socially constructed meanings of fundamental legal terms (e.g., property), and so on. The issues not surprisingly typically take a legal form but they are enmeshed in, indeed arise from and have significance for, a larger social context.

Project: On the basis of Macaulay, Friedman, and Stookey; the readings on the compensation principle; and any other materials, identify and analyze the social context of the takings clause-compensation problem.

Whichever topic is chosen, the paper will be long enough to accomplish the foregoing assigned tasks, *possibly* approximately 20 to 30 pages long, typed double-spaced, *plus* notes and reference list. The sophistication of the paper will reflect the level of the course. The student is advised to prepare the paper with a view toward possible submission for publication. It is very important that each student opting to prepare a research paper discuss his or her prospective topic with me early in the course. Please try to submit the paper at the time of the last regularly scheduled class period before the final exam.

Texts: 1. Werner Z. Hirsch, *Law and Economics: An Introductory Analysis*, 2nd ed. Boston: Academic Press, 1988.
2. Warren J. Samuels, *Essays on the Economic Role of Government*, vol. 1, *Fundamentals*, New York: New York University Press, 1992.
3. Warren J. Samuels, ed., *Fundamentals of the Economic Role of Government*, Westport: Greenwood, 1989.
4. Nicholas Mercuro, ed., *Taking Property and Just Compensation*, Boston: Kluwer, 1992.
5. Stewart Macaulay, Lawrence M. Friedman, and John Stookey, eds., *Law and Society: Readings on the Social Study of Law*, New York: Norton, 1995.

1. INTRODUCTION TO THE STUDY OF THE ECONOMIC ROLE OF GOVERNMENT: ALTERNATIVE APPROACHES TO LAW AND ECONOMICS

1. Hirsch, prefaces and ch. 1.
2. Warren J. Samuels, "Edwin E. Witte's Concept of the Role of Government in the Economy," *Land Economics*, vol. 43 (May 1967), pp. 131–147.

3. Samuels, ed., *Fundamentals of the Economic Role of Government.*
4. Warren J. Samuels, "Law and Economics: Some Early Journal Contributions," in Warren J. Samuels, Jeff Biddle, and Thomas W. Patchak-Schuster, *Economic Thought and Discourse in the 20th Century*, Brookfield, VT: Edward Elgar, 1993, pp. 217–285.

2. LAW AS SOCIAL CONTROL AND SOCIAL CHANGE: LEGAL FOUNDATIONS OF THE ECONOMIC SYSTEM – THE PROBLEM OF ORGANIZATION AND CONTROL AND THE INTERRELATIONS BETWEEN LEGAL AND ECONOMIC PROCESSES

1. Macaulay, Friedman, and Stookey, *Law and Society.*
2. Warren J. Samuels, "The Idea of the Corporation as a Person: On the Normative Significance of Judicial Language," in Samuels and Arthur S. Miller, eds., *Corporations and Society: Power and Responsibility*, Westport: Greenwood Press, 1987, pp. 113–129.
3. Samuels, *Essays on the Economic Role of Government*, chs. 1, 2, 3, 5.
4. Robert B. Seidman, "Contract Law, the Free Market, and State Intervention: A Jurisprudential Perspective," *Journal of Economic Issues*, vol. 7 (December 1973), pp. 553–575.
5. Warren J. Samuels, "The Economy as a System of Power and Its Legal Bases: The Legal Economics of Robert Lee Hale," *University of Miami Law Review*, vol. 27 (Spring–Summer 1973), pp. 261–371.

3. LAW AND ECONOMICS OF PROPERTY, CONTRACT, TORT, AND REGULATION

1. Hirsch, chs. 2, 3, 4, 5, 6, 7, 9, 11; chs. 8, 10 optional.
2. Warren J. Samuels, "The Coase Theorem and the Study of Law and Economics," *Natural Resources Journal*, vol. 14 (January 1974), pp. 1–33 [*sic*].
3. Robert D. Cooter, "Coase Theorem," in *The New Palgrave: A Dictionary of Economics*, New York: Stockton Press, vol. 1, pp. 457–460.
4. Warren J. Samuels and Steven G. Medema, "Ronald Coase and Coasean Economics: Some Questions, Conjectures and Implications" (distributed). Published in Warren J. Samuels, Steven G. Medema, and A. Allan Schmid, *The Economy as a Process of Valuation*, Lyme, NH: Edward Elgar, 1997, pp. 72–128.

4. APPLICATIONS AND FURTHER CONTRASTS

A. The Compensation Principle.

1. Samuels, *Essays on the Economic Role of Government*, chs. 10, 11, 12.
2. Lawrence Blume and Daniel L. Rubinfeld, "Compensation for Takings: An Economic Analysis," *Research in Law in Economics*, vol. 10 (1987), pp. 53–104.
3. First English Evangelical Lutheran Church of Glendale v. County of Los Angeles, CA; June 9, 1987.
4. James Patrick Nollan, et ux., Appellant v. California Coastal Commission; June 26, 1987.
5. Donald Black, "Compensation and the Social Structure of Misfortune," *Law & Society Review*, vol. 21 (1987), pp. 563–584.
6. Mercuro, *Taking Property and Just Compensation*.
7. Lucas v. South Carolina Coastal Council, 112 S. Ct. 2886 (1992).

B. Regulation and Deregulation

1. Samuels, *Essays on the Economic Role of Government*, chs. 6–9.

C. The Principle of Wealth Maximization

1. Warren J. Samuels, "Maximization of Wealth as Justice: An Essay on Posnerian Law and Economics as Policy Analysis," *Texas Law Review*, vol. 60 (December 1981), pp. 147–172.
2. Warren J. Samuels and Nicholas Mercuro, "Posnerian Law and Economics on the Bench," *International Review of Law and Economics*, vol. 4 (December 1984), pp. 107–130.
3. Richard Posner, "Wealth Maximization and Judicial Decision-Making," *International Review of Law and Economics*, vol. 4 (December 1984), pp. 131–135.
4. Warren J. Samuels and Nicholas Mercuro, "Wealth Maximization and Judicial Decision Making: The Issues Further Clarified," *International Review of Law and Economics*, vol. 6 (1986), pp. 133–137.

D. Inequality and the Equal Protection Clause

1. San Antonio Independent School District et al. v. Rodriguez et al., 411 U.S. 1 (1973).

[Discussion of assigned readings]

Hirsch = neoclassical/Chicago approach; also will be institutional approach or Marxist approach.

The fifth book by Macaulay, Friedman, and Stookey is a different book; places law in context of society, causal factors, and consequences.

[The US] Constitution is linguistic frame of reference. Terminology – needs substance. The history of constitution = history of interpretation.

Spengler's "Problem of Order"

1. Freedom vs. control (autonomy vs. control)
2. Continuity vs. change
3. Hierarchy vs. equality

Must work out these problems within society to resolutions, this is a process.

[John R.] Commons: Valuation/valuing is a process. How it is organized/ structured governs valuing and leads to values. Keep this in mind.

Preliminary Points: Dichotomies that are false dichotomies:

Polity and economy. The modern mind is a dichotomy of compartments. This dichotomy is false; it is useful to talk about them for certain purposes. Specific topics can divide the two, but it is still part of something larger.

Polity and economy are two aspects of the same thing. Reified notions given to certain understandings. Is the right to vote economic or policy? There is no pure policy vs. economy that is independent. Body of selective perceptions that divide: reality is that there is a legal economic nexus.

Linguistics of polity and economy
Terms and concepts = variable content = aspects of nexus

Government is important because it is a part and parcel of legal-economic nexus. [John] Locke and [Adam] Smith both wrote that the chief function of government is to protect rich from the poor.

Laissez-faire vs. reform dichotomy: Intervention signifies introduction of government into a situation where it had been absent. Government is never absent from a situation; there is also legal change of law. It is not a matter of government or no government, or more or less government, but whose interests it [government] chooses pursue. Laissez-faire is a sentiment; naïve as a description or explanation and empirically wrong. To go from intervention to nonintervention is just changing the interests that government will pursue. In a market economy = lots of government. So it is not about how much government, but what interests government protects.

Society = abstract individualism, but government is important; protects some interests. There is no area of life in which government does not have a law in a legal sense, e.g., surrogate motherhood, is it a contract or slavery? There is no direct law until court cases and legislature create one; new circumstances = new law. Need law to provide control, settle disputes.

Same people often perceive different roles of government in economic vs. sociological (e.g., Republicans vs. Democrats).

Laissez-faire = attitude that does not say much; sentiment, but perception is important to construction of reality. The belief and acting on that belief is important.

Commons distinguished between value and valuation. The same is true for law and "lawing." Tend to reify law: traditional religion = absolutes (absolutist ontological position); sources of legitimation and the privileged status of law. Psychological source: most people, most of the time, desire closure and determination. Some people accept ambiguity, but very important things need some idea that law is concrete, given, final.

In every society there are two mentalities:

1. Law-making mentality: Mindset of those who understand that law is made by people – it is important who makes the laws.
2. Law-taking mentality: Believe that law is beyond them.

There is a psychic balm function at work in this ⇒ obfuscation; clouding that government is important as a mode of social control and change.

1. Governance = making of important decisions: death, taxes, military service, opportunities. It is power exercised by various people who may not have public office. Commons said that sovereignty = governance. Property is sovereignty; to have money is economy.

2. Public purpose: Alpha ⇔ Beta rights situation (or who has the right?) One has the rights; other has non-rights, pollution vs. environmentalist. Life is a combination of positive-sum and zero-sum games.

Alpha; Beta: Government must choose between Alpha and Beta over who has rights. On what basis is the choice made? Some notion of public purpose is the basis of choice. Alternative possible bases include egoism, bribery, corruption; these can eliminate the inevitable conception of public purpose. Ends/means, e.g., old vs. new welfare systems? Which is the best means to the end?

<u>Introduction to Lectures</u>

Specific objectives:

1. Insight into the fundamentals of economic role of government and the different ways of understanding fundamentals.
2. Insight into problems of inquiring into the fundamentals of the economic roles – conceptual, ideological, and substantive.
3. Introduce to several approaches to the economic role of government.

Lectures will be heavily institutionalist: systemic issues, conceptual, and theoretical problems.

1. Course will explore fundamental importance of government to economy.
2. Course will not attempt to reach conclusions about policy of government. What government should do = irrelevant? Affirm that government will promote certain interests over others and this is important, even when intending or trying to appear not to.

<u>Explanation</u> vs. <u>justifications:</u> Explaining why is not a justification of difference in language. Difference between language that describes vs. language that motivates.

Emphasis:

1. The legal system and economy are not independent and self-sufficient but are socially constructed.
2. There is a legal-economic nexus with economy and polity spheres.
3. Need to appreciate that much of what is written is meant to be either
   a. psychic balm, or
   b. social control.

4. In much of literature, the terms law and policy are treated as different, but our course's theme is that law embodies policy, e.g., maternal/family leave (topic for paper?) plus or minus court decisions, legislations, collective bargaining, corporate decision making. All of these are policy, but only some are law.
5. Process: It is helpful to see law as a process of social construction where the result is policy. The process is like "partisan mutual adjustment," essentially Common's collective bargaining state. Bargaining among interest groups, but who gets to participate and on what terms?

Samuels, Biddle, and Schuster's *Economic Thought and Discourse in the 20th Century* (1993) does not address Marx or Commons. Looks at vast literature of articles.

1. There is an enormous literature.
2. Rich background and discussions.
3. Very different ways that things can be modeled.

Themes continued: There are a number of different schools of thought, alternative conceptions of law and of economics, as well as legal-economic analysis.

Approaches:

1. Neoclassical Approach: Gershwin textbook. Characteristics include:
   a. The market is pure and abstract, independent and self-subsistent. How related to law? Market is an *a priori* starting point.
   b. Research protocol – schedule producing unique, determinant, optimal equilibrium solutions.
      - Unique means one; a single solution; recognizes a core of possibilities, narrow or broad.
      - Determinant in that instead of many factors, it deals with the determinant solution, not a possibility of several solutions.
      - Optimal is capable of multiple interpretations; the most common is that there are no further gains from trade.
      - Equilibrium; modeling such that you get the result of equilibrium is a balancing of forces and initial conditions.

Richard Posner has an alternative version? Advocates wealth maximization but rejects utilitarianism as too narrow? Welfare maximization is complicated; are you dealing only with goods or with other things? Must decide range of discussion and research protocol; law as an optimizing process that leads to optimal institutions?

Approaches to law:

1. Law is a wealth maximizing process (more later). Law contributing to wealth maximization is a unique developmental approach.
2. Here is law; then what is its impact? The impact approach.

Dilemma: Conservatives want to damn institutions. If you follow this research protocol and law is driven along an optimizing path, then law cannot screw up; this is a serious problem.

There are two ways of looking at institutions that are subsets of Classical Approach:

1. The Pigovian
2. The Paretian

Paretian is dominant in economics; it is the idea that welfare is maximized; optimality occurs when the gains from trade are exhausted – essentially where marginal cost = marginal benefit. The Paretian approach defines optimality in exhausting gains from trade.

Pigovian is the tradition of [J.S.] Mill, [Alfred] Marshall, and [John Maynard] Keynes; it is associated with Cambridge.

a. Pigovian equivalency
   Private marginal cost = Social marginal cost
   Private marginal benefit = Social marginal benefit when there are no externalities and welfare is maximized. If they are not equal, then under- or overproduction, which require taxes, subsidies, or regulation.
b. Marginal utility$_i$ = marginal utility$_j$, where person $i \neq j$. This is equating people's marginal utilities across incomes. Utility between people is based on the assumption of the diminishing marginal utility of income. The goal to maximize utility is a conception of welfare maximization.

Problems with this include:

1. Problems measuring utility; Do we assume people are the same? Different?
2. Assumption of equal capacity to derive utility.
3. Disincentive problems create opportunities for reform.

Both approaches are neoclassical and have very much in common. They assume markets, the integrity of private property; thus, market solutions are the best.

2. Institutionalist Approach: They are not interested in unique, determinate optimal results, but in the factors and forces at work that determine whose interests are to count.

The laws are dictated by whom? One must understand the law that establishes the structure and the positions in the market.

Most fascinating topic is Pareto; also known for his theories of power and behind the scenes analysis. Powerful and cynical approach.

Institutionalists see processes by which the economy and law coexist and coevolve; they focus on factors and forces at work.

3. Critical Legal Studies: This was movement among law school professors and people of 1960s. It was a time of student rebellion; some of the scholars are lawyers and understand the cognitive dissonance and intellectual schizophrenia.

Critical: Take law as laws over self-rationalization, class context, gender context, social construction. Contemporary equivalent between legal realism and Marxism (marriage – Holmes, Pound).

Legal realism is the antithesis of analytic jurisprudence. (Law is a system of logic. Form premises that lead to fundamental decisions; self-subsistent, logical deduction.)

[Margin note: legalism + Marx, variety of Marxism, more emphasis on conflict, class.]

In 1880, Oliver Wendell Holmes, in his *Common Law* states that "life of the law is not logic but experience." It is how experience is interpreted and acted upon.

Legal realism: Law is something that originates from people, especially judges who reach decisions based on experience and whose judgments have multiple interpretations. It is a deductive process.

Marxian approach: Government is part of the superstructure (dependent or even autonomous variables). The state is a representative of the ruling class.

1. "Executive committee of bourgeoisie" allows the ruling class to dominate and exploit the ruled class.

2. Facilitates the accumulation of capital.
3. Rationalizes the system and protects it from external and internal threats.

Law is socially constructed

1. All groups share an <u>instrumental</u> view of the state. The state is a tool, an <u>instrument available for control</u> (to be captured and used.) All schools share this perception.
2. There are groups that have different values, and perceptions of reality. Some accept reform and some do not accept it.
3. Each approach contains <u>an affirmative theory for the use of government.</u>

The first and third points are very important; look to neoclassicals and their affirmative approach; even conservatives.

Approach this area of studies (regardless of schools)

– Fundamentals of government
– Analyzing and identifying fundamentals

Need to be able to think in terms of each of the schools, work within schools and appreciate them as theories and as modes of discourse. Texts are subject to selective perceptions: all texts are a matter of interpretation, which leads to hermeneutic circle problems.

$$\text{basis} \Rightarrow \text{theory} \Rightarrow \text{basis}$$

Real problems are the usual sentiments about government. Real choices have to do with the use of government $\Rightarrow$ who uses it for what purposes? Who has access and to what effect?

Economics is not a mystery; law is not a mystery. They are theory, description, and social control.

Multiple Schools of Thought there are

$$\left\{ \begin{array}{l} a \\ b \\ d \\ \vdots \end{array} \right\}$$ Matrix approach:
important is the nature of ideas and interpretive problems and competing ideas.

Further Thoughts:

Neoclassical approach is primarily a research protocol.

1. The fundamental concern is of <u>resource allocation.</u>

Marx was concerned with this as well, but he was more concerned with the system of capitalism. Alternative schools have little interest in the allocation of resources. These schools are concerned with the factors and forces of who uses government and to what end.

2. Economy is independent and self-subsistent = neoclassicism view.

Accept it as an abstraction, but basically that the economy is independent ignores the legal foundations of the economy.

3. <u>Definition of Economy</u>

Neoclassicals: economy = markets
The rest say that the economy is more than the market,

But the operation of institutions and power structures affect and influence markets. Take the Hayek example from the History on Corporate law. Rebuttal to Hayek: if stock holders don't like it, they can get out.

4. <u>Terminology</u>

<u>Methodological Individualism</u>	<u>Methodological Collectivism</u>
≠ Normative individualist approach to study of man + society that can <u>only study individuals – only individuals act</u>	to know what is going on must <u>study group processes, structures + interactions</u>

Irony of this is that individuals act within systems, groups, organizations. Problem is which individuals count and within what processes? You cannot escape this problem; both approaches must confront the same problem. Individuals act only within system + structures and systems + structures cannot be without individuals.

Market: <u>Methodologically collective</u> concept; not merely derived from looking at individuals. "The market works." What does works mean? Inputs + institutions = performance results. To work does not mean much. Optimality is a collective concept, exhausting gains from trade and efficient allocations on basis of market adjustment are not with regard to single individuals.

Cannot be only methodologically individualist. The individual position is a function of the system. To make a distinction between individualism and collectivism misses a great deal.

5. Rationality Assumption: That people know their interests and strive to achieve it single mindedly. Problems:

  a. Whose self-interest is to count? That is what law is all about.
  b. How do people come to have self-interest? What is the process of development?

6. Paretian Criterion: Assumes structure of trade, and that power is already specified. It is reinforcing the existing power structure and set of preferences. It avoids interutility comparisons, whereas other schools are interested in this.

7. Definition of Output: What is output? The output of auto industry is transportation. What about fuel conservation, safety, environmental protection? These are costs that redefine output. Output of a police department or a school system is a matter of selective perception.

8. Positive vs. Normative

This course is a positive discussion on normative topics.

  Positive: attempts to explain or describe objectively, the intent, "is"
  Normative: attempts to evaluate and is should or should not, "ought"

Basic proposition in logic is that you cannot derive an "ought" from an "is" alone. That requires one to read additional normative premise because it "is" does not mean it "ought" to be.

Positivism 1	Positivism 2 = Conditional Normativism
Pure "is" statements (see above)	What is to be done to achieve a particular end?
	What is necessary to accomplish it?
	Normative = end for the mean

It is very important to distinguish these two issues. If preoccupation of neoclassicals with market leads to the perspective of significance of laissez-faire, private sector; market in the private sector.

Commons: Value vs. valuing ⇒ "working rules." Response to human tendency to verify important concepts. Valuing is a process of determining what the rules will be. Commons is not referring to the exchange value of goods, which is important. [But rather] the rules and institutions that give purpose to the market = process of valuing. It is not price, but the price structure that is important, plus the process of valuing. The allocation of resources is important; not price, but "what is price." This is a fundamental theme of Commons' *Legal Foundations of Capitalism* ⇒ quest for value/valuing or that value arises from the process of valuing.

Note: Normative = choices. Prices in neoclassical economics are fundamentally normative, but objectively determinable. Price = "coefficient of choice," [from] Schumpeter.

Positive vs. Normative Continued:
Post materialism, the distinction is erroneous. It is difficult to make a purely positive proposition. Modern economics = rationalization of laissez-faire economies – psychic balm and social control function of economics.

Institutionalist Position: Although the neoclassical approach is a research protocol of unique, determinate, optimal solutions, the institutionalist emphasis is on process, factors in the process, and not on particular result. Emphasis: organization and control, power structure.

Institutionalist has a wider scope of variables and a longer chain of variables

  neoclassical = harmonistic
  $\{P_x \leftarrow \Delta \leftarrow$ market$\} \leftarrow$ legal rules $\leftarrow$ government $\leftarrow$ uses of government
  $\downarrow$
  allocation of resources

whereas the institutionalists see conflict.

Commons was not interested in prices and optimal allocations at a point in time; he was interested in determining rules of the economy. Institutionalists see no unique optimal solutions; only solutions as a function of the power-rights structure.

  Power structure$_1$ ⇒ Rights structure$_1$ ⇒ Optimal solution$_1$
  $PS_2 \downarrow \Rightarrow \uparrow RS_2 \Rightarrow OS_2$
  $\downarrow$ government

The Edgeworth Box solution determined by initial position $\Rightarrow$ that is the rights structure.

Must talk about <u>law and government</u>; interests of government. Neoclassical harmony is undermined/underpinned by conflict.

1. Principle of the Ubiquity of Law. Every aspect of life has a body of law pertinent to it, with rights, responsibilities, and duties, e.g., surrogate parenthood, foreign embryos. This illustrates

    a. The ubiquity of law;
    b. Novel idea, leads to entering in legal process for rights. Technology does not imply rights; courts create rights.

Laissez-faire = misconception; choice of interests, sentimental. Favored or opposed to law: government sides one way. Common law? Courts and juries determine/make common law, e.g., [Jack] Kevorkian.

Proposition: Government is deeply involved in definition, creation, and structure of the economy. Must realize that the Western mindset is individualistic and antigovernmental. The pretense is that where is "The Law," rights are absolute. That government can be limited is an obfuscation of the importance of government. This leads to a motivation to manipulate the recreation of the economy, which is part of economic process, the process of valuing.

Limiting the Economic Role of Government, e.g., the gold standard, inflation, quantity theory. Hayek says so explicitly, which is instrumentally useful, but these instruments are active government.

The critical immediate issue: Is law to be changed? Not that we have a law, but whose interests represented by law leads to government. The interests [protected by] existing law or opposite interests? Laissez-faire does not define reality.

<u>Reject distinction between economy and polity</u>: The state and the economy are often perceived as self-contained, self-subsistent. Interactions are a necessary evil in some veins of thought, which means that they must recognize there is a nexus out of which both emanate.

Private vs. public = matter of <u>self-selection, selective perception</u>
    $\downarrow$

Private vs. public law; all are law. All that is one is simultaneously the other. Property rights = private + public (law, collective action). More empirically and logically defensible story than the others; this is not necessarily ontological and reified. Relative stories; "one man's terrorist..."[1]

No attempts to present solutions of policy, was not intentioned. Material of this course is complex; not linear in presentation. In sum:

1. Process of working out optimal solutions
2. Work out restructuring rights, changing the rights structure

History of economics has examples about how different economic theories lead to alternative explanations of changes that happen to the economy.

Theory + normative paradigms $\Rightarrow$ how economy operates + changes

Examples:

Law of rent: Ricardo vs. Malthus. Malthus provided a defense of landed aristocracy (and the Corn Laws). Ricardo rejects the Corn Laws (business and working class perspective).

Labor Theory of Value – conservative vs. radical (Marx)

$$\begin{array}{ll} & \text{policy implications} \\ (\text{Ricardo}) & \uparrow \\ \text{law of rent + value paradigm} & \\ (\text{Malthus}) & \downarrow \\ & [\text{different}] \text{ policy implications} \end{array}$$

Lessons from article on history of legal economics:

1. It is important how you define the economy and polity; law vs. market, interactive or separate?
2. Law is a function of the economy.
   Economy is a function of law.
   Private = a function of private, which is a function of public, which defines public.
   Mechanisms of functions vary in alternate economies.
3. Property rights
   a. Property exists independent of law.
   b. Property as what emanates from and through the legal process.

Under (a), the police power of government is relatively meaningless; all is a matter of taking. Under (b), almost anything goes – historically. "Protect property" is the language of Locke and Smith, "protect rich from poor." Is it protected because it is property, or is it property because it is protected? The latter is the approach of this course. Belief in both (a) and (b), as are empirically present.

> property = f (values, population, technology, etc.)

Problem of order (Spengler): not to established verified order; order is worked out:

1. Autonomy/freedom vs. control
2. Continuity vs. change
3. Hierarchy vs. equality

All are a concept of governance and power; always are these things. Freedom within system of control ⇒ freedom for whom? This is an empirical proposition. Continuity vs. change ⇒ always both; many not clearly one. "Protect capitalism" meant extending system to other people.

> Mechanism change = real world
> Continuity = continued old mechanism

Hierarchy vs. equality: all societies lead power spread (diffuse) and power concentrated. Example 1: France 1960s – De Gaulle wanted locally elected senators, rather than centrally by party that lead to a diffusion of power. But, it concentrated power in hands of De Gaulle (only power center). Example 2: Richard Nixon's structure for welfare problem. Turn welfare over to the states vs. welfare rights lobby. Power was diffused to the people, but disenfranchised welfare people. [Bill] Clinton changes power structure.

George F. Will: Fundamental issues? Problem of what it takes to be constitutional? The Constitution has to be interpreted to have meaning. The Constitution organizes government, individuals, subgroups. It is what we make it out to be, but many ignore that this is all open to interpretation. You can have differing historical interpretation; interpretive government.

The constitution is shaped by history, but whose history? How do we deal with change? What about national traditions? Which of Framer's content/intent matters? This is a rhetorical proposition, with inevitable enormous elasticity. Justices' preferences = methodological individualism.

George F. Will is a conservative who rejects judicial review (although typically conservatives like judicial review) ⇒ even Scalia accepts multiple meanings ⇒ writing plagued by decisional bias; internally inconsistent? If the constitution "disappears," this implies that the constitution has an independent existence.

[Joseph] Sobran is a conservative libertarian who opposed the Iraqi war because it supports big government. Constitution causes conflict and judgments must be made. That the First Amendment strongly enforced by Supreme Court has enormous consequence. But is the Tenth Amendment an independent restriction or tautology? Problems of constitutional interpretation; it is generally not treated as independent on power of government (by mainstream liberals), but this is a matter of interpretation.

Contemporary example: Right to bear arms, what arms? Does this mean tanks or fighter jets?

Moral relativism – can a book be evil? Pegelf [unidentified]: religion + evil? What is the meaning of evil? True religion = problem path; guarantee free exercise of religion, but what about the range of religious practices? Sobran's libertarianism ⇒ moral absolutes.

What is government authorized to do? How broadly should we define commerce? Was initially to limit beggar-thy-colony practices; multiple monies, manufacturing. Is this commerce?

Articles of Confederation = slippery slope to centralized government, development of national markets.

1. Failure of Jefferson's formula: All are property owners and participate in local government and local markets. National markets = failure (political externalities)
2. Modern warfare
   Spanish–American War, WWI, WWII, Cold War = national government activism
   "National Security"

What about "Coin Money?" Now only the central banking system controls money. Extra – constitutional money control (90% of the money supply is bank credit). Idea of governance (not just government but multiple sources)?

Federal	Judicial
State	Legislative
↑	Executive
Local	Administrative

There are conflicts between all combinations – intended or not, including lots of built in conflict in the system such as "checks + balances." All is part of the nature of the system, and it is impossible to be consistent as writers; lexicographic system.

Introductory Discussions

1. Theories
2. Theories vs. worldviews/ideologies
3. Different analytical or modeling techniques

X = multiple interpretations

Blind men and the elephant story.
The object of study is multifaceted, which allows multiple interpretations, and makes the subject look different.

One fact: Different schools of thought interpret the government's role in the economy differently because it can be interpreted differently.

1. People have different concepts of law.
2. People have different concepts of the economy.
3. The relationship of individual to the law and economy.
4. Definitions of commodity.
$\downarrow$

> Is it a physical object? Common law and Administrative law imply that all important commodities have legal definitions that enable consumers to make choices, e.g., the legal definition of ice cream. A commodity is a legal-economic phenomenon.

Different conceptions? There are different paradigms and modes of discourse, views of what a theory should be, including

Neoclassical $\Rightarrow$ optimal law
Institutional $\Rightarrow$ relativism
Marxism $\Rightarrow$ to gain the revolution

Three sets of paradigms:

1. Harmony vs. conflict paradigm
Classical, neoclassical have marginal utility of both

       Mainstream = harmonistic
       Institutional = conflict ("tendency toward entropy?)
                     solutions need to be continuously worked out

Most significant issues are conflict issues (interesting issues), but this is a judgment.

2. Productivity/exploitation/appropriation paradigms
    a. Production and exploitation $\Rightarrow$ combination of positive + normative
        (see history notes) $\downarrow$
                    Attempt to describe + explain, but all has normative implications.
    b. Appropriative is essentially only positive, that operation of economy is a function of who can get what; jockeying of position for wealth $\Rightarrow$ contest
        class which leads to an appropriation paradigm.

3. Free will + Determinism
        This has problems; discussion has floundered upon types of determinism (opposite of free will) and philosophical realism vs. scientific realism.

Determinism neglects reasonably empirically relevant $\Rightarrow$ people may be constrained because people make choices; absolves individuals of responsibility to pursue free will. People don't have complete free will. Cannot choose what alternatives you have; these are not absolute because of deterministic constraints.

Combination of constraints + choice (compromise position), when who gets to choose and under what circumstances?

Philosophical realism: Ontological position that there is a world that exists independent of us and must accept that this reality exists. This does not explain very much with institutions. Are they reality or a perception of reality? Can you discover reality from perception? This is not a conclusive solution to its problems:

1. Is a reality commanding to us? If we all assume this reality, there no choice. But all
        disagree to formulation of reality, then all must choose.

Scientific realism: Attempts to avoid ontological discussion. There are principles and laws that characterize human activity and these have explanatory roles ⇒ enlightened program.

Problems: 1. Natural laws (ontological), but most are tendency states
                    Marshall: This is likely to be the behavior under circumstances
            2. Does not preclude possibility that if laws exist they cannot be manipulated
                    Malthus' Law

Free will is always a matter of constraints, both institutional and physical ⇒ which constraints and distribution on individuals?

Legitimation: Different theories of property ⇒ origins, workings, developmental positive propositions. Also, theory of legitimation that can justify institution or particular aspects. It is important to isolate normative = legitimation from the descriptive and explanatory.

   1. It is difficult.
   2. It is an inevitable problem.

Chosen on basis of power, ideology, selective perception, normative status then legitimation = important process. Free will requires legitimation effect (?)

Fundamental: What do we mean by this? There are different authors = different levels of abstraction. Is "real" fundamentally separate from ideology, perception, models, discourse? Do we know what the word "real" means?

Fundamental: Deepest and most general thing can say about a topic?

   1. Selective perception
   2. Process of working things out

Selective perception explains lots. A process must be worked out, then that works out other things, e.g., most political theory and commentary. Where should lines be drawn? One must recognize the conception of choice: people who want closure and determinacy vs. those who are content with open-endedness and ambiguity.

Creating vs. defining Social Reality. Is law found or made? Sports rules analogy ⇒ rules change over time, e.g., forward pass in football. In economics, National Income Accounting was controversial.

Behind everything are rules. Law, as opposed to sports, is treated as a global, transcendent and given, but law = intrusion on natural liberty; political bargaining ⇒ not everybody treats all law in the same way, e.g., property law vs. the internal revenue service (IRS).

Why is law said to be <u>found</u> rather than made?

- Inheritance of medieval philosophy; ontological validation.
- It is the best way to order things.
- Legitimation ceremonial sanctification to gain acceptance, social control.
- Psychic balm = comfort that there is law, some bedrock body of law.

Why is law said to be <u>made</u>? For the opposite reasons. It is that rationalization = legitimation; empirical view; nontranscendental. There is lots of pretense in this issue, including the following:

- People with power often don't feel they have power.
- Power is not seen as power.
- The burden of seeming to have power.

They would rather say "that's the law." This has made of discourse of decision making, late 20th century courts are more open about it, but there is still pretense.

Analytical vs. realistic jurisprudence ⬊
↓　　　　　　　　　　　　　　　　decision-making process
law = matter of deduction; automatic because it is axiomatic

Modern judges have exposure to legal realism: tendency to legitimize. <u>Intentions</u> of <u>Founding Fathers</u>? This is a <u>rhetorical stratagem</u>; it serves to give them privileged status or a view of their intentions attributed to them.

<u>Law</u> as <u>Language:</u> What is being described in the constitution?
Not science? NOT statements of distribution of power

↗　　　　　　　　　　⬊

Language is descriptive　　　Language is exhortative
What is it? Is this the case?　It induces people to act in certain ways

Constitution seems to be describing language. Concepts are selectively definable and applicable in law = different precedential sequences. Law is language, and therefore defines reality. It is a tool to define and remake reality; words do not have independent meanings. Words are instrumental in making and remaking our world. Legal system + economy = artifacts influenced by words.

Fallacy of misplaced concreteness (verification): Most constitutional interpretation commits this as all texts permit alternative readings (and place in the scheme of things), e.g., the Constitution, Smith, Marx, etc.

Roscoe Pound on "Common law and legislation." Law from legislation is a problematic idea because law is from courts; that was the idea. Important is that people's belief system(s) are matter of selective perception.

Part II. Models

Model: Set of variables that is structured in a particular way, with dependent and independent variables. Models allow lots of variations: inclusion/exclusion, specifications, social space, statements of theory, data use to test, decision rule. → They all leave stuff out, especially processes by which numbers are reached:

$$Y = C + I + G, \text{ so how do I find } C, I, G?$$

Most models leave out processes by which certain things are determined, e.g., Malthusianism. For there to be a complete model, we would need to find causes of population pressure. Malthus even simplifies. Models intended to elicit processes by which things get determined.

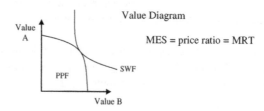

A, B = values. What about specification of freedom, peace, unemployment?

Four facts of variables:

1. Process of values are the axis, how to value A or B?
   Politicians with issues tell you what should be on the axis; it is not a given! Most economists and political scientists assume them, but in practice must find the values = lots of what legal-economic process is about.

2. Shape or slope of Production Possibility Frontier (PPF)
   Tells us about the trade-offs. Hard to make sense in this context; limited work done. Politics matter; the price will be visited on somebody else, votes are interpreted. How much of value *A* lost to get more *B*? Power, image, jockeying, relations, etc., e.g., St. George Tucker = second American professor of economics, appointed by Jefferson. His preferences vs. constituent preferences on the big issues = slavery and protectionism. His constituents wanted both; he opposed both.

PPF = pressures to bear. ⇒ All is relative power; trade-offs that must be made (e.g., unemployment vs. inflation). Also Social Welfare Functions (SWF) = preferences and their weighting.

3. Determination of preferences is a complex process; economists want preferences as given.
4. Determination of their weighting, both in people's own minds and within society = question of power structure.

Most analysis takes for granted some aspects of this; can be any of the four. This is legitimate, but in the real world all is up for grabs.

Note: SWF is not an assumed SWF. Intended to represent the actual given, ongoing evolution of preferences and power structure.

System Working Out

1. General interdependence
2. Cumulative causation (consequences ⇒ causes)
3. Joint determination

You do not get determinant results.

<u>Opportunity Set Model</u>

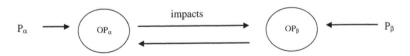

- Opportunity among which can choose
- α = an economic agent
- β = another or all other agents

What governs opportunity sets?

1. Power: participation or basis of that participation in decision making
   a. Rights: also the right to change rights + change law
   b. Persuasiveness
   c. Etc

More money = larger opportunity set

2. Choices: if you invest wisely, you get more money
3. Impacts: your choices affect other agent(s), externalities

These are all relative (α relative to β). This is true in all organizations: churches, government, corporations, family, models collective decision making. This is a complex process, as <u>opportunity sets = variable things</u>. Who is the community $\Rightarrow$ who is β? This is determined by rights and distribution.

Composition of opportunity sets and structure relative to each other:
$$\downarrow$$

$$\text{have} \left| \begin{array}{l} \text{dependent + independent variables} \\ \text{joint causation/determination} \\ \text{cumulative causation} \\ \text{general interdependence} \end{array} \right.$$

<u>Power</u>: Want a positive analysis not pejorative.

Propositions

1. <u>Power is necessary to accomplish desired ends.</u>
   a. To get value A on the axis.
   b. <u>How</u> to get desired ends is another matter.
   c. What ends should be is also another matter.
   d. Power is a neutral, necessary tool.
2. <u>The quest for power</u> is not only for particular ends, but it is also for its own sake; e.g., identity reasons.
3. <u>Power is reciprocal.</u>
   a. More for α = less for β.
   b. Power is a zero-sum game.

There is an overwhelming preoccupation with zero-sum games $\Rightarrow$ and these are the really critical games because of the reciprocal nature of power. Neoclassical emphasizes positive-sum games (Pareto optimality) with minimal treatment of zero sum. Game theory is interesting because of interest in zero or negative sum games. Politics + legal-economic nexus are mostly zero-sum games.

4. There is a tendency for powerful to seek further power. "Power corrupts and absolute power corrupts absolutely."[2]
5. There is a tendency for power to provide its own rationalization.
6. Pluralism as a good requires the division of power as a check on power in order to diffuse power.
   a. Want to render power innocuous
   b. Adam Smith, Federalist Papers

Dualisms

1. Decisions $= f$ (power structure) and the power structure $= f$ (decisions)

   $PS_1 = DS_1 \Rightarrow PS$ The power structure does not just exist

   $PS_2 = DS_2 \Rightarrow PS$ as decisions determine its reconstitution.

   $\quad\quad\downarrow$

   [decision set]
2. The working rules of laws and morals govern the acquisition and use of power.
   a. The distribution and use of power govern law and morals, i.e., "moral majority" wants to use power to control morals.
3. Values depend on the structure of the decision-making process and vice versa.
4. The income and the wealth distribution $= f$ (power structure) and vice versa.

Back to models

1. Take your standard Production Possibility Frontier model
2. Values for action; process of trade-offs, preferences; weighting system
3. Models tend to assume above processes
4. But these are really a process of working things out, and the process is interesting; not necessarily temporary result. This applies to all decision-making situations and institutions.

Opportunity sets model
   a. Persuasive power
   b. Opportunity set $= f$ (process of rights, power; choice by each actor within opportunity set; impact of choices)
   c. Included are rights to seek changes in law = changes in rights $\Rightarrow$ rights subject to interpretation and revision

Model 3: Weber + Pareto combination; multiple interpretations as to variables pursued and included. Power, knowledge, ↑ Psychology → policy.

Power variables: Participation in decision making and the basis thereof.
Knowledge: Whatever people accept as knowledge or truth, important that beliefs are true.

   Pareto: Two kinds of knowledge
      1. Logical experimental: objective, confirmable, replications
      2. Nonlogical experimental: beliefs, sentiments rationalizations, values, ideological formulations, wishful thinking

For example, Social Contract. Pareto's example is a seaman and Poseidon. Accepted as knowledge because it is acted upon = important. People's definition of reality.

Psychology: Motivations, attitudes, psychic processes and mechanisms, self-interest vs. altruism. Freud: economy of psychic energy; ego, id, etc. Internal motivating processes and internal control. [Karen] Horney[3]: types of attitudes, aggression, withdrawal, compliance.

   – People's psychology = key factor in decision making ⇒ policy.
   – People's psychology is complex.

Pareto believes that people are driven by instincts; what becomes important is then which instincts operate when.

Note: Three sets of variables

   1. Also the interaction of variables within them
      a. Interdependent
      b. Jointly determined
      c. Cumulative causation
   2. Each set of variables can be given different interpretation and different modeling, there is no single way of modeling.
   3. Propositions made in one set of variables can be reformulated in terms of others.

For example, Richard Nixon biographies: can explain him as a power player; as knowledge (what he accepted as true); internal psychology and his need for approval, thus not which is true, but any object of explanation can be interpreted in terms of each/all ⇒ statements can be reformulated in terms of alternate sets of variables ⇒ ubiquitous normative choice. Underlying it all is selective perception.

[Herbert A.] Simon's *Reason in Human Affairs* (1983)
- Democracy has a happy perception
- Politics has an unhappy perception
- Labeling is problematic because of selective perception

Samuels: Labeling $\Rightarrow$ solutions; goes far to influencing solutions
$\downarrow$
theme of working things out and reaching accommodation

1. Role of the Expert? Two basic approaches to decision making, and all US administration is both.
   a. Inevitability of subjective decision making.
   b. Importance to technical details $\Rightarrow$ experts.
   Vast literature on the expert in social affairs. But professionals also = selective perception, schools of thought, methods of modeling, beliefs. What should be the role of the expert? Selective perception as to the public interest; normative judgments. The expert is not about facts but look at the normative domain.
   Back to power, knowledge, psychology
   $\downarrow$
   Is what we believe that defines reality, values. What we expect: taken as given, possible, desirable. Variables = enormous in scope and order; this is important because people act on these beliefs.
   Myth, symbols, metaphors, ideology $\Rightarrow$ Pareto. These are always subject to selective perception*.
2. At any point in time knowledge is heterogeneous, composed of multiple facets.
   What we accept as knowledge $\Rightarrow$ policy choice; policy problems, and solutions is tautological to knowledge, e.g., how we define the "farm" problem leads to a solution; the particular solution defines problem.
3. If a set of variables = knowledge = product of information flow, then the process of information is manipulated; politics is the manipulation of information.

*Pareto's central arguments: power players manipulate psychology to manipulate knowledge and therefore policy. Once you understand Pareto $\Rightarrow$ never understand politics same way.

Psychology: Sets of variables; each individual = complex combinations, and a multiplicity of competing pressures.

For example, Freudian Oedipus complex, which is the situation where a child has a sexual longing for a parent and antagonism to the parent with same sex. It is incipient/ subliminal. What is a satisfactory working out? Must mitigate feelings. When you do not work it out, you have problems with authority figures and sex. Can also talk about the "adolescence problem," the child wants the security of parents, but also wants autonomy, which leads to conflict. A satisfactory working out is that the child is in the family but has autonomy; therefore can accept power/authority figures.

Psychological: Freedom and control. The problem is which is which and to whom? Attachments are object of manipulations of politics, e.g., policemen are friends or foes?

Power: Conflict over distribution of wealth = heart of policies, e.g., tax burdens (trickle down?) Government is a vehicle for groups to promote economic interests.

- Schmoller: Upper class increases income through control of government, lower class = unfavorable.
- Ruldolf Goldscheid[4]: Classes and power structure affect wealth distribution, and where the state = instrument of ruling class.
- Schumpeter: Taxes = f (social structure), taxes are a handle to control social structure.

Capitalism, Socialism, and Democracy: Most definitions of democracy are wishful thinking. Democracy is a system of choosing leaders who then decide what policy will be.

Politics are process of manipulation of psychology through manipulation of perceptions of reality. This is cynical and empirically accurate. "Politics is economics carried on by other means" [Paul] Samuelson. Samuels: economics is politics carried on by other means.

Problem of Order Model: Freedom vs. control, continuity vs. change, and hierarchy vs. equality.

- All societies are engaged in a process to decode freedom to and freedom from; and control over or control under. All economies have the problem of Freedom vs. control, which affects opportunity sets.
- Definition of continuity and processes of change.
- All societies have tendencies to both hierarchy and equality.

Defining terms; criteria make issues problematic.

1. Four models apply to all decision-making circumstances.
2. Legal-economic nexus is the process of working out and solutions.

First Preliminary Paradigmatic Case Study

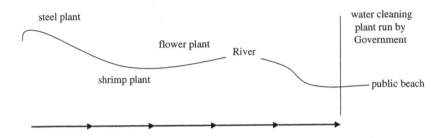

Suppose we have an α–β rights conflict. Who has a right vs. a non-right?
Steel plant can or cannot pollute

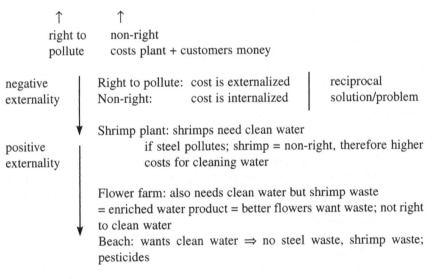

Complex relation of dual nature of rights → reciprocal character of externalities.

Coase 1960: The problem is whether α can harm β or whether β can harm α ⇒ have dual nature of rights. The actual externality depends on who has which rights. The waste cleanup plant ⇒ depends on where you put it along the stream and who to tax ⇒ rights.

1. Inexorable determination of rights
2. System of taxation (e.g., water cleanup plant)

What is the impact of models?

- Knowledge: Must know about pollution; is it toxic? For steel, shrimp, flowers ⇒ determine values and whether each type of pollution should be on axis?
- Identification process; subjective identification; pretenses. This is model 1 = working out of solution.

Opportunity set model 2: The opportunity sets of all actors = f (law, others decisions). Everyone will attempt to change laws in their own favor. The other two models also apply.

Coase Theorem: Zero transaction costs implies

1. markets internalize externalities,
2. rights = neutral.

Coase says that the real point is that transaction costs are not zero ⇒ institutional theory of production. Paper is coercion by Samuels; this is a [history of economic] thought paper because uses resources of historical materials; use of economics = multiple.

Paper relating all theories of cost:

- Theories are treated at mutually exclusive ⇒ approach cost topics from different angles therefore not mutually exclusive.
- Add another theory of <u>cost = f (rights)</u> ⇒ much like Coase. The things that we call costs are or aren't registered in markets depending on rights.

    Consistent with Coase.
    1. Registration + market
    2. Valorization
- Latent objective: the relative nature of costs ⇒ economic argument. The situation is that cost is conclusive; however, maybe costs are not absolute but depend on rights; does not invoke cost as an absolute.

Not saying that costs "aren't so," must pay prices, but that costs are what they are = f (law).
⇒ law that says restrooms must provide plastic gloves, etc. creates costs.

Price is determined by demand and supply. Revenue for some is costs for others; therefore, cost is related to demand and supply, behind which operate institutions, laws, rights. The paper has lots of case studies and examples from all aspects of economics.

Case Study of Pollution

- Multiple actors with different interests, as with factors of production or consumption.
- Behaviors impact each other.
- Rights = dual nature, and externalities = reciprocal, e.g., the α–β rights problem.
- Phase of status quo: state of rights and non-rights held by people.
  1. Status quo = ambiguously defined in rights and non-rights.
  2. Heterogeneously definable, and where law is silent = multiple interpretations.

     Pretense can be made about what law means

new circumstances = complications

Selective perception driven by ideology/material interests. Status quo point definition realized externality. Proposition: externalities are costs not registered in markets

$\Rightarrow$ meaningless propositions

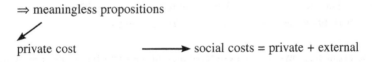

private cost $\longrightarrow$ social costs = private + external

Costs not internalized by markets? They are internalized in <u>some market</u> (where externality is realized); in which market are the costs realized?

This means that there is no unique Pareto optimal result: it depends on initial starting point, and allocations are specific to initial entitlements. Note how this incorporates the models $\Rightarrow$ power, rights, opportunity sets, value diagram.

<u>Second Paradigmatic Case</u>: How do people get rights? Nature? Omnipresence? This is a complicated story.

1. Individual bargaining and private contract
2. Legislation that gives rights with certain specifications and by alternative methods

3. Litigation or bringing suit under equal protect clause; e.g., laws failing to provide maternity leave do not provide equal protection; court law determines $\Rightarrow$ constitutional law. What about maternity leave to the father?

Rights are produced; they are manufactured artifacts and institutional; shouldn't mystify rights = matter of processes $\Rightarrow$ contracts. Rights are situational specific; down to earth; and the sources of rights are multiple: contract, litigation, legislation.

Red Cedar Case ($\approx$1914)

Virginia = statue for red cedar rust
    The fungus lives on trees but does not adversely affect cedar trees.
    It does harm apple trees.
        ➤ industry   decorative

Apple owners are unhappy, so legislature passed a law to destroy the red cedar trees that live too close to apple trees (taking case where taking is not the issue). The cedar owners lost up to Supreme Court; they argued that their property was taken to benefit someone else. But, the Supreme Court held for the legislature. Had to make a decision; ineluctable necessity of choice between laws of property. The old law was sound but silent about red cedar rust, with the effect to give cedar owner rights to decide and apple owners non-rights.

The cedar tree owner has a coercive advantage (payoff); apple tree owners exercise right to go to legislature, which resulted in a new law = coercive advantage to the apple tree owners.

$\left\{\begin{array}{l} \text{Two sets of rights + non-rights} \\ \text{Two structures of mutual coercion and coercive advantage} \end{array}\right.$

In either case, we could have a market solution and found gains from trade eventually exhausted. The state is invoked in either case; no reason to privilege old or new law $\Rightarrow$ state had to choose.

1. Inexorable necessity of choice.
2. Could have been a technology solution; fungicide $\Rightarrow$ further problem? rights = f (technology) or legislative decision

3. Organization
   a. Dominated legislature (apple growers)
   b. Apple growers = intense economic interest that allowed them to organize easily, whereas it was hard for cedar owners to organize ⇒ material interest compared to an aesthetic interest.
4. Is a structure of mutual coercion; coercion = burden of other's choices. The law changed the burden of coercion ⇒ different power structures = different market solutions; result contradicts Coase theorem.
5. Objective point of view; cases are noncomparable by way of economic theory; cannot choose between Pareto optimal results._
6. Intervention: cedar owners felt government intervention; not laissez-faire = bad government. By not intruding in a situation where it was absent before, this is not a case of intervention because had a law of property ⇒ if define intervention as government into absent areas, there are interventions. This is usually the case; just change in interests where government gave power.
7. Legal change of law by law.

Two different conceptions of property:

a. Property exists independent of government.
b. Property is what it is because of the actions of government.

If (a); then government = problematic ⇒ is an attack on property. If it is (b) = change in government interests, if there is a change of law ⇒ eventually eminent domain vs. police power, which is a later topic.

Political + Legal System ⇔ Market System

- Mutual causation in influence
- Grow up together (Commons' *Legal Foundations of Capitalism*)
- Not separate, independent processes, legal-economic nexus are mutually defining

Footnote: Notice that in 1990s, you would ask to fully define rights to do economics, but rights are not, cannot be fully specified. Dualism (caution) property ⇔ politics. Politics and property are part of the legal-economic nexus.

Fundamental Points

1. Law is part of the social (re)construction of the economy. All have agendas for government with any change in law; using government to

promote laissez-faire, marketization is not the absence of government. This sounds statist but it is true $\Rightarrow$ reality.

2. The economics is part of the social reconstruction of the economy. Policy = changing economy = f (reality); all schools of economics is to social control function.

Platonic element	Aristotle element
Idealization of the economy	To believe and act on, so that one can
Conception of the economy =	separate fundamental from selective
the basis of policy and reality	perception, subjective, normative

No Platonic element, but is Aristotle as fundamentals exist (Samuels interpretation).

3. Paradoxical intertemporal characteristics of law and legal process
    a. Common law + Constitutional law is ex post law; do not know in advance, only after the fact, legislation is not retroactive.
    b. Mode of discourse that courts use is the language of precedent and choosing between precedents $\Rightarrow$ law after all is not consistent.
    c. Law really means the future = operational meaning. Commons $\Rightarrow$ futurity as a constituent element of economics.
    d. Law has both a public and private goods characteristics; decisions because of litigation = private pursuit law = private good pursuit of advantage by some people public good dimension (i) nonexclusion, (ii) additional MC of supply law = public good as it applies to all which means rights are both public and private.

Amend an Omission: Question of material leave $\Rightarrow$ number marks of right generation, such as private contract; are collective bargaining $\Rightarrow$ unions negotiation. Also, e.g., homosexual marriage and "equal protection." Hawaii is considering this, IBM grants, as do many universities.

Fundamental Points: Possible to talk about fundamental points.

1. Law = made social construction
2. Economics = mode
3. Platonic vs. Aristotelian
4. Law = legal process; temporal issues
5. Public good nature of law

6. Status quo point ⇒ rights and non-rights
7. Selective perception principle
   ⇒ Al Schmidt[5] states that selective perception is involved in everything
   e.g., family values? Language of political models, divorce?
8. Dual meaning of "intervention"
   a. Intrusion of government into a situation where it hitherto has been absent.
   b. Change in the interests to which government is giving support, assumes domain where government has been absent. Or assumes no domain; government is changing interests to which is giving affect.

This is terribly important. <u>Laissez-faire = sentiment,</u> political is not analytical value. Government = total system of social control, but also nonlegal social control.

- Presidency = bully pulpit ⇒ legal social control
- Smith in Theory of Moral Sentiments: that moral sentiments are applied through approval and disapproval, therefore nature of society to enforce action through internal and external passing judgment ⇒ common moral rules

Smithian view of world, world = <u>ubiquitous intervention;</u> all about nonlegal social control (religion); why should religion intrude into an area? ⇒ whether it is sensible, accurate to talk about intrusion vs. changing interests.

- Government is ubiquitously present; when it isn't, will be called to act.
- Involved is the meaning of intervention and meaning of government and legal change of the law by law.

George Will: "... choice of any tax program ... special social consequences ... discourages particular behavior ... change." Conservative attempt to obfuscate using government to promote values through political change; which interests government to support ⇒ unequal distribution of incomes and wealth.

a. The <u>economy is an object of legal control</u> (political); law controls everything.
b. The <u>law is an instrument of economic advantage;</u> people use the law to gain economic advantage. This is an empirically correct statement.

Model of Social Control or law within the Model of Powers + Society: is that the same institutions that are social control are also power players – e.g., church, political parties. Problems or issues are the proposition that government is an instrument, a tool available to whoever can control it. Metaphor = tool, or government = arena in which the contest to control takes place. Power is worked out; "principle of the use of government." Selective perception of "the" economy and "the" polity prevents this recognition.

Role of government = object of inquiry. Examine different approaches that use to understand government. Approaches:

1. Government = exogenous "black-box, treatment that government is a process that is independent of people and mankind ⇒ transcendent system". That is perfect and nondecisional (like law of gravity); "slot machine theory of justice." Government is marred by politics; gives effect to what is really, truly there.
2. Government as a neutral extension or aggregation of private choice. Government exercised neutrally through rules (once rules exist). Government = accounting device; balloting box, not a black box.
3. Government as a preference aggregation process is a decision-making situation and it is not neutral, this is in contrast to both 1 and 2, control of Government = control of decision making.
4. Government as an instrument of the powerful tautological element in defining powerful social, political, economic bases to identify power not God, nature, neutral, but government = powerful.
5. Government = instrument with which to check the power of the powerful study; Commons' Legal Foundations of Capitalism on theory of state, government, private property understands that both 4 and 5 operate.
   - Bourgeois law came to dominate government .
   - Private property = protections against the state and those who control the state.
   Janus faced character of private property. The Magna Carta was checked by barons (landowners = power); private property ⇒ non-landed property (bourgeois). All = selective perception; however, define government depends on perceptions of who is powerful and depends on the power distribution.
6. Government is the source of problems; government as inevitable.
7. Government = source of progress and solutions; these two at the bottom of dichotomy of US system of government. United States has the best system in world vs. the view of the US government = coercive + source of problems. Extol and minimize.
8. Government is a preference aggregations process; no assumptions about neutrality, e.g., direct or indirect democracy, monarchy, etc.

9. Government exists to serve the public interests. Law and economics ⟹ jux-taposition differentiating between public interest approach: government exists to save public as if something called public interest; private interest: no public interest, all private but whose private interest dominates.

⟹ Public Choice literature has a long-standing interest in political science; economics to talk about "public interest" and how to determine this approach promises a public interest. This is that regardless of democrats or republicans ⟹ US national interests. Geopolitics remain the same; internal vs. external interests; geopolitical interests that transcend ideology. Question: Does market economy ⟹ democracy/pluralism? Does China decide? Japan or Vietnam?

10. Government = matter of self-interest, but whose self-interest?
    a. The individual
    b. Group self-interest (Bently's group theory of politics)
    c. Government is a matter of self-interest of politicians (Buchanan, Wagner)

    Problem with this approach is what totally destroy belief in democracy if politics = self-interest. Can this be a market? Is that good or bad? Are elections a method of reaching a temporary equilibrium? ⟹ How do we interpret particular politician actions? Nixon = democracy because Nixon was self-interested; "median voter issue." Weber's idea of "politics as a vocation;" politicians = transmissions mechanisms; therefore, waffling is fine. The problem is what is the self-interest of politicians? This is an approach to government ⟹ analytically this have empirical evidence to support; normative = nature of politics in democracy.

11. Idea that government = single or complex decision-making process. "The government" vs. agencies, checks + balances. Use this in combination with other theories of government.

12. Government as a dependent + independent variable. Law = independent at a point in time, but is dependent over time.

13. Market-plus-framework approach. Dominant approach in economics; social sciences. Can separate market from the framework? You can, but often it doesn't make sense to distinguish market from institutions that form markets. Also, relative weight to be given to legal and nonlegal components of the framework.

How to distinguish government actions as framework filling or nonframework filling ⇒ in practice, it all becomes framework. This is a serious problem of identification. Is it possible to distinguish framework filling vs. nonframework filling? Samuels doubts it.

For example, antitrust laws, markets, private property, competition. But does a right of property = right to monopolize? Are these laws framework? Or what about pollution laws? Maternity benefits? ⇒ Are laws that change institutions of property framework filling or nonframework filling? Without selective perception, once cannot use this dichotomy.

Is the framework static or dynamic? Can framework be established once and for all time? If morality can change over time, then law can change over time. This is a powerful and predominant approach that can combine with other approaches.

Main Points:

1. It is important to recognize that government = arena of power, participation in decision making and the basis thereof.
2. Valuation process: economy, polity, society.
3. Two ways of looking at things/phenomena:
   a. In terms of powers and power play
   b. In terms of social control
   Both have pejorative connotation ⇒ anathema to harmony and freedom; typically don't look at things this way; empirical and positive.
4. Government is an institution of collective action = important to the process.
5. Collective bargaining state (Commons): what takes place in government is collective bargaining of interests.
6. Politics = mode of self-government; politics easy to characterize/characterize method of governance; if no politics what would you substitute?
7. Government is not exogenous but both an independent and dependent variable; not a given thing; neither is policy.
8. Stress on difference between law making and law taking:
   Makers = aggressive
   Takers = passive
   Consequence of natural law is to protect law makers and induce passivity in law takers.
9. Let X be a government function; distinction between identifying a particular role of government and determining its substantive nature. Whether it is to perform a certain role and how to constitute the role.

10. Principle of the use of government = instrument or a tool.
11. Whether government change interests that it supports "change of law by law"; not if "intervene" but how.

Question: Assuming government is important in defining, creating, and structuring elements of the economy ⇒ requires normative direction. As a positive proposition = government is important. Normative: some normative direction is necessary. Discussion chosen by selective perception of government, what government is doing, freedom, coercion. Most discussion about econ role of government = part of discourse in waking out normative direction. What drives selection perception? Psychology; social beliefs; manipulation of beliefs by power players; power. All = mutual independence, people interaction, e.g., healthcare, welfare. Manipulation of beliefs to obfuscate importance of government; all are engaged in this. See the value diagram: politics = method to determine values. On axis, trade-offs, weights. All = form direction of government. Big government debate = sentiment.

Must distinguish between the role of government and substantive content of the role of philosophy = notion of "primitive terms" given substance by practice.

1. Law
2. Economy: market mechanism; inclusive or exclusive of government?
3. Private ⎫   Enormous variable content ⇒ tend to go in tandem
            ⎬   but relationship is complex and must be worked out.
4. Public ⎭
5. Property: not have an independent existence of social content that defines it
6. Free enterprise: combinations of terms "fine" = market and "enterprise" ⇒ conflicts between
7. Regulation ⎫   Analytically equivalent = matter of changing interests
8. Deregulation ⎭   It supports substantive = what are these regulations
9. Commodity: no ethical transcendent existence; defined by custom, practice, law
10. Economic units: individuals; content worked out in practice $= f$ (law)
11. Costs: multiple concepts, perspectives

Costs$= f$ (rights) as a cost to others; substance of all terms worked out in practice. Must assign particular substance if not key questions.
        ↓
        Result is ambiguous without clear substantive definitions

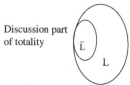

Discussion part — What happens with regard to $\overline{L}$, is reflection of
of totality — $\overline{L}$ — rest of L;
L — Any term => gives effect to lots of other stuff.

<u>Nature or status of terms</u>: Not "natural" or transcendent, not real or independent of social practice; they are created with episodic, temporary meanings. They are worked out; they are insubstantial symbols.

Part III. History of Law and Economics

This is an old and new topic $\Rightarrow$ ancient thought; Plato and Aristotle; a central topic or set of topics throughout history of thought and economics journal articles literature until 1960. In 1960 = Coase's work and the modern movement from Coase.

Treatment channeled by

1. Preconceptions of economy + polity interrelationships that require preconceptions
2. People's attitudes about what government should do
3. People's particular attachments or identifications
4. Effects to change distribution of income and wealth, e.g. [Presidential candidate Bob] Dole's tax cut; Stockman in reference to Reagan tax cuts

Target of some and basis of other ideologies. All = agenda with regard to government.

<u>Four basic approaches post-1960</u>

1. Economy $= f$ (law)
2. Law $= f$ (economy); economic determinism
3. Market-plus-framework approach
4. Nexus with interrelations

Within the neoclassical mainstream:

a. Pigouvian = pro-reformist
b. <u>Paretian = antireformist</u>

Both emphasize the market ⟹ identify sub-Pareto optimality and government action to correct (market failure). Paretians define welfare maximization through exhaustion of trade without alternative to problems of power.

Marxian approach: State = instrument of domination and exploitation. By definition communism ⟹ classlessness ⟹ statelessness. Private property is part of the superstructure that enables the ruling class to achieve their goals (exploitation). The state = instrument of the powerful, rule, classist. Class directly and indirectly controls government; level and structure of government budgets directly relates to who controls government and how to bring about accommodations between classes. What about how spending and not spending works? Who benefits, compromises, conflicts? Key = idea of state as domination and exploitative function of the state.

1. Legitimize + reproduce the system (public education)
2. Facilitate capital accumulation in private hands

This advances certain class interests; functions of government is to perpetuate, legitimize, reproduce the system of rule and exploitation. Focus of Marx? Capital, factories. Why is there conflict in the capitalist system? Because of

1. Legitimization needs of the system; functions of welfare state = renders the poor docile.
2. Facilitation of accumulation, over taxes, with regard to consumption. There are not singular and obvious methods to do this; conflicts for spending on military, education, welfare.
3. Imperialism, buying off the poor, macro policy to limit instability, e.g., price stability decreases profits.
4. Within capitalist class with regard to distribution of surplus value across sectors ⟹ e.g., pollution laws.

How to explain the growth of government spending? Marxism stresses

1890 G/Gross National Product (GNP) ≈ 3%–5% ⎫
⎬ How did this take place?
1996 G/GNP ≈ 35% ⎭

1. Growth of capitalist powers + control of state
2. Growth of crisis and conflicts within capitalism; instability, impoverishment

Government budget tells us that

- war, defense, national debt from war = matter of capitalist imperialist policy
- welfare state to buy off the poor
- subsidies to businesses
- educational system to perpetuate hierarchy

These are not neutral categories, but deterministic of capitalism.

Alternative Marxian Theory
The standard: State = part of superstructure based on models of production.
Alternative: De-emphasis of state as a derivative phenomena and de-emphasis of idea of state as class domination = more/less autonomous power, functioning to perpetuate to system and to serve as a vehicle for accommodation of conflicts of interest. The state = autonomy; class not basic definitional foundation.

Since 1960: Three main developments with variations

1. Neoclassical Chicago approach seeks to identify optimal law, rights, solutions standard neoclassical research protocol ⇒ utilitarian idea; this is what economists should do = very, very common.
   a. Variation asks: Suppose government does things, what are the consequences? Are they optimal or suboptimal? Econometric methodology; descriptive and interpretative ≈ Coase.
   b. Examine how legal system necessarily produces the optimal result. This is Posner's approach; not just that government should do this, but does this.
2. Critical legal studies ⇒ in law schools. Combination of legal realism: law in a sociological way; not transcendent, e.g., McCauley Book, Marxist history. Motivation was that young in the 1960s ⇒ reacted to Vietnam, Civil Rights, radicalization, feminism focus on power + ideology in Marxian way.
3. Institutionalists = diverse group
   a. Description, interpretative = most work on role of government
   b. Problems of labor, poverty, development
   c. Problem-solving strategies
   d. Corporate system vs. textbook markets
   e. Samuels, Schmid theories about role of government, alternative model of welfare economics. Cynicism = Samuels last chapter of Pareto

Words in general: Words have meanings and attachments that we give them; they are not independent. The invisible hand = metaphor for the market = metaphor for equilibrium, competition. For example, "arbitrary" has many connotations; typically pejorative nuance, though defined as unbiased, or if it is biased, the base and use of the base is arbitrary ≈ coercion faces same issues. The purpose of the coercions article is that the different respects that can be interpreted as coercive; the operation of valuation in society to use some definitions rather than some others. Antitrust and coercion, structural vs. behavioral considerations, the railroads problem ⇒ Microsoft vs. Netscape.

Converse of coercion = freedom ⇒ books on freedom; lots of literature.

⇒ Selective perception of coercion + ideological attachment.

Fundamentals Book: Categories and class, fiction

Legislators pursue strategies

> 1. Ideological ⇒ integrity + internal consistency
> 2. Immersion: read as much as possible data, issues, info ⇒ sensible solution
> 3. Trading – negotiating for votes

Law Schools
Keith Tribe explored the 17th, 18th century history of economics in Germany ⇒ sociological insight. Germany = different from United States, Great Britain in 20th century. Economics was part of law schools and was taught as an administrative science ⇒ to staff government positions; trained for monarchial bureaucracy. Economics came to be very different = intellectual discipline, science, denigrates government, highly academic, inward looking.

Law schools: Trade schools, training in a profession involving technical expertise for sale to settle suits; contracts ⇒ network of impersonal interactions. Law schools are laden with professional scholars for whom law = object of study; law = intellectual exercise. Training in law school = training in governance.

Law and Rights: Law is an artifact, law as language. Language defines the world. It establishes and articulates institutional regularities, norms, and values. Read constitution: what does it mean as language? Descriptive, proscriptive, normative? Law = concepts, definitions of words give effect to various concepts and are selectively applied. Commons, Johnston spelled out the transformation, the meanings of various terms; e.g., property. Physical, corporeal, incorporeal, tenure = property. Every term = history at point in time verify the definition of the word chose selectively to use. You cannot refer to THE LAW because it will change; interpretations change, or are applied differently.

$\Rightarrow$ Conflict between <u>proscriptive</u> + <u>prescriptive</u> approaches to language

Cannot use certain definition   Permissive use can be
                                                made of words
The word is only what it is   Words are what we will

= Dilemma; words at point in time are standard, but change over time. What is true of law = true of language in general; <u>selective process.</u>

Relationship of <u>language</u> and <u>social construction of reality</u>

{ 1. Social construct = creation, e.g., economics created
   2. Construction = creation of meaning; in reality grew a set of meanings

Language serves function in defining reality and serving as a basis for further construction. Look at constitution = words that define economy; reality = textual framework for decisions of the transformations and further reconstruction.

Legal system and economy are both artifacts; influence and are influenced by language by the concepts ensconced in words $\Rightarrow$ reification: more finite and definitive than in fact; words have independent meaning. Process of language, institutional evolution; verify denies the process.

Reading of Texts: Any text can be interpreted in different ways. Meaning of text is the reading that is given from hermeneutics. Stigler: Consensus of economists can judge what the *Wealth of Nations* meant. Multiple interpretations; care only to defend on base on which the interpretation was raised $\Rightarrow$ hermeneutic circle. Professional consensus, Stigler says, should determine. See how different people get different things out of same book $\Rightarrow$ varies.

        a. Different readings
        b. Empirical fact that we do get alternative readings
        c. Because of approach from multiple standpoints

Framers intent = arguments; not facts. The constitution means multiple things and has been used in ways never contemplated. The arguments = mores in a linguistic game.

<u>Constitutional and Legal Juxtaposition</u>

1. Constitutional text revisions = multiple meanings
2. Issues that go before the Supreme Court involve clash between constitutional clauses; clashes over meanings of clauses.

For example, government ⇒ full employment; inflation = taking of fixed, saved income or fighting inflation = increased unemployment = taking of income. Takings = Fifth Amendment Takings Claim, but government has the power to issue currency and declare the value of money from the Constitution. One of readings and applications of the Constitution and choice of clauses.

Also true of Common law: courts = different lines of reasoning = array of precedents; stream of options. Courts/judges must choose to cite one precedent over another.

Heterogeneously constructed, interpreted, applied: question of what the courts will hold.

<u>Constitution and Economics</u>: Varying valuational paradigms; positive paradigms of how economy <u>is</u> organized.

Oliver Wendall Holmes: Constitution does not embody Spencer's social statics; people will read law in conjunction with some book; some perception of society is, ought to be organized and controlled.

Fundamental question: How to take rights in relationship to government. Independent of government = limit government/law; dependent on law for meaning. There are psychic balm reasons and tradition of naturalism; supernaturalism. Must discriminate between the Economic Role of Government in general vs. substantive content, e.g., property rights. Problem is the desire for certitude = natural law + rights = "nonsense on stilts."

Police powers vs. eminent domain ⎫ Process that determines rights
Regulatory power   ⎬ or limits to rights
Regulatory interstate commence ⎭

If rights are determined, then no takings

If rights = transcendent existence, then there is a taking. This is the most crucial issue before Supreme Court. Eminent domain: people with property, rights can be taken given certain procedures and compensation. Police power: power to regulate in interest of public health, safety, morals, welfare, or regulation of property and contract.

"Petty larceny of policy power": assumes property rights, Supreme Court.

Attitude toward rights and rights to government = fundamental to legal-economic policy questions. Typical terms in legal/economic discussions = primitive terms, so to avoid questions of definition. All these discussions are laden with primitive terms that have selective usages. Law, economy, public, private, free enterprise, regulation, deregulation, produce definitions. Treated as if had substance, but substance is variable.

<u>Complex Intertemporal Characteristics of Law</u>

Most/all legal discourse looks backward to precedence, rights; real meaning of law has to do with the future.

P.S. 1 (precedential sequence) $\Big\}$ Decision which affects future
P.S. 2

⇒ Future making as a prelude to present reconstruction. Ex post nature of law; court law is ex post – do not know if a statute/behavior is constitutional until the courts have spoken ⇒ pretense that courts prediscovering an actual, real law really making law through decisions.

Public good character of law: (i) law applies to others at no cost and (ii) they cannot be excluded. Situations:

1. Contempt of court ⇒ in that court or should another court review about behavior of lawyers and courts; all court decisions affect behavior.
2. England's National Secrecy Act vs. freedoms; especially freedoms for national security; government malfeasance – question about underlying order of control.
3. Ordinance that all night grocery requires two people with the objective to deter robberies; some studies show decrease of robberies, but does this conflict with the nature of free enterprise? ⇒ trade-offs; = law as selective perception, interpretations.

4. Universities have two conflicting modes of decision making.
   a. Contract; specifics provide for our reformation in the future.
   b. Managerial discretion, who decides what causes, how many, how to make decisions? Who makes decisions? Legislature = power to managerial; practical = faculty. Student participation in academic governance – what form and what weight?
5. Case in England 1920s. The House of Lords sustained a legal district auditor who said would decrease the cost of living raises; wages of civil service should decrease.
   a. What does employment contract explicitly call for? Some have cost of living clauses? What if it is silent?
   b. What is legal context within which to be interpreted? Nominal vs. real dollars? What if an increase in the price line?

Contracts of adhesion ⇒ possible paper topic. Contrary to imagining and ideology, people do not bargain over contracts (command idea of contracts); others accept or reject ⇒ standardized to consumers. Exceptions are big companies with multiple suppliers; suppliers take or leave. Freedom to negotiate is very very limited over most of life. Contract protects seller's interests; limits consumers. Protections law (warranties, lemon, fraud) are contrary to images of free enterprise. Common law provision that enabled court to overturn a central clause if it is too one-sided. *Laesio-enormis.* Today overturn if gross disparity (e.g., three times price).

Futurist nature of law: Most discussion of law is retrospective, whereas the operative significance is the structure of economy in future and the future behavior of people.

Sovereignty: Problem of governmental immunity ⇒ governance. The ability to make decisions that count, of importance to families, institutions, economy, polity ⇒ making decisions that affect people.

"Enlightenment Agenda" included a cosmopolitan view of humanity as opposed to nationalistic view. Smith in his *Theory of Moral Sentiments* – appreciated that the value of others, the further removed, the less they count ⇒ distance function.

Smithian Economics – others values and interests count on par with ours ⇒ especially international trade. Mainstream = cosmopolitan; considerations of nationalism runs counter to cosmopolitan economics; modern enlightened economics.

UN = threat to a sovereignty? Attempt to project idea of international sovereignty, but have nature, courts, trade, all with sovereignty. International sovereignty involves perception of autonomy; all are interacting economically and politically. Political sovereignty = historical conception; rhetorical.

> Internationalism vs. Nationalism

↙   ⟶   – Isolation = nationalism to some

Continuation of The Enlightenment– Insulation
Ubiquitous externalities   – Aggressive stance

Historical significance: End of feudal period, and had a diverse number of landed aristocrats vs. a king ⇒ uneasy relationships; became king by beating others. *Pax Romana, Pax Americana* ⇒ results from exercising to hegemony. States are what they are because of internal/external conflicts. Nation, form of nation, elite structure come to define sovereignty.

Sovereignty = Governance: Political conception. Irony that countries can have a self-perceived proclivity for political sovereignty but economic sovereignty washed away.

1. World economy: developed Pacific Rim, EU, multiple centers of power; countries connected economically. That economic sovereignty is lost is a fact of life, "more or less" free trade.
2. Growth of MNCs = chief rival to nation-state = multinational corporations

Sovereignty in a nation-state system is not self-subsistent, but is sentimental agreement.

Commons on *Sociological View of Sovereignty* talking about governance. Property = sovereignty; to have property get to make decisions that affect other people; distinction due to breakdown of feudalism = proliferation of sovereignty; disaggregation; division of governance, also functional equivalents to property with legal protection. How deal with sovereignty? It's a political theory. Political vs. economic decision making; form of governance, religion, and the relationship between the two = more complex with the modern nation-state, MNCs.

Case study: Governmental Immunity. So long as official involved = governmental function is immune from liability. 1907 Hawaiian Supreme Court case. Holmes addresses government immunity – sovereign exempted from suit because of authority to make the law.

1. The government the sovereign? Sovereignty in the people.
2. Why not legal grounds against law make the law ⇒ for what is sovereignty, a metaphor? It is a floating term/game, therefore multiple interpretations; legislature can establish liability, can a court? Legislature vs. judiciary.

Holmes does not make a judicial matter; desirability vs. logical necessity. You must make liable to affect behavior; source of law subject to the law that it makes? Holmes says this is illogical. Any difference in sovereign immunity when king, sovereign people, or sovereign people's government?

Most doctrines = situational conflicts; particular conflict, e.g., Locke's *2nd Treatise on Government*. English king, 13th century – could be sued and sue. Sovereign immunity from Stuart/Tudor doctrine to avoid liability ⇒ due to Enlightenment thinking.

What is Sovereignty? It is not absolute; not in a nation-state system; abstracting from this: is sovereignty anything more than hegemony?

– In every institution = variety of perceptions, power, interests
– Not a categorical absolute but a characteristic of opposing forces

Why Holmes? Because 1907 cause was anachronistic ⇒ a clause celeb. Becomes a continual topic in his correspondence. State will do what it can only constrained by concessions of the populace that are necessary to maintain power; Holmes acknowledges limits, e.g., Japanese internment was OK for 40 years, then we decide to compensate.

Sovereignty = balance of forces and sense of legitimacy. Government in opposition ⇒ Journal. Dichotomy in government. Power: If Holmes is right, then government is both officialdom and these who are willing to fight; think of making decisions. Holmes = lots of metaphysics but a practical question as to the threat of rebellion. English Parliament in 1770s – have the right/power to legislate American colonies.

Governance – process of working this all out. One distinct characteristic of government, chief function of government is to determine division of power between public and private. Government = locus of decision-making process. Government is an important process of working all this out. The concept sovereignty = post-medieval residue and application. Is it a question for the legislature or courts? The critical issue is the autonomy of judges; courts are/do legislation. Who declares law as an exercise of sovereignty? Holmes says that "the law is not a brooding omnipresence in the sky." Sovereignty = metaphor of ultimate power, legislative, people, but if people fight, the sovereign must give in.

If prices are based on costs, how calculate costs: as original or reproduction costs, if rising prices, consumers want original and firms prefer falling prices and vice versa. Marginal utility = f (circumstance). There's a tension between the levels of government and compartments of government; court checks legislature, which is too subject to population pressures.

Charon Editorial: Conflicts within government are eternal; now conservatives are using "traditional" liberal arguments against courts, judges. It all depends which side the bread is buttered on. ⇒ Poverty questions = very important issue/old issue. Old Testament had distributional issues.

Practical Cases

1. 1980s = instances of student newspapers trying to report on pregnancy and divorce, political connections, homosexuality; schools like to keep away from these subjects = multiple handles.
   a. Privacy – should students do investigate work and report on people = big issue privacy vs. freedom of information; has to inform students of grades?
   b. Educational policy: schools argue that this form of activity is not a matter of university educational policy, therefore not allowed.
   c. Student newspapers are the property rights of the school authorities, therefore they get to make the decisions.
   d. Can replace school board with another through voting if there's disagreement.
   e. Behavioral consequences of student journal.
   f. Free speech and the First Amendment; does going to school mean giving up free speech right?
2. Professor unilaterally changes location of the course to have air conditioning from North to well South of the river = inconvenient; problem of governance and sovereignty. Should students vote? Professor decision unilateral?
3. Supreme Court Case Green vs. Frasier (1920): long history of interpretation of state and Federal constitutions with regard to the kinds of state commercial activity allowed.

Xenophon's study of government's role in development now (1880s post) lost of state provisions that spend no money except for public welfare courts uphold and reject/develop public role.

In 1920, courts upheld North Carolina tax statute that provided taxes to finance marketing and manufacture of farm products. Question: What is a public purpose?

Law: What is, what mean, sources?

1. Ubiquity of law; law is not aberrational, not part time; whatever define law to be.
2. Historically in Western Civilization we have two legal systems: common law and civil law; elements common to both are interpreted differently.

Common Law	Civil Law
Law is promulgated by the courts	Law codified in a code
Judges decide between parties	Court is to morally administer the law with code
Long and complex history with English kings	Systems of law making

United States = 49 Common laws   } Also uniform commercial codes; Constitution

Civil law = Louisiana/French }
Continental countries = Civil Law Systems with code

Common Law Systems = dichotomy. Circumstances hold that courts make law, also hold where judges find the law. Natural law, legitimacy, law as transcendent. Civil Systems: Courts applying the code, but lots of room for discretion. More or less superficially common and civil ⟹ in practice judges make choices.

3. Common law
   Constitutional law   } In United States, we have these sources of law.
   Statute law
   Administrative law }
   As long as we have federal systems; legislatives ⟹ multiple forms of law.
4. Divine law, natural law, positive law; people have had a belief in conception of natural or/and divine law; some claim natural is derivative to divine; also vice versa.
   God cannot violate natural law.

Most thinking here is not very rigorous
   e.g., miracles = god violating natural law   }   Sloppy theologi-
   "miracle of brain" ordinary occurrence   cal language

Divine and/or natural assume law given to man; antecedent, transcendent. Pragmatic: government violates divine/natural law with torture?
Law is not transcendent; creation of mankind; content of law changes =
empirical phenomena, not transcendent. Roscoe Pound: lawyers trained
in law schools = case law but legislation is also law that gives a heretical
view for law school. Conventional view = unsophisticated; that legislate
makes law, execute enforces the law; judicial makes the law, but discretion at all stages; what is the law?

5. Useful to understand law as a process rather than a fact; not a priori, not
found; but a process to be worked out. It is a matter of selective perception and rhetorical motivation inevitability of the normative nature of
law; subjectivity; objective facts but what is the nature of objective facts,
e.g., price is objective and also subjective valuation. The law is portrayed
as objective for political purpose, etc. = psychic balm as transcendent
source; legitimation through is what it is at a point in time; reification;
the law is politics.

Politicization

1. Put into politics what was hitherto not in politics.
2. Make explicit as political what was political, all along but what wasn't
   explicitly recognized as such.

Reification: Treat something as if had intended, transcendent existence, ontological
naturalistic fallacy in philosophy. This telescope is and ought ⇒ ontological "is."

Rights: Language of rights = three senses.

1. Claim ... I have the right to ...
2. Adjudicated conflict determining who can do what to whom, conflicting
   claims that have been evaluated in a system in which two inconsistent
   claims are determined, therefore rights have to do with other people – the
   α, β rights conflict.
3. Sanctions = means by which adjudicated claim is supported, protected.
   Statutes = sanctions, but must be enforced.

What is law

"Complex subject – the Law" implies know what we're talking about. Discussion = court law (common, civil), legislature and administration, but ultimately determined by the court.

1. Decision of the court – holds for α over $\beta \Rightarrow$ law involves the holding of the decision.
2. *Ratio decidendi*: grounds, basis of decision. Courts holds for α over β on the basis on line of reasoning, some grounds.
3. The sequence of precedence of the decision latest in a sequence of decisions and law = that articulated through the sequence.

Problems with 1–3 are particularistic but given the impression of something not particularistic multiple judges = multiple reasons for voting a particular way; therefore "a" ground vs. "the" ground $\Rightarrow$ same issues with sequences; multiple precedential sequences, construct, or distinguish precedents?

4. Overriding principles or rules: first there (1–3) are merely manifestation of overriding principles or rules; problem is that courts attempting to articulate these. Principles disagree to what they are. Roscoe Pound believes in basic jural postulates. Pragmatic legal realist = in a bind, law is a matter of deduction from basic legal principles; recognizes this.
5. These are themselves overriding principles or rules, and are still more general to higher level of principles; layer more general rules $\Rightarrow$ desire for something transcendent.
6. Natural law: multiple forms of law; argument not necessarily progressive.
7. Legal realists idea of law: distinction between law on paper and law in action.
   Law in action = what is done by prosecutors; by way of discretionary at every stage = exercise of discretion, especially criminal law: police, prosecutor, court law is what the law person says/does. For example, meat inspection law.

Sources of law

1. Custom: Conflict between revelation, custom, law, including what religious, noncodified and codified, leader say.
   a. Law in England is very much based on this conflict.

b. Origin of law of business, 18th century = law of merchants;
Burgher law not covered by federal land law ⇒ private commercial
courts.
Meaning
a. Merchant courts ⇔ common law courts; decisions look at what
other courts do.
b. Law of merchants cemented interests of business and there the
legitimized law of business ⇒ law for everyone else; commercial law from merchants. Whose customs? Choosing between
customs?

Q: structure of the market for control:

Sources of Law Continued.

1. Custom: Law does not emanate from vacuum, but exists within and
   reflects society that depends on custom, therefore custom ⇒ law is logical. Because law codifies belief systems. When law is faced with custom
   ⇒ conflict within or between customs, law chooses between claimants
   of custom status. J. R. Commons: courts deal with landowning society
   when conflict with urban industrial financial society ⇒ customs of working class and control of jobs, conditions.
2. Considerations of morality and equity: Same ideas as customs.
   Dominant notions of morality ⇒ influences law, but law must choose
   between claims of equity, questions of preconceptions, reality ⇒ conflicting conceptions of morality + equity, tail-chasing game; lawyer ⇔
   preachers.
3. Public policy: 18th, 19th, early 20th century is in law a concept of public
   policy = more philosophical, deeper than ordinary public policy time
   honored public policies such as protect of property protections of corporations, public safety, welfare, and morals ⇒ generalizable public policy.
   Smith lectures on jurisprudence – 18th century language = "Police"; to
   policy = police; establish policy in deep, broad sense.
4. Statutes: Source of court law; not until 20th century that common law
   judges accepted statute law as a source of law; common law always
   superior to statute law previously – see Pound. Recognition that statutes = source of law is recent. Question: What law is? Whose source
   they are?
5. Force: The will of the sovereign; sovereignty = matter of force. Modern
   politics = substitute for force; historically force= source of law. Was

determinant in determining shape of the law for US Civil War, European settles vs. Native Americans, Quebec succession movements, former USSR, Eastern Europe. The Napoleonic Code = obvious example not mentioned.

6. Past Judicial Precedence: assumes judicial authority; past decisions = law; decisions how must choose precedence.

7. Opinions of Experts: Authorities; Brandeis on Brown vs. Board of Education; law and social significance of law authorities testified upon; to be authority, must be recognized as such – attributions made by others, publications? Great deal of this in court decisions ⇒ signed and unsigned law review articles.

8. Legal Theory: Analytical jurisprudence; emphasis on logic courts like to present decisions as if followed logically difference between reaching a conclusion and exposition on the conclusion; logically expositive = persuasive but "not say much" because about what are you being logical? Problems = use of a model; set of variables structured in a particular way; logically is separate from the model but also not tell us about the real world. Difference between logical validity and truth, or is truth conditional?

For example,

$$\frac{\text{\_\_\_\_}/\!/\text{\_\_\_\_}}{\text{\_\_\_\_}/\!/\text{\_\_\_\_}}$$ This Euclidian assumption ⇒ angles of a triangle, geometry of a plane.

Non-Euclidian geometry ⇒ curve space; geometry of multidimensions, but which is true is a separate matter? Question: Can you expect answers from logic above? NO! What are the premises? Whose premises?

Holmes' *Common Law* states that the "life of the law is logic, but it is also experience." Can you base economic role of government on narrow theoretical premises? Yes, but does not mean ⇒ truth. Only a model; selective perception. Legal theory can be the basis of law; law static morality of justice? Yes, done all the time. The problem is to recognize that it is being done.

Legal Realism + Sociological Jurisprudence

Roscoe Pound was for the law equivalent of institutional economics, with an emphasis on experience, practice, empiricism ⇒ directly opposes analytical jurisprudence; recipe approach. Legal realism: choice to cook, choice of recipe and lots of relevant choices to choose between = matter of practice, selective perception, therefore whose experience, whose premises, whose goals, whose preconceptions ⇒ powers and policy of choice. Analytical jurisprudence obfuscates choice problem = choosing your premises.

Question: What does legal realist say? "Is law an expression of certain set of economic conditions? Is there economic determinism? Law = f (economy). Some say yes = law of industrial capitalism, but then is economy = f (law)? Some emphasize both; conflicts.

Alternative to whatever way system reflects economics, there is still within the system lots of choices.

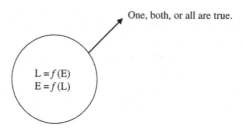

One, both, or all are true.

$L = f(E)$
$E = f(L)$

Within existing system, decide α/β rights conflict.

Marshall's economic laws this morning in history; introduction on natural laws. Natural law = reification of existing law; law ontologically given. Tendency characteristic of taking certain historical accounts/events ⇒ categories ⇒ details from which they arise ⇒ reification "cow-ness example"   ↓

Done because of a generic tendency to think like this; verify to legitimize.

Question: What are we dealing with here? Reality or particular premise; transcendent or given in Constitutions? Or an operative premise? Often treat premises as given rather than hypothetical starting points ⇒ all boils down to choice; basic assumptions to verify begs question of choice ⇒ given society in which you're operating or not.

All theories = combination between positive and normative, but still a useful distinction.

Theories of Law: Theories tend to become not descriptors but actual participants in working out solutions. ⇒ Epstein on law and economics movement in law schools is both positive and normative, embodies ideologies and an agenda.

Is one example of many theories that are positive theories with deep normative implications ⟹ part of process of working out most people do not do this except for Schmid and Samuels; ideas not intended to be of use in making decisions.

Basic normative premise: better to have deep matter in the open rather than hidden. (1) ⟹ normative position (see Pareto, Knight); limited because it is not intended or in fact useful analysis is overwhelmingly agnostic. Criticisms: left – doesn't go far enough; right = statist, Marxist. Things look different from different standpoints.

1. What is the author's positive theory?
2. What is the motivation or intent behind the theory?
3. Of what use if any is the work for determining legal policy?

Second normative premise: since government has been used in the past to establish rights, it is presumptuous to say government is not doing so in the present; both values = Enlightenment values. Theories become part of working out of nature of problem. Epstein = neoclassical law and economies to find right answer to law ⟹ to be useful for policy implications need additional assumptions to convert positive to normative interests. Privileging one position over another, inexorable government choice, then legal/economic analyst makes choice.

Analytical jurisprudence and neoclassical economics = such a lengthy chain of reasoning that normative gets buried or is too remote that seems positive. Neoclassical = footnote to Hume's "cannot derive on ought from an is alone." Opposite = unequivocal position. Law = method of making choices; forms social preferences. You need identification, selection of whose interests are to count; more than describing ⟹ policy process. Description = different impacts, therefore also policy; some benefit and others don't benefit. Positive analysis = structural, distributional consequences.

Theory ⟹ policy: joined by normative assumptions; theoretical premises, e.g., Malthus and Ricardo's theories of rent = same theory but differing normative premises. ⟹ Conflictual process working out what law is to be theories = part of it overtly or inadvertently.

Language: Conceptualize law as language = important; law = instrument or check on power but it is both an instrument of power; law = shabby. Is both a check on power; law = good/bad; e.g., α/β rights conflict; rights to monopolize.

Law = symbol manipulation; law and discussions = manipulation of symbols. What is property, governance, rights, etc.? ⟹ When read cases ask "what are all these things the court is saying? Symbol manipulation? Are they metaphors

for anything substantial?" How much of what is said is derivative of perceptions of what the economy is, e.g., Freidman that businesses not have social
obligations ⇒ playing rhetorical role in modern politics.

Metaphors: Economics is an array of metaphors; market = metaphor. [Small note: if
all = artifacts, then the only goal is to manipulate policy = ultimate]. Fact: All dealt
with by law and economics do not have an independent existence; the world is an
artifact of symbols and metaphors but not abstracts ⇒ true enough so that Pareto
has seen fit to say so, is important. If accept this ⇒ come to grips with it.

Critical distinction between law vs. policy: law semantics vs. policy semantics
holds law in higher esteem ⇒ "that's the law." Law has a higher standing, law is
given, is more substantial. Policy is made not found; lesser.

Context

1. Philosophically tend to treat law as absolute and policy = pragmatic.
2. Policy = lower line esoterically but practically law is not an issue, law is
   passed policy law as given = legitimizing function.

But law is policy; the distinction breaks down; law against killing: manslaughter,
first degree, negligence, self-defense, war, death penalty. Not an unequivocal
absolute. There are societies in which killing is the moral thing ⇒ medieval,
postmedieval, duels; law is policy and is not universal.

Prefer laws because of policy it implies ⇒ ontological law verifies the policy of
existing law; converts law of time and place into natural law of the universe; telescopes is and ought; rhetorical established as normative as inexorable. ⇒ law is
policy, therefore is a matter of a division of power, social control, power. Grander
than policy verifies it; legitimizing fashion, e.g., freedom of speech precedents
reality from being defined by people in power, in totalitarian regimes; differ from
government = jail. Government support one set of interests or another.

Judges make the law or find the law ⇒ waste of time; legitimization purposes.
Really working out process of $F + C$, $C + C$, $H + E$. Law is found = metaphysical ⇒
nature made = empirical, pragmatic therefore is an artifact; there no position on
transcendental, but psychological significance, political motivational significance.
⇒ Meaning of conflict between Idealism + Realism

Realism = philosophical realism; reality independent of perception of it and must
act in conformity with the reality.

<u>Idealism</u> = what matters does not mean a preexisting reality but our own concep-
tion and must choose between conceptions; part Kantian that if reality cannot
know it; ideals from us and not from reality.

Realist criticism: is a reality but many alternative idealisms; choice must be made.
Idealist: choice must be made; realists choose too because don't agree on what
THE reality is. Platonist; real exists but important is the ideal we have of it ⇒
action ⇒ changes what is real. Idealist: more than one ideal.
Bottom line: How do people treat the status quo; status quo is important because we
start from there (J.M. Buchanan); but how specify status quo? Doesn't say much.
Status quo verified or treated as an artifact, matter of policy and subject of change.

Behind Law = implicit is metaphysical conceptualization: conceptions of what law
is, what society is, whose interests are power structure specific, economic system
specific, ideology, religion, e.g., law of post-feudal agrarian vs. urban industrial;
metaphysical premises were very different – standard use of comparative method.
Holmes: "general propositions do not decide concrete cases/ends." Determine
A–B rights conflicts; same point = St. Thomas Aquinas "reason needs not only
general but particular principles." Holmes states that "the decision depends …
more particular than major premise."

Holmes: also that people prefer to have premises remain inarticulate, e.g., politicians' claims to tax cuts all have different premises of distributions; studies on tax
burdens and distribution that distribution ≠ very different.

Rights: can see law as social artifact/socially constructed, not categorical absolutes
⇒ deconstruction and pragmatic method. Rights = multiple meanings/levels:

1. A <u>claim</u>
2. <u>Acceptance of claim</u> by court or statute; established right
3. <u>Enforcement of acceptance</u> of the claim

Semantics of rights = discourse; often not very helpful ⇒ to claim a right is to claim
a privileged position and a policy that exercised right gives effect to. Statement in
terms of rights ⇒ treats as absolute starts with concept that is universally compre-
hended to be an absolute; all rights relate to other rights at any of the three levels.

Rights not tell us much – e.g., I own the money in my wallet, but what to do with
it = f (prices, economic structure, The Fed, etc.); positive and normative connotation. Rights tend to be treated as absolutes when they're usually highly relative.
Language of rights intellectualizes established positions, modes of enforcement
by treating as categorical absolutes.

Different <u>authors model rights differently</u>: some that affirms/condemns rights based discourse define rights discourses differently ⇒ problem that exists.

1. [Wesley Newcomb] <u>Hohfeld</u> – writer beginning of century states that people use terms in question begging ways; difficult to make sense of legal writing that uses same words in different ways. ⇒ talked about rights, duties, exposures, immunities complex set of jural pairs. Commons very impressed with this therefore able to interpret what is going on in technical ways ⇒ complex and powerful nuances.

2. <u>Robert Lee Hale:</u> big effect on institutionalism and legal realism; uses Hohfeld's models but treats rights in opportunity sets model.

 Functions of power and rights and interactions, e.g., Red Cedar tree case.

Larger more generic sense in <u>context of mutual coercion.</u>

Book review in October 11 issue of *Science* and a letter to the editor.

1. Social-biology = work in multiple fields
2. Too large extent social-biology known by view of its cites; any particular discipline ⇒ food for mill on both sides of ideology

⇒ Knowledge to social action and social policy (Review): *Portrayal of Science and Reason* by [Paul] Ehrlich. Population problem, lots of data and interpretation of data; difference mostly in interpretation. Related to knowledge to social policy, where there are two points of view: (1) policy based on knowledge and (2) knowledge does not lead to policy unequivocally. The "is" does not always give "ought"; use of ignorance argument. That debate over interests, priorities and values of society at large is larger than environmental debate = actual relationships are very complex.

<u>Rights Continued</u>: dealing with language ⇒ three connotations of rights:

1. Claim of a right
2. Affirmation of claim
3. Enforcement

Right without protection and enforcement = right? ⇒ mode of discourse is the value of policy supported by rights and who makes policy, but task in terms of absolute rights. Rights = multiple modeling.

Hohfeld model ⇒ opposites + correlatives, requires rigorous adherence to definitions. Hale, Samuels = opportunity sets model on a basis of power.

Rights = instrument vs. check on power; Commons view on property. Meaning of statement that "*X* has a right to ..." depends on who makes the statement.

1. By court and legislature this "is" statement [becomes descriptive]; is actually an "ought" statement; language has a metaphysical underpinning = pretext; in practice telescopes "is and ought."
    Holmes quotes distinguish "is" and "ought"; ordinary language is a conflation of "is and ought"; by a court is an authoritative ought statement. Is the law ≠ should be the law, but "is" by an authoritative voice means ought proposition.
2. Participant in world means is and is statement that is the law ⇒ descriptive proposition.
3. Intent vs. consequences of statement; intent is that "*X* has the right" over *Y*, but effects is another matter ⇒ rights distribution implies results = f (intent as to who, logical consequences).

What does having a right mean? Enhanced decision making ⇒ opportunity set model, power. Rights are relative to government agency that makes statement and relative of other rights ⇒ enable participation in economic system.

Law and Economics Field: fundamental tension:

1. Rights antecedent to policy; such rights ⇒ such policy.
    $R_A \rightarrow$ optimal solution *A*
    $R_B \rightarrow$ "   " *B*
    Institution govern allocation of resources ⇒ rights matter, but remember Coase Theorem then rights irrelevant (not Coase view).

2. Use economic analysis to determine rights; Posner's view. Circularity argument ⇒ cannot use economic analysis to determine rights because economics = optimal solutions = f (rights). Posner accepts reluctantly.

Property Rights

1. In general; in particular to economic analysis; expositive of issues
2. Specific role of property rights in economics
3. Controversial fundamentals; what fundamentals are; Samuels view

What is property? Proudholm says that property is theft. Analysis does not mean consumption goods; produce durables and capital because from expropriation of surplus value by capitalists
⇒ agreed with Marx on this issue.

What is Property ⇒ Samuels says that property is power = participation in decision making = form of rights (equivalent in opportunity sets model); power not in the negative pejorative sense. Property becomes one way that people participate in the decision-making process.

Property absolute or relative phenomena? Most discussion = absolute, although misinformed. Property = bundle of rights relative to government recognized end and other rights; property rights = name to certain actions of government to determining that people have certain decision-making power ⇒ certain protections of interests over other interests.

Property is what it is because of what you can do with it, e.g., tea kettle. Law defines what rights are – limitations.

Rights dual because have both private and public aspects ⇒ Economic significance of any right is contingent and problematic; paradox is that treat property rights as absolute but with value contingent in market. As absolute = psychic balm, social control ⇒ rhetorical aspect, but economics shows value relative.

Commons and Courts ⇒ use value → market value. Property protected from some government competition but not market competition. Capitalism as "creative destruction" by Schumpeter.

Transformation of Property and Distributions

Smith in *Wealth of Nations, Lectures on Jurisprudence* ⇒ transformation from feudal to commercial property; property government; law change from one stage to another. Empirical and historical account on property and government. Also Commons in *Legal Foundations of Capitalism.* "Use value to market value" is what transferred economy to capitalism ⇒ see also Herowitz, Nelson, Lawrence Freidman. All books on this topic have found out complex multitrend; was that law changes over time:

> Property = dynamic institution; changes over time (Commons!)
> ↓
> Conflicts between established and claims; property claims

Charles River Bridge (Boston): Monopoly to erect a bridge, but then later another bridge allowed; first company sues.

Property must be given legal status, e.g., stock options. Creative destruction of feudalism to capitalism; also particular rights destroyed or become secondary to other rights; this is not an exogenous phenomena but an endogenous evolution $\Rightarrow$ means that <u>inevitability of noncompensated losses.</u> Any government action affirms some interests over others, therefore something is taken if *B* previously had the right whose interests are protected? Logic of eminent domain that rights = absolute therefore compensation; is ideological strategy to minimize legal change. Takings inevitably about noncompensated losses; therefore, Lockian view of world is that government exists to protect property = sentiment, selective perception; particularly case in world of dual rights; reciprocal externalities.

$\downarrow$

Protect property if government = inextricable necessity of choice, e.g., pollution stream example deny arguable claim = easy way out. $\Rightarrow$ Property is a name to certain protection of interests by government and is property because it is protected, not that it is protected because it is property. Locke and Smith beg the issue. Government always employed in support of some interests; cannot be silent or inactive; therefore, welfare reform still protects some relative to others.

Then problem with Night Watchman theory of Government – that government compels night watchman. Where are police?

1. Highways
2. Marginal cost, rich neighborhoods
3. Poor neighborhoods
4. Commercial and industrial property

Allocation problem; solution determines what property the night watchman watches $\Rightarrow$ <u>government determines property it is said to protect; property in empirical pragmatic sense.</u>

<u>Private property = participation in decision making; therefore property = part of the process in society and economy because other rights of protected interests</u> (e.g., labor legislation, consumers). $\Rightarrow$ Government protection of interests; property only part of total problem of order.

Freedom/Control, Continuity/Change, Hierarchy/Equality

Have property = rhetorical claim to reinforce some position; ongoing process on who has what property.

Property Rights Continued

Private property and efficiency/optimality [change school, Hirsch]. "Private property is necessary to yield optimal outcomes" statement; what is meant by optimal?

- Exhausting gains from trade?
- Individuals adjust activities in pursuit of their self-interest?
  optimal = specific to individual self-interest?
  = specific to individual actions?
  = on basis on through trade?

Statement is a <u>tautology</u>. Define optimum in terms of individual adjustments which private property allows people to make therefore is obviously necessary to yield such optimum.

1. What is the defense of that definition of optimum?
2. Limitations of "private property" to reach that result?
   $\downarrow$
   Market failures?

Taken to be on a priori premise; simply acceptance or interpretation of existing system, e.g., Marx example from history this morning for Marx = part of the whole.

Optimum makes private property meaningful: 1. Belief in freedom and self-choice
                                              2. Defense of existing interests

$Power\ Structure_1 \rightarrow Rights\ Structure_1 \rightarrow Pareto\ Optimum_1$
$PS_2 \qquad\qquad\quad \rightarrow RS_2 \qquad\qquad\quad \rightarrow PO_2$

No unique, Pareto optimal result; achieved result = f (existing power structure); therefore core or set of optimal solutions specific to some initial setup. Allocation of resources = f (distribution of rights).

Definition by legal decision making:

$Resource\ Allocation = f\ (\Delta + s) = f\ (rights,\ power) = f\ (government) = f\ (who\ controls\ government)$

Whoever controls government influences who has what rights $\rightarrow \Delta + S$; long chain of determinism.

<u>Central Problem</u>: whose interests are to count as right? How? (See Schmid). Let markets work give effect to power structure that governs markets; how = through what institutional/power structure.

Anti-methodological individualism agreement = collective process through which individuals are to count ⇒ only individuals, fact that always individuals who are to count; <u>therefore, question really is whose interests and through what institutional structures.</u>
   "Individuals preferences to count" does not imply particular/specific institutional structure. Means that property and government are interdependent variables (dualism); <u>government is what is because of what controls it ⇒ property power and property is what is because government recognizes it.</u> ⇒ Larger context of Locke, Smith argument; "government protects rich from the poor," e.g., Reagan's tax cuts. Government is driven by those who can control it. Government and property are both dependent and independent property ⇒ positive proposition, although radical.

<u>Operation of Selective Perception</u>: of benefits, losses, what is property, "taking cases," injury due to government = defensible law, activities of government = ordinary doings therefore no damage; selective perception of property, comprises property ⇒ loss and reason for loss? For example, natural disaster relief.

All interests that are property rights that are not protected rights they because cannot be transferred but are protection of interests: labor laws, consumer liability laws, etc. Legal significance is that property is protected by due process but other rights are not, e.g., cannot take land, but no problem with inflation taking purchasing power.

Conclusion: avoid obscurantist thinking; recognize inevitable; necessity of choice (<u>Miller vs. Shone</u>); even in Marxist society; individuals preferences to count is whose? ⇒ Antistatist in Soviet Union, but statist in Western civilization ⇒ bugs people, but is true.
   Rights = <u>transcendent then not worry about government</u>; rights verified but rights really protected interests.

<u>Summary</u>

1. Ordinary problem of order: all must work out power; freedom vs. control, tendencies toward hierarchy vs. equality, and balance of continuity vs. change. No simple formula for this; all societies have social control. Question is on what terms maintain freedom/control, hierarchy/equality, and continuity/change? What to promote? For example, supply side economics ⇒ "prosperity for all."

Stockman claims that language was a "Trojan Horse" $\Rightarrow$ redistribution in favor of the wealth but no method to determine "right" path. At any point in time there is a structure and all decisions = working out; order and also f (distribution). Cannot ignore economic role of government because it is fundamental and because it determines whose interests are to count $\Rightarrow$ rights = protects interests.
Rights = honorific connotation
Dual nature α right = β non-right means "whose rights?"

2. Laissez-faire = set of sentiments (useful to protect against perceptions of arbitrary behavior of government). Attitude – no different from adolescent attitude – obfuscates role of government.
3. In process, government is a dependent and an independent variable. Important to see government is dependent variable $\Rightarrow$ output.

Critical issue is not whether law is, but whose interests to support and when to change the law (legal change of law). Therefore, whose interests to which to give support? Objection is that this is statist; it does not tell us who should have what rights but focuses on "is" propositions; we need normative assumptions to get "ought."

Historical Elites that Control Government

Right: Unions, welfare = elitist
Left: Right is elitist

Pluralistic society with wide range of problems/interests/issues. The configuration of elite groups changes but there are elite groups. For example, Republican parties, Eastern Establishment vs. the West and Southwest, economic conservatives vs. social conservatives. Democratic: Continue to use government to protect interests vs. change position of disadvantaged groups. Conflicts among elite groups.

US society: Pluralism and hegemonic control, which is dominant? Cannot neglect either.

$\Rightarrow$ Economy is an object of legal control; law is an instrument of economic advantage

   – Legal-economics nexus; but [treated] separately is also true
   – Cannot avoid legal control
   – Government and law = objects of economic advantage

Government $\Rightarrow$ interest protections
    Interests protected as rights
    Legal change of law by law
        This is why leadership is so important, chosen, replaced, e.g., term
        limits

The problem is who uses government for what purposes given that government is an instrument for control.

Government is

1. An arena of power play; therefore, special interests try to combat this.
2. A valuation process; government is a participant in the social valuation process.
   But, which and whose values?
3. An institution of collective action; it forms the social welfare function and changes the social welfare function.
4. A system of collective bargaining (J.R. Commons); vote trading, interests bargaining.

Government is a process rather than a completed thing $\Rightarrow$ it "becomes" rather than it "is."

The Market
Milton Freidman claims that the market "works."
  – On an ideological level; social decisions through markets.
  – Market failure?

It does work, it does produce results $\Rightarrow$ but it doesn't just exist. The market is a function of institutions and power structure. There are a <u>number of possible markets</u>; institutions matter because they form markets and give effect to power. Most import institution = government $\Rightarrow$ no unique Pareto optimal solutions.

"Government operates within the market"
  – True must borrow, buy imports, etc.
  – Form markets
  – Operates through markets, e.g., money market

This is hard to see because people have an <u>ideological filter</u>; "works" does not mean much – does it produce what you want it to?

Selective perception to where markets work and don't work

1. Chicago = markets work and are optimal
2. Others = welfare economics and market failure

Two Joint Processes

1. Rights formation and reformation
2. Working out optimal solutions

⇒ both go on simultaneously. This is the deepest connections of welfare economics.

Rationality = huge topic given many different definitions. Paul Diesing[6] = many different forms of conception of rationality. Economics = procedural, substantive; there is the problem of identifying the basis of how people learn self-interest.
Economics = particular functions

1. Escape from problems of human nature and preference creation by pos-tulating people know their own interest and seek to achieve it; this is the nature of humans. There are problems with this, e.g., Arrow Impossibility Theorem.
2. Build in individual decision making; self-interest maximization builds in a principle for making decisions. Problem: what is the individual? Physical? Family? The enterprise is largely finessed.

Rationality = complex. Experimental economics demonstrates that pursuit of rationality is complex and has dubious philosophical implications (Thaler, Frank, in theory).

⇒ Useful assumption: Samuels emphasizes the social construct in which prefer-ences are formed, institutions. But will assume people have interests and a will pursue them. But the real world is more complicated than utility or profit maxi-mization. ⇒ What about objective functions? Terms are easily hypothesized, but in practice you get varied specifications.

⇒ Constrained maximization is what's going on here. People practice within opportunity sets which are a function of forces, including power, rights, actions taken by government, the choices of others, the consequences of choices, etc. An individual learns in this process their goals; means/ends process, in which opportunity sets are formed and reformed.

Rationality and Uncertainty

Radical indeterminacy ⇒ we do not know future because we cannot know it exists since it (the future) depends on what we make it. ⇒ post-WWII economics is dealing with uncertainty; the existence of uncertainty impacts unique, optimal, definite solutions ⇒ rational expectations theory.

Rationality projects deliberateness (Alfred Marshall) ⇒ business domain. Two kinds of decision making (terminology is Frank Knight).

1. Deliberate: means/ends
2. Nondeliberative: the subconscious, wisdom/folly in institutions, including, for example, habit, custom, religion, and received law. But, who will make decisions?

Curious tension within Austrian neoclassicism (Hayek). That both deliberate and nondeliberate decision making are in the domain of rationality assumptions is limited. Herbert Simons bounded rationality ⇒ people's knowledge is bounded (not available, resource costs), and that people have knowledge/sufficient information. The rational expectations response is that people acquire optimal info = correct expectations = don't worry.

Even deliberative decision making = composite choice (Solow). Competitive markets: large number of buyers and sellers, all with constrained maximizations. This yields an equilibrium price and quantity combination. No one chooses this equilibrium price and quantity; it emerges as a composite choice emerges as a result of individual choices. For example, consider the allocation of resources to education. Federal and state government, school boards, teachers, parents, charities all help determine this outcome.

Two Public Finance Textbooks Compared

Musgrave and Musgrave[7] suggest that the proper size of the public sector (e.g., level of government spending) is a technical rather than ideological issue. Burkhead and Miner[8] claim that there is no conclusive principle.
Issue: There is a fundamental conflict in whether the decision making is technical or subjective. (For example, that the level and structure of spending can be determined technically like taxation – but can it really be?)

35% GNP = matter of government spending on goods and services. In Europe, we see the mid- to high-20%; some as high as 45%. Is this objective determination?

| Developed | 25%–45% GNP |
| Least developed country's (LDCs) | 14%–17% GNP |

Implication is that government does not hinder development. Samuels does not accept a technical determination of government spending, arguing that instead power, ideology, and trade-offs also determine outcomes.

Essay on costs not at issue here. Rather the issue is

1. whether the level of government spending is given by system or ideology (subjective);
2. whether the level of government spending is technical.

And there's an element of truth to both

1. Definitions are everything

Private and social costs: is wrong to define private costs as costs borne by an individual and social as borne by many. The Pigouvian Marginal Private Cost = Marginal Social Cost doesn't work because you can't have 50% = 50%. The social costs = total costs borne by producers, consumers, and everyone else; this can't be equivalent to only the private cost.

2. Book Review

Poetic Justice: the Literary Imagination in Public Life by author Martha Nussbaum. Review by Bromwich.[9]

More to the world than rational choice ⇒ ethical and esthetic considerations are part of literature.

Richard Posner goes to her class:

a. "Rat choice"
b. Uses George Herman Meade to critique rational choice
c. Adam Smiths' *Theory of Moral Sentiments* – uncautious spectator
   – Little narrow but not wrong; justice as a mere writing down of propriety but Smith = benevolence and/or justice. Justice is more than just benevolence.

- The main point that impartial spectator = projection of first persons' good sense; individual sentiments enforce common good sense.
- Individual sentiments depend on that common sense of society is just.

Smith = matter of consensus, no absolute test. Sympathy is an important notion to Smith. Bromwich misapprehends Smith's in personal sympathy . Sympathy = "invisible hand of social morality." These words grew to Smith and are not equal explicitly to Smith. It is a matter of interpretation.

Charles Dicken's *Hard Times* – conflict between legal social control and nonlegal social control. Posner believes all seek to wealth maximize, though he understands nonlegal social control ⇒ paternalistic ethic – both legal and nonlegal social control.

Human agency in context of this course ⇒ voluntary vs. volitional ("give me your money or your life"). There's a big difference. Free-agency operates within an opportunity set = volitional. Commons, Hale claim it is voluntary – you have the opportunity to choose what's in your opportunity set. In context of Dickens this is the ability of individuals to choose their own life as separate centers of agency.

3. Dissertation by a student in Auckland, New Zealand[10]

⇒ White vs. Maori. Treaty states that the Queen is sovereign but Maoris can retain their own customs ⇒ there are multiple interpretations of terms (what they mean, how to employ them), but white men's interpretations are the ones that count. But in the last 25 years, New Zealand courts have turned around and tried to make restitutions.

Cost Essay

1. Rescue standard theories of cost (Note that costs are relative in nature).
2. Costs = function of rights, which are in turn a function of power. Thus, institutions matter.
3. Invocations of costs in making decisions is relativist because whose interests are to count are valorized in the market.
4. Recognitions of costs = selective perception.

[Margin notes: that the private marginal cost = the social marginal cost is an incomplete and inaccurate statement. Institutions matter in how they are recognized by the market and valorized.]

Neoclassical economics ⇒ managerial economics. There is the discursive nature of framing the issue? Is it implicit? Consider an externality – it could be generated by production or consumption. The externality is a cost that escapes the market. This is wrong because we only talk about that particular market = misleading by narrowly defining the market. Then there is the matter of Pareto relevant vs. Pareto irrelevant externalities, namely if people bargain or if they don't bargain or don't really care.

Part IV.

Equality

Equal protection clause. The objective is to explore the ramifications of equal protection ⇒ purely positive analysis, not what the clause really means or really should mean.

Equal protection clause – Fourteenth Amendment "equal protection of the laws." It was written in part with a view to class legislation because England had legislation that treated propertied classes differently. ⇒ Later, it was modified by the Civil War associated amendments to include race = attempt to tell all states that people should not be treated differently.

| *Plessy v. Ferguson* (1896) | Separate but equal schools were ok |
| *Brown v. Board of Education* (1954) | Separateness creates inequality |

Problem that we need to confront is that different school districts have unequal financial capacity = unequal educational experiences. Counties, cities, school districts = political subdivisions of states. Therefore, when a state divides citizens up among districts ⇒ unequal facilities. The same law applies to all because some are unequally situated; cannot be solved. The history of economics, politics cannot be ignored because ⇒ unequal distribution. Wealth is not an exception.

General Points

1. All are <u>unequal in various ways.</u> We cannot escape this fact; then the ways in which are unequal are to matter, e.g., athletic teams for sports-gifted students and the Florida case of handball vs. softball. ⇒ How much inequality is natural and how much institutionally based given naturally. Inequality? How do institutions affect this?

2. <u>Treating unequals equally means that you are treating them unequally.</u>
   Per stirpes is dividing an estate into equal share in wills = problems.
   Fundamental questions: if they are unequal and if you treat them unequally ⇒ equality? There is no escape from this conundrum.
3. <u>Dual nature of rights</u>
   a. Literally impossible to give equal protection
   b. Necessity of choice
4. <u>Difference between formal and substantive equality</u> (formal – equal legal
   standing; substantive meaning whether you're rich or poor). We can also
   talk about De jure equality vs. de facto inequality. What kind of equality are we talking about? Is it a matter of equal opportunity or equal
   results?
5. <u>Universal rights</u> (declaration) Against who are they sanctionable?
   Distinguish between claim, protected, sanctioned? There are many different games: business, society. If all are unequal, choice of game influences which inequalities are important.
   a. Unequal advantage
   b. Game chosen gives advantage
   Choice of game means some inequalities are more important than
   others.

6. <u>Hierarchy vs. equality</u>: Tendencies exist deliberatively and nondeliber-
   ately, and both are inevitable ⇒ similar point to 5.

Guest lecture: Nicholas Mecuro[11]

Orientations: only teaches law and economics to law school students, and this is
a vocational course; must retain relevance.

Law ⇒ justice, "fairness"
Economics ⇒ standard neoclassical economics of efficiency in exchange and
production, Hicksian cost–benefit analysis.
Review, scrutiny, precedence: does concept of efficiency lead to/create law or
legal decisions? Can lawyers and judges import it or use it? Because it is true
that many do.

1. Nearly 800 judges through this school with J.G. Manning (Yale)
2. Dispositions of Reagan and Bush ⇒ appointed this kind of judges
   State ←→ economy
   Comparative institutional approach to law and economics

Law, Economics, and Public Policy

Anarchy ------------------→   Constitution -----------------→   institutions
                              (form of social contract theory)   (working rules)
                              Rules for making rules   Rules by which
                              are determined   agencies operate

For example, Newt Gingrich knows working rules but cannot change rules of Senate.

Other examples: these are worked out by institutions themselves ⇒ form our working rules:

1. Rules of evidence
2. Committee procedures, power
3. Procedures for standards, and rules to make decisions ⇒ mechanism
4. Who gets to intervene

Not given once and for all and are not set in stone, but once they're in place the question becomes what property rights structures can be employed?

Institutions - - - - →   1. Communal property rights, e.g., seas, fisheries, space. The government gives illusion of committee, but not really. Is private sector property rights?
                            2. Exclusive, transferable, enforceable ⇒ "efficient" results, e.g., assigning rights to air pollution = efficiency but what about least cost vs. best cost?
                            3. Public sector property rights. What are the status rights = maze of complex of regulated state. Take, for example, eligibility requirements for food stamp or public housing. There is nothing inherent to yield an efficient solution.

This is the economic impact of choice = constant necessity of choice.
Conclusion that public ←→ private arguments are nonsensical. Never very much of a movement, e.g., telephone deregulation.

At each stage of choice is that character of economic life is from revisionary, evolutionary process.

McKenzie and Tullock, *New World of Economics*

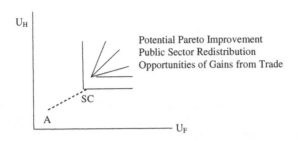

People fearful of *x, y* so subject *x, y* to cost–benefit analysis.

Otherwise, only promote choices within Pareto-improving options. Therefore, can see that private sector ⇒ trickle down ⇒ charity as solution to failures. Minimize the role of government ⇒ this drives economic conservatives in politics. If must help people, fall back on welfare economics with earned income tax credit ⇒ powerful ideology.

Executive branch is minimal in law and economics. Judiciary = Chicago view of the role of economics. They look at case law ⇒ e.g., Posner, which is really a focus on judicial law generating efficient outcomes. If it is not efficient, should create laws to make it such. Conflicts could be resolved better by relying on judiciary instead of the legislative or constitutional changes.

One critic = James M. Buchanan (public choice theorists). See his critique of Posner's first book.

Tort literature: How many accidents are such that society realizes are background risk and how many are compensated risks?

Cx	*Cx*	*Cx*
Cy	*Cy*	*Cy*

Limited liability	Negligence rule	Strict liability
"it's your problem"		Few things uncompensated

Guido Calibresi[12] (and even Ronald Coase) looking for a remedy that will decrease costs. Not all liability laws cause same sum damages.

500	360	200
300	240	800
L.L.	N.R.	S.L.

Judges ought to know that they're both *ex post* and *ex ante,* that they affect future choices and cases. Law and economics chooses least costs (in this case negligence) as the most efficient solution.

Tension is that justice vs. efficiency. Even worse, how to combine the two? Average? It is a quick leap from "is" to "ought" in law. ⇒ Posner and Easterbrook very much decide on efficiency over precedents.

Samuels: That even Clinton's health care only changes the working rules, regulation of the market, this does not equal much change of public and private. Logic that underlies this ⇒ Schmid type. Change the working rules or rights. Easterbrock emphasizes that you're just changing incentives ⇒ change behavior ⇒ change economic performance.

> Change law ←------→change economics
> Concern of law and economics movement
> Much of literature tries to estimate this empirically

Problem of equal protection clause continued:

1. Are all unequal; unequal in various ways.
2. Treating unequals equally is a conundrum without solutions.
   Problems of political and economical equality
   Process of working out solutions
3. It is impossible to give substantive equal protection of laws.
   Cannot protect each party equally = choice
   ⇒ Formal equality vs. substantive equality
4. Human rights and sanctions.
   Fundamental claims against who?
5. Inequality arises in different games/situations.
   Rewards different people differently. Problem of equal protections within Spengler's Problem of Order and tendencies of hierarchy vs. equality ⇒

equal protection clause has as a function = working out and resolving conflict of hierarchy and equality.

6. Standard left-wing is that inequality per se is wrong ⇒ offensive in presence of great wealth. Economics = defense/ criticism of inequality. Question: The proprietary rights by which people become wealthy?

   a. Tough problem ⇒ Samuels core is that people have unequal access to government use, and use government unequally ⇒ different unequal results. For example, the big issue with Affirmative Action redresses rights inequality. Changes $\alpha\ \beta$ to $\beta\ \alpha$ rights distribution
      ⇒ access to and use of government.

   b. Wrong people are getting the distribution of income.
      Distribution is wrong ⇒ Gini Coefficient. Or distribution is OK, but wrong people get high incomes ⇒Ruskin's "nice guys finish last."
      Question: Distribution per se is wrong; or wrong people, then what is the mode by which distribution is made? Institutional arrangement ⇒ distribution = function of power structures.

7. Institutionally Produced Inequality
   But really all is influenced by institutions = more complicated is this. How do we identify what is due to institutions rather than persons? And not everyone believes this is bad; in fact most don't because of the Protestant Ethic.

8. Equal Opportunities vs. Equal Results
   Sequence of time $t = 0, 1, 2 \ldots$.
   Distribution$_{t=1}$ ⇒ f (distribution 1) = distribution 2 ⇒ etc.
   The conflict between opportunities and results is incomplete and misleading.
   The problem is that different people are unequal in different ways ⇒ criteria?!

Historical cases:

Aristotle distinguished arithmetic vs. geometric equality. There is within level = equality; as ascend the pyramid = increase inequality = empty, unexplainable model but used as legitimating, e.g., Orwell. Defined the problem, but no solution.

Locke and Smith: Both accepted the structures of our time but were also revolutionary. Smith says that one function of government is to defend the rich from poor ⇒ but rich control government = defining rights.

Bentham: Greatest happiness for greatest number. This worked against policy of government and control defines rather than solves the problem. To whom government is responsible? Intensive vs. extensive margin?

Pigou: Maximize social welfare, equalize the marginal utility of the last dollar of income. With identical utility functions ⇒ equal incomes. But unequal utility functions ⇒ inequality but how do people get capacity to derive utility? ⇒ J.S. Mill = how rank activities?

Distribution is a personal matter = function of institutions, function of power, law, structure, and rights. There is a tension between hierarchical and egalitarian tendencies.

Role of Equal Protection?

Not solve the hierarchy vs. equality problem. Gives legitimacy of whatever ongoing hierarchy-equality solution there is currently; there are always uncompensated losses, therefore taking clause legitimacies. This means of seeking reformulations and protecting against change = framework of discourse.

Sen ⇒ problems of equality and inequality. See Sen's book *Inequality Reexamined* (1992). He is in favor of "equality of what"? Why does the modern state profess some notion of equality?

⇒ it continues to exist in modern world that rejects traditional forms of authority; equality = allegiance = considerations of equality (socialistic?)

Need to find a practical conception of equality, but need to know the purpose = different notions of equality.

Also John Rawls's *A Theory of Justice* (1971). Includes themes that bear on problem of equal protection.

1. Policy not adopted unless helps most disadvantaged.
2. Some goods that society should provide to all people because they're alive.

Last topic technical vs. ideological issues (subjective). Role of expert in policy making; relationship between ends and means and that continuum.

Examples:

1. Externalities: economists distinguish technical vs. pecuniary externalities. Technical includes smoke and pollution. Pecuniary are those that affect prices and incomes.

Literature limits to physical externalities; nonphysical ruled out as they are funneled through the market. This is an impressive distinction because physical is just through different markets. Economists (technicians) apply this distinction; what makes a professional decision correct? Consensus, whose?

Pareto relevant vs. Pareto irrelevant externalities. To eliminate the discussion of externalities = rhetorical strategy ⇒ Buchanan does recognize small numbers, large numbers problems; issues of organization. Posner believes all law is predicated on a wealth max.

1. Courts do this automatically, legislatures do not [Margin note: law is an optimizing process, which leads to optimal institutions. Does this mean that law cannot screw up?]
2. This is what courts should be doing. However, you would need to convince people that
   a. There should be a market for anything
   b. Judges should reach welfare maximization approach.
   ⇒ Market for rape and for babies; if accept this, accept anything. [Margin note: assigns rights to the rapist, then women must buy off. Alternative as status quo rights situation.]
2. <u>Fines</u> vs. <u>Jail</u>. People are wrong and need to be punished ⇒ more efficient to choose between jail and a fine, but unequal distribution of wealth means some must go to jail = unjust?
3. <u>Rights to parties in best position to minimize costs</u> (transactions)
   Problems: a. How should we measure costs and benefits?
   b. Differences in defining and weighting = different solutions.
   c. Costs = function of the system in place. You may disagree with the system ...
   ⇒ real estate property: title search and insurance = different systems = different costs.

All are examples of policy as technical solutions on a subjective element. The bottom line is that there is no conclusive rule; but there is a large role of technical policy making.

<u>Coase Theorem</u> and the work of <u>Posner</u>

What we know so far!

1. Rights are dual in nature.
2. Externalities are reciprocal. Coase makes both points "problem is whether alpha can harm beta or beta can harm alpha."
3. There is selective perception of rights, costs, benefits, injuries.
4. Different rights structures will create different externalities and the same for alternative resource allocations, income distributions, etc.

Need to work out difference between Paretian and Pigouvian externalities. Also how to solve – solutions.

1. Education; how to behave is a form of social control; moral suasion = behavior.
   Influence. This was the Ford and Carter administrations solution to inflation.
2. Employ a tax or subsidy. A tax penalizes for pollution, which leads to increased costs borne by polluter; need to be large enough. Logic is to induce the pollution to change behavior by punishment. Subsidy works exact opposite ⇒ taxes and subsides are essentially symmetric, equivalents. Issues of attitude – why reward pollutions?
   Psychodynamics.
3. Could adopt user-fees to use a river or to use the air/pollute.
4. Regulation – there are two kinds. We could prohibit the activity or establish standards.
   Economists = pro-market; don't like regulation because prefer fees or taxes or subsidies.
5. Invest R&D to get new technology, e.g., nuclear power or solar power.
6. Government to produce the solution. The government cleans up the water; user charges to finance.
7. Merger solutions of polluter and pollute. This internalizes costs of pollution/impact.
   Results depend on relative weights of industries ⇒ conflict within merger solution.
   For example, metropolitan government: city vs. suburbs creates externalities. This is the rationale behind metro government, to have it all combined to provide internalization of externalities = tendency for ever larger government.
8. Coase solution. Create a market for externalities via property rights.
   a. Can have a market for externalities and this will solve.
   b. Zero transactions costs; rights distribution is irrelevant, as the resulting allocations are the same.
   All we need are fully defined rights ⇒ Buchanan's Pareto relevant externalities.
   Pigou is just fine, but that you have a market does not mean that the marginal private cost = marginal social cost. There also needs to be fully developed, institutions – both are costly and take resources, e.g., trains, sparks, and farmers.

There are issues and costs of organization, numbers problems, and the zero transaction costs assumption is not real world $\Rightarrow$ Stigler's version of the Coase Theorem meant that there is no externality problem; mainstream focus that this was a solution. $\Rightarrow$ Coase eventually argued that he did not mean what the Coase Theorem had come to mean and not believe in zero transaction costs, but rather that institutions matter. Coase waits over 20 years to refute that institutions and costs systems were involved.

Version II: The allocation and distribution of rights is locatively neutral. Alpha can buy off Beta or vice versa $\Rightarrow$ some assignment of rights either way. Coase also rejects this for same reasons: (i) transactions costs, (ii) the large numbers problems, (iii) wealth and capital distribution, asymmetrical power.

Original article was in the *Journal of Law and Economics* (Coase, 1960)
- *A* allowed to harm *B* or vice versa but must recognize the system influences this (p. 2).
- Costs are reciprocal.
- If factors of production have the rights, then to do something that has a harmful effect is also a factor of production (p. 44).
- Maximum value of production $\Rightarrow$ optimal pollution = neoclassical research paradigm, but Coase now rejects this.

Article in *New Palgrave* by Rober Kultor. The zero transaction cost interpretations of Coase theorem = false; they're a tautology. Samuels agrees with this view.

Coase Theorem

Coase also did a Theory of the Firm $\Rightarrow$ focus on transactions costs. Why was it formulated the way it was? Especially interesting question because Coase argues that the lessons from his work are the opposite of Stigler's interpretation.

Calabrasi says law of welfare economics:

1. The Coase theorem comported perfectly with the neoclassical research protocol.
2. Chicago libertarian view is that you don't have to worry about government.

What Coase means is that the world does not have zero transactions costs: rights, institutions, costs matter. The focus on zero transaction costs is an idealization of world that rules out variables. Coase claims that this is not the real world ⇒ alternative world of policy and analysis than Stigler.

Other Assumptions

1. Takes the existing distribution of income and wealth as given. Coase theorem assumes existing distribution = irrelevant, taken as given but really different distributions of income = different abilities to buy off even with zero transaction costs. Assignments of rights depend on the distribution of wealth ⇒ impact.
2. The individuals buying and selling are the same. Experimental data shows that buying and selling prices differ depending on if you own it or don't own it. Decreases demand at higher prices. Schmid wants to test neoclassicist who believes Coase Theorem if rights irrelevant: "give me your wallet." ⇒ indifference to consequences of the distribution of income and wealth. Different price/cost structures and Coase must assume away.
3. Assumes existing law of property – reifies law of property.
4. Assumes indifference toward status quo structure of social power, as well as existing technology, resources, tastes.
5. Optimal results achieved solely through individual adjustments through trade.
6. Markets for externalities. Must assume there's a market; no trade = optimality; trade = optimality; no market = optimal. Whatever happens is *ipso facto* optimal.
7. A bounded consumption set.
   Koopmans: Pareto optimality is a matter of marginal adjustments, but some decisions are not marginal so the analysis does not apply. What about actions/choices where survival is threatened; theory assumes survival for adjustments. To assume against survival must assume
   a. Dealing with a farmer whose means are already provided for, who works in a factory
   b. Welfare state
   c. Protection of the environment = planetary survival
8. Perfect Competition – or large numbers case, or indifference to market structure but clearly different institutional structures = alternative solutions.
9. Actors have sufficient knowledge – but this is costly to acquire.
10. Informational asymmetries: neoclassical economics = assumptions of equal status.
11. Coase = local optimum rather than social or universal optimum.

What is the significance of the Coase Theorem: fits into sentiments and research protocol.

1. Produce unique results that fit the neoclassical research protocol
2. Conducive to laissez-faire

Coase = counter revolution to Pigouvian economics, which gives an opportunity for government to correct externalities, prima facie case for government actions. Coase = no externality problem at all = Stigler interpretation.

Coase is aware that usual treatment leads to "casuistry," eliminating all variables that prevent reaching desired results. This logic only yields valid conclusions, but is not equal to true conclusions, e.g., Ricardian vice. Adopt all necessary assumptions ⇒ valid conclusion, but assumptions are finessed, are variables that enter in the real world to make solutions nonunique.

Central Issues

1. Desirability of market solutions: both Pigou and Coase agree here; Pigou = conservative.
2. Sufficiency of market solutions: Pigouvian position ⇒ Coase. But whether in the real world markets are sufficient, is another question. Not all can or should be handled by markets. Pigou and Paretians recognize that markets will not suffice.

Legitimizing the market – abstract from all variables that prevent one from extolling the market. Coase says:

- Rights = factors of production
- Externalities are reciprocal

Maximize the value of output/production. Coase uses this language as if it is a simple scale to compare alternative arrangement toward maximum value of production. ⇒ Coase: since institutions matter, you must really compare institutions. Criticism of cost–benefit analysis to compare institutions, when really they're noncomparable.

Posner

Younger, American comparison to Coase. Posner = more prolific; outgoing and abrasive ⇒ completely different from Coase. Different orientations to same material, Posner is competing for status with Coase.

Posner:

1. Law should maximize the value of output/wealth.
2. Common law does so.

This counts even though one doesn't always know it; courts have always chosen to do this and they should. Do not need other considerations of justice. But, the problem is that this position is circular.

> Rights structures $\Rightarrow$ price structure $\Rightarrow$ resource allocation = max value of output
>
> $RS_2 \rightarrow PS_2 \rightarrow RA_2 \rightarrow MVO_2$

Count decision is given the existing rights structure, which is noncomparable with other rights structure. You cannot say that $MVO_2 > MVO_1$, then you should choose structure. 2. Cannot use result to argue which rights assignment is to be made = circular.

Posner is coming around to this.[13]

1. Does not affirm argument same way anymore.
2. I am not a potted plant; judges are decision makers.

Posner does not use this explicitly in his court decisions; e.g., economic value of life. Potted plant quip = response to Robert Bork's idea that counts should not legislate and only give interpretations to original constitution. Rather, Posner = inevitable judicial action. Judges = whose interests are to count?

Problem is that Posner was too exuberant in youth, e.g., that there is a market for everything. Probably won't be nominated to the Supreme Court.

Credit

Between him and Coase = tremendous impetus and legitimacy to the Law and Economics movement. To become a lawyer now = Chicago law and economics.

Regulation	vs.	Deregulation
dirty word		nice word

Connotation of government, nuances of freedom and discretion = enormous psychological and motivating power. Deregulation is the logical equivalent of regulation; analytically, they're the same thing.

⇒ Contrary to belief system, logic.

1. <u>Dual nature of rights.</u>
   Rights vs. non-rights.
   Not so easy to identify non-rights, no immunity.
2. <u>Where rights come from</u>: court cases, statutes.
   And right regulates the other party's non-right, e.g., stream model.
   Steel = right to pollute and the rest have a non-right.
   Change regulation ⇒ deregulated, and now steel = non-right and others
   have.

If you regulate an actor and then deregulate, all you are doing is changing the
<u>interests to which government gives support</u> ⇒ <u>Changes rights structure.</u> No
escape from this: in whose interests government will act? Regulation= fundamental; not epic phenomenal, not pejorative.

Not so easy to see in practical applications; the usual arguments are analytically
meaningless. Regulation is given a bad name. Analogous to police – some you
like, and some you don't like. It is a matter of selective perception = mobilization
of political psychology.

Whose interests should government promote?
Government is an arena in which it is worked out; who is regulated and unregulated. Government = contest for control. Law, morality, market, interpersonal
interactions all = systems of social control, therefore regulation. People will be
regulated.

Medieval = concentrations of power.
Modern = wider participation in decision making ⇒ special interests.

Process of determining relative rights and whose interests are to count ⇒ critical
is selective perception.

<u>Compensation Problem</u>

For example, airport expansion vs. population expansion

Airport

City

Issue: Whose expectation is to be protected by law? Who has a reasonable interest? Expectations of no noise or expectation of community = necessary airport?
Increase in community size leads to an increase in airport usage.

If, think, people should recognize the issue ⇒ will not or cannot lose anything,
vs. if people should be allowed to enjoy their own property.

Eminent Domain: power of government to take land for a public purpose for just
compensation ⇒ historically = land. Issue is defining public purpose and just
compensation ⇒ include capitalized value of future use? Historically, this has
been a way to take private land for public use. Also companies; e.g., public utilities have this power, but use value ⇒ exchange value. Expanded eminent domain
to the taking of value.

⇒ Involves taking (Fifth Amendment). What constitutes a taking is at issue. This
is as opposed to police power – opposite of eminent domain. Government action
promoting public health, safety, welfare, morals, etc.

OPTIONS: Take property = eminent domain
                Condemn property
                Regulate property restricts the use of land⇒ taking vs. police
                power?

Smith v. Ames (1877)
Munn v. Illinois (grain storage)
        Some industries signaled out for special treatment.
        But how regulated? Fair return on fair value ⇒ determines level of
        proper compensation
        Protect the equity of the owner?
        Value = capitalized value of income of the property?
        Police power vs. eminent domain changes the values.

Is regulation intended to be a taking or to prevent a public nuisance? Interpret
intent of legislation. There are two different paradigms

1. Eminent domain ⇒ view of property. Property is independent of government. Therefore, adverse to property = taking. Government compensates
   unemployed?
   Widows and orphans? Anything government did could seem as a taking
   requiring compensation. If draw the line, eminent domain = irrelevant.
2. Police power ⇒ no compensation.

Issue is all about where to draw the line. Welfare between two conceptions of property rights.

Takings Clause

Just compensation. Need a theory of constitution, law, rights are all about private property; exists antecedent to law and any government taking requires compensation ⇒ what is property; eminent domain? Narrower version: property taken for public purpose must be paid for = land; socialized burden of costs. This is reasonably compatible with police powers.

Most who are interested in Takings Clause are interested in working out values/ principles for what constitutes a takings and what does not (make coherent discussion) ⇒ important endeavor.

Samuels: what goes on in process of working out? No particular feelings for one side or another

⇒ arrays of principles; distinctions made which are not conclusive = why and how happens?

1. Ordinary conduct of government = benefits and costs are ubiquitous. How do people operate if ubiquitous potential takings ⇒ decrease in opportunity sets.
    a. Principle of selective perception applies to governmental actions; injury or not; evidence of injury; injury constitutes damage = taking, e.g., theft vs. competition, or permissible vs. impermissible injury.
    b. Different people are differently situated to make decisions that affect other people. Government acts ⇒ injury; opens or closes military base, highways = nothing government does that does not injure someone, especially courts.

Problem is not protecting property, but to define what is property that you are protecting. Working out of takings clause = injury. Inevitable and ubiquitous injury by government ⇒ levels and degrees. Fifth Amendment only applies to government; all that private person does or has is because of government.

Shelley v. Kramer (1948): sale of real estate property = clauses that prevented sale to particular people [based on race]. For government to enforce contract = government action = action violate Fourteenth Amendment, but this did not stop owners for selling to whom like. Government not enforce, but really government is behind all actions of private property = ubiquitous applications, analogous to school finance; unequal wealth or interest in education violates the equal protection clause.

Takings clause cannot prevent all takings. *Miller v. Schoene* (1928)[14] government choice is inexorable, therefore someone will be hurt.

What constitutes taking and what = compensation? Wide ranging field: selective perception, process-determined activities of government, government agencies unfairly compete with private.

When compensation is just:

> Government use = most valued ⇒ owner, or
> market value as a general rule = theory of appraising property (have different theories to govern value of property).

What constitutes a taking?

1. Utility theory
    Compensation paid on basis of efficiency gains, de-amortization of costs, settlement costs paid whenever settlement costs are lesser than de-amortization of costs and efficiency gains. The problem is that all = selective perception.

    Kaldor-Hicks compensation test: should an activity be undertaken? The answer is yes if after compensation, there is still a surplus.
    a. Fool-proof formula
    b. Not paying people = injuries

    What are the costs? To whom? How do you measure these? Settlement costs? Pay people's costs but costs = function of rights, and rights are what is in question.
    > Costs = f (system) ⇒ alterative systems = alternative costs
    > Which are legitimate costs? Pain and suffering?

    Torte law reform compensation for pain and suffering
    Is not conclusive sense. Schmid argues that you cannot = efficiency without talking about rights and rights are the point of issue. You cannot

compare efficiency gains between systems; the only way out = selective perception. Selective perception is not a limitation.
   a. Fact of life
   b. Way in which the process works
2. Fairness Test
   Principles: a. Social arrangement should assure each participant the maximum liberty consistent with like liberty of every other participant ⇒ only applied on basis of selective perception clause, e.g., equal protection clause.

   But very sensible, meaningful argument
   But what is the reach of its meaningfulness? ⇒ equal liberty requirement

   b. Rawlsian *Theory of Justice*
   If treated differently = ok so that (1) all = equal chance to attain the different positions and (2) the arrangement can reasonably be supposed to work to everyone's advantage and especially to advantage of the least advantaged. Also makes lots of sense, but what does equal chances mean? Or reasonable likelihood to benefit? How do we know this rule is best? Compare rules?
   ⇒ What about person who does not get compensated? Is the takings clause then advantageous? Not compensated = not unfair if it is a consistent application of Fifth Amendment? Wide range to handle losing. Joseph Sax (1971) of Michigan = following rules:
      i. Should not be compensation where government action = resolution competing private interest. Desire property broad enough so that it covers almost everything because rights = function of law; necessity of choices.
      ii. Public interests and rights on par with private rights; flood and erosion control, economic structure, scenic and historic areas. When have this, we do not need to compensate.

Government must choose between conflicting rights. But Epstein argues this could apply to everything and allow government to do whatever it wants:

   If conflicting spillovers = no compensation
   If not conflicting spillovers = compensation

But government is involved if there are spillovers or eminent domain? Set of cases with no conflicting spillover = government taking to build a school, etc.

Sax = maximize total value of resource base, but not just individual parcel, e.g., regulation to maximize oil flow vs. sustainable yield ⇒ how quantify entire resource base when can only maximize on efficiency claims and efficiency = matter or rights? No independent calculus or test, this requires selective perception.

*Inexorable, ubiquitous losses and selective perception always create a question of how the test is to be applied. Burger (1974) wants fairness and efficiency that lead to a more specific minimum sum of (i) nuisance costs/harmful externalities, (ii) prevention costs, and (iii) administration costs. Fairness depends on the community's common sense; multiple interpretations, not unequivocal criteria. Depends on recognition of injury and evidence of injury, therefore what is to be compared, costs, depend on the law. Whose costs? Government? Firm? The steel plant or the people downstream? This is the same position as Coase, when wants cost–benefit analysis for different institutions, but we do not have all that data and the data is subjective.

First-in-time Approach by Burger. Alpha = first, activity is legal ⇒ Beta, who also has legal activity fairness and efficiency require Alpha protected from Beta and costs borne by Beta. ⇒ First mover = privileged position; could work to determine position, conflicting reasonableness of expectations between the two original landowners. Really a matter of density.

Epstein (1985): Any removal by government of any right = taking that requires compensation except for very limited police powers. But what is a right? What about *Miller v. Schoene* (1928)?

    Measure compensation for red cedars true owner?
    What about a government fighting inflation or unemployment?

Epstein ⇒ Lockian. What interests protected as rights? Simpler if you're only taking land. To apply any rule, selective perception is inevitably applied.

Even Epstein = exceptions for when some benefit for the public exists because of long-standing custom or overtly utilitarian calculation. ⇒ makes test more difficult, not to get compensation. Define rights broadly or narrowly; what is reasonable? And what about the reasonableness of expectations?

Blume and Rubenfeld (1986)

Economic argument is strongest:
a. Where risk of loss is large, relative to the wealth of the individual.
b. Risk of loss is large relative to the magnitude of the loss, e.g., underground coal mining.

But is this conclusive? Multiple interpretations and subjective elements. Every principle applied in different ways because of selective perception and when these principles are applied, they are the means by which rights are determined. Test that determines whether they have rights = ironic and most important process that some interests are affirmed and some denied.

Donald Black (1987): interested in what actually happens. Modern trend = compensate individuals for their misfortunes. If from organizations ⇒ corporation vs. individual (gets protected), this is not equal to normative, but rather to observative. Strict liability is more applied to organizations. Liability varies directly with social, cultural, status distance, etc.

McCauley and Friedman book = sociological jurisprudence = law in action. Law on paper describes intended outcomes; actual outcome are different.

Boulding and Pfaft "Redistributive to the Rich & Poor" examines government programs to find out the benefits ⇒ sociological variables = law in practice.

Cases dealing with Taking Clause = mode of determining property rights ⇒ rights are socially constructed by, in part, court cases. The decision of Takings Cases ⇒ rights. Ex post facto nature of law but determined for the future.

Resolution of compensation problem requires deciding which interests the law is to protect. Ubiquitous externalities, Alpha/Beta rights conflicts, uncompensated losses lead to a selective perception of loss, evidence of loss, and decision on whose interests to protect. Joint determination of rights and whose losses go uncompensated cannot protect against all losses = Lockian interpretation = part of process of rights. It also serves in framework of a larger matrix of principles of law. Serves as a check by courts on arbitrary and tyrannical power of government – or does it? Selective perception ....

All checks on government are on tyrannical use of power, including the check itself that is subject to selective perception. A clause can equal check and the clause is also the exercise of power by people who haven't been elected.

Psychic Balm: In face of radical indeterminancy. The idea is that there is a clause, obscures necessity of choice, and gives people a confidence of their rights ⇒ allows them to accept uncompensated losses = sense of comfort and legitimates decisions made under its aegis ⇒ creation and destruction of rights. Paradox: government must pay compensation; but clause legitimizes legal change = check on legal social control, but itself is a mode of social control and a means to or by which the injured are induced to bear losses. Demand for compensation = demand for rights.

Lucas v. South Carolina Costal (1992)

Analytical issues:

1. Market valuation is the only mode of valuations.
   a. Lawyer protecting use vs. exchange value.
   b. Loss is partial or total and its significance.
2. Context of police power or eminent domain.
3. Expectations: is the law based on certain historical understandings or are historical understandings a function of law?
4. Common law vs. statute law. Determination is by courts and legislation on who makes policy.
5. Police power over issues of public health, welfare, safety, and morals.
   – Noxious use a nuisance?
   – Public health?
   – How far police power extend? Is police power only for preventing public harm or does it extend to creating public benefits?
6. Who has the status to bring suit and determine the "ripeness" of an issue?
7. Definition of property.
8. Ideological gains on property and economic role of government.

Supreme Court Antonin Scalia's opinion:

– Case is suitable for review because of an injury in fact, which is not equivalent to a prospective injury.
– Prior to Mayhor [unidentified] case, issue over direct appropriation of land regulations goes so far as to constitute a taking. Same uses cannot be allowed.

- Cases are not helpful in laying out "going too far." Why selective perception is so important.

Two cases: 1. Physical invasion
2. Regulation denies all economically beneficial use

What about restricted uses? Trial court found regulation of South Carolina Costal Conference rendered the lots value less.

Regulation of harmful use is not equal to a taking. Preventing a harm vs. conferring benefits; this is selective perception. Deprives owner of all beneficial use means what exactly? No compensation is unless it does not equal part of property nature, then look at background uses. This is not relevant here. In this case, goes beyond all principles and applies even if only a temporary taking. Scalia is trying to carve out an area of compensability. ⇒ Kennedy concurs but addresses permanent takings.

Regulation leaves any significant market value or use to own.
What is a reasonable expectation for investment vs. states' interest?

Justices Harry Blackmun and John Paul Stevens dissent:

1. Scalia launched a missile to kill a mouse; damage will spread.
2. The case not appropriate for review.
3. South Carolina pursued federal legislative mandates.
4. This property has been underwater for half of the last 20 years.
5. All property is held under the rule not to injure others or the community, and is not limited by the takings clause.
6. The landowner never faulted the legislative claim.
7. The existence of facts supporting legislative claim is to be assumed.
8. There is no basis for placing a burden on the state to prove there is no taking ⇒ the burden is on owner.
9. The case is not "ripe" for review. Lucas failed to achieve/pursue available administrative options.
10. No basis for claiming the land is now valueless, rejects that owner has right to highest and best use of the land as he perceives ⇒ may be unreasonable.
11. Court has affirmed the power of state to regulate no matter how restrictive.
12. Deprivation of all economically valuable use depends on how property is defined and this is not objective, but rather subjective.
13. Scalia is criticized for his interpretation of case history ⇒ history of no compensation, therefore is not reasonable.

248 MARIANNE JOHNSON AND MARTIN E. MEDER

Law creates new expectations? Blackmun = narrow conception of the takings clause. Stevens dissent:

1. The case is premature, a permanent taking is the only real issue.
2. There was no showing of injury in fact, and the plaintiff has the burden of proof.
3. The court is not observing <u>judicial restraint.</u>

This is a broad question. Problems: Is it even possible for judges not to be restrained? What does it mean? *Roe v. Wade* court, judgment as right of privacy but that is not explicit in the constitution. The court can be unrestrained and creative. The Tenth Amendment gives power to states ⇒ what? How much? Inevitable interpretation; no way judicial restraint = misleading. We do not like courts to complain of no restraint ⇒ semantic issue.

Stevens' judicial restraint: Court should not follow a rule, which is to not anticipate a question of constitutional rule prior to the necessity of decisions. Sometimes courts are political or sometimes courts make decisions on narrow, technical grounds in making law? What is a necessity is a matter of judgment; subjective.

Claims that Scalia has a categorical rule that regulatory takings must be compensated; anything more than nuisance law is already a limitation. But why only nuisance law? This is a categorical but impossible rule; must consider facts of every case. Post decisions are the opposite of Scalia that Steven's quotes; what you are doing is defining property ... the rule cannot be categorical. Courts can avoid the rule by manipulating the meaning of property. Given the rule, can market special estates take advantage of rule by falling within the takings clause? If defined narrowly enough, anything can be a total taking and this is not desirable in takings law.

Landowner perception is not sufficient to justify a rule. Regulation may single out or not property owner and eliminate uses. New rule by Scalia is unsupported and unsound. Scalia's exception is irrelevant.

Eminent domain extends taking clause ⇒ conservative. This is a stratagem vs. police power, which creates an opportunity for legislature and courts to regulate broadly.

*The rule would freeze the common law of state. Legislature historically has the power to define property, changes in property, and to define uses of property.

Analytically unwise in the face of changing circumstances; property is always a matter of weighing public and private interests, but Scalia wants property as an absolute.

Courts rule will hamper states and local governments in coping with environmental problems:
   And investment expectations are not the only pertinent expectations.
   Cost borne by owners or the many?

Even if total destruction of value, this is a risk inherent in investment, risk of regulation?
   Justice David Souter's statement is not equal to a dissent.

   1. Idea of total loss is questionable.
   2. No review on procedural grounds, therefore it is not topical.
       A court cannot help but assume about loss even though cannot address directly.
       Question of loss is a superficial and one-sided treatment.
   3. But past decisions = past total takings and in the past, have not compensated both.
   4. Nuisance inquiry is equivalent to conduct, not on the character of property, therefore other reasonable uses, cannot have property that is only economically nuisance.

No data, therefore not consider. Scalia: not conduct but property. Claim vs. State, but no claim vs. nature. All of it is a manipulation of legal reasoning to determine property – working out meaning to property. This is true even if you adopt a complete eminent domain approach. Still have uncompensated losses and it does not apply to all government action.

CASE 2: A business as property.

Landowner, businessman, employer. The government condemns or regulates for eminent domain.

        Landowner has a loss.
        Businessman has a loss.
        Workers have a loss.

Who do you compensate? Traditionally only landowners, but more recently compensated business for moving costs and in some cases, even compensated workers. Practice extends the range of interests under eminent domain.

[Spengler's] Problem of order
   Freedom vs. control: who decides?
   Continuity vs. change: past vs. present
   Hierarchy vs. equality: not so much, but it lurks to extent that property is
   narrowly held, therefore you have inequality, so that any issue is within
   all the three.

Even with a broad Scalia eminent domain, there are always uncompensated
losses; but other things government can do that never create an eminent domain
issue (e.g., change monetary and fiscal policy). Process of defining property;
working out property.

Part V.

Public Expenditures

Problem: universal ⇒ common belief that the more you spend, the bigger government, hence a more important government.

1. But, you can't measure the importance of government by how much it
    spends; courts are important and they do not cost much due to antipathy
    of paying taxes ⇒ $.
2. Statutes create a nationalization of real property is a radical change with-
    out a change in spending.

Two questions:

1. Level of spending, 1900–1996
    Grew from 3.5% to 35% of GNP
    Range varies 25%–45% across developed countries, LDC's 12%–17%
    Why did it happen? What accounts for this? Determinants? Not a simple
    answer; long list of variables.
2. Existence of interpretive problem

Interpretive Problems

1. Growth is a normative or a positive?
    How inevitable is growth of public expenditures?
    Is it a policy matter?

That developed countries have two times as much spending, therefore developed means inevitable growth of expenditures.
- Economic growth
- Nuclear family breakdown
- Longevity of people

Can make a case that growth of spending is plausibly a positive matter. Or of course it is also a matter of policy. Can repeal; not have to enact; perceptions of problems ⇒ discretion in a range of spending choices within constraints.

Government spending driven by policy or driven by variables ⇒ inevitability.

2. Different kinds of economic systems
    Comparative economic systems; classifications but how meaningful are the qualitative comparisons?
    Because some like government spending; others do not.
    Interpretation base some conceptions of economic systems?
    Take distinctions for granted is not clear.
    For example, Schumpeter: Capitalism is socialist because there is a concentration of ownership; elite running the system ⇒ corporate capitalism. Former USSR was state capitalism, therefore the analytical equivalent of corporations. Qualitative differences that are more ideological than substantive on the process of leadership selection. Weber's political capitalism; differential opportunists for gains based on political power.

3. Pigeon holes for accepted and unaccepted government activities, differentiating framework filling and on-framework filling activities.

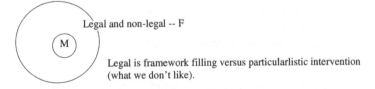

Legal and non-legal -- F

Legal is framework filling versus particularlistic intervention (what we don't like).

This is not a useful analytical device, no independent test to determine framework filling vs. intervention.
a. Legislature that changes property rights could be either framework filling or an intervention.
b. Antitrust laws – cannot distinguish if intervention or not, then not a meaningful analytic device ⇒ rhetorical.

4. Difficulty in making distinctions between:
   a. more intensive performance in a traditionally government area and
   b. extension of government into new areas.
   Government defines and assigns property rights; can be seen as both.
   Worker safety rights? Product safety rights?
   Is this property rights as "protected interests" or is it getting government into new areas?
   Not clear in a conclusive sense; selective perception. Is the welfare state legislation or an extension of property rights? $\Rightarrow$ Some activities cost more than other activities, e.g., courts vs. inspectors. And there are different ways of instrumenting rights that have alternative costs.

5. You can make sense of a long list of factors.
   Growth of expenditures attributed to:
   a. Power and power play
   b. Belief systems
   c. Psychological attitudes toward government
   d. Technological imperatives
   e. Force of population growth
   f. Force of population density
   g. Force of population interaction
   h. Aggregate income level
   i. Distributions of income and wealth
   But difficulty distinguishing between these $\Rightarrow$ great inconclusivity. $\Rightarrow$ Power and power play and belief systems. Interpreting New Deal is whether it is due to the power of liberal democrats and Roosevelt's coalition, but how is that different from belief systems? Impact WWI and elevation of government, excesses of 1920s (speculation). Force of Great Depression leads to changes in belief systems. These were not homogeneous.

   Alpha value = more power $\Rightarrow$ court
   Beta value= less power $\Rightarrow$ loss

   But also say that a change in beliefs $\Rightarrow$ transformation of core values lead to the New Deal. Cannot discriminate between these two.

   Question: What is a filtration system in economic thought?

   $\Rightarrow$ Psychological attitudes toward government
   How have these changed? Government is always a necessary evil.
   Look to government to solve the problem.

But can argue that Great Depression lead to profound influence on psychological attitudes that are difficult to identify and distinguish.

⇒ Technological imperatives
Modern society is urban, industrial, capital intensive.
Logic of industrialization? Significance per se? As a differential variable.

Galbraith sees technological imperatives, but not everyone.
Veblen and Mitchell argue that the modern economy = pecuniary state of mind.
Matter of fact; nonteleological, bottom line is a growth of deliberativeness.
Is this new? In some respects modern world is fundamentally different.

⇒ Population. Malthus and population growth:
1. Income tends to the minimum subsistence level.
2. This decreases quality of life.
3. This increases reliance on formal over informal social control.

= Growth of policy system ⇒ level, density interaction. Can we distinguish between these ideas? How much is ideology ⇔ population. Affects institutions, distribution of services.
a. Identify variables
b. But difficult to separate consequences from one another
   Growth of fire department because of power or due to increased population?

⇒ Aggregate income levels
Microeconomic income effects; increase in income affects inferior, normal goods that now affects new goods. Selective perception of what we can affect leads to subjective demand. Parallel development is a labor/leisure trade-off. Institutionalized coffee breaks, vacations – are these a failure of the Protestant work ethic or due to a growth of income?

Distribution of income and wealth
   How much people spend on government; property taxes change
   Increased income classes = increased money on government

Increased education = increased money on government
Not possible to distinguish effect, therefore explanations for government spending are very weak.

6. Different budget items have different explanations. Cannot explain in totality, but individual items categories. Government spending is not a single dependent variable, therefore there are different explanations.

7. Definition of output is a ubiquitous problem. The auto industry produces transport, fuel efficiency, status, safety = vast and complex. Output of police force = arrests, level of crime, cars, surveillance, community safety.

    – What are the goals of institutions? How operationalize these goals?
    – Multiple goals: additive vs. substitutable.
    – Consequences are complex and include fiscal, psychological, behavioral.
    – Complex causes, definitions, and complex consequences = problems of evaluation and measurement.
    – Causal sequences of public sector actions can lead to complex political externalities, multiple conflicting decisions between cities.

Example: Ambiguities of dealing with quantities and qualities and causes. Assume there has been a higher level of expenditure per person on fire department and police, which is a consequence of behavioral activities.

1. Change in preferences for people for law and order may be due to increased income.
2. Increase in crime, therefore to get same protection, need more police.
3. Production characteristics of police have changed now; increased urban vs. rural; now want professionally trained, college educated.
4. Shift in the provision of protection between public and private supply, e.g., private security guards.
5. Empire building by police chiefs.
    Unless it's possible to distinguish these ⇒ really don't know.

Growth government spending
Interpretative issues: must resolve before looking at growth and how we answer these questions influences what we say.

Two fiscal problems

1. Realist vs. idealist conceptions of the public sector how it is to be defined? Central specification? Or is it whatever it is? Interpretation and purpose? Wittgenstein says that language is not correspondent with reality ⇒ we have built in preconceptions. Understanding of public sector ⇒ determine and measure.
2. Unit determination: government is not equal to a single coherent entity, therefore the level of expenditures is not attributable to a single reason ⇒ different explanations required. In different states or countries, units sometimes single and sometimes consolidated. For example, in New York, the state is responsible for public welfare throughout the state and New York City handles its own ⇒ metropolitan government. Government units are not homogeneous in units or responsibilities.

Causal factors:

100 years ago = 3%–5%
Today = 35%.

1. Scarcity
External factors: war and increased costliness of war and preparation for war; four major wars that are more capital intensive. The United States is also a more conspicuous part of nation-state system since WWI, WWII, Cold War. The world has shrunk.
Internal security: FBI, CIA, military industrial complex; noncompetitive bidding lead to a war party, e.g., Lockheed.[15]
It is difficult to make rational decisions about weapons. Technical; to understand tactical significance of weapon systems.
1. What can it do?
2. Place in strategic plans of war?
3. Place in strategic plans of opponents?
Used for coercion ⇒ inefficiencies or realities? Also need money/funding for the aftermath of war, including benefits, debt repayment, rebuilding.

2. Change in values/belief system
Not clear this happens – if so what is it?
Nineteenth century liberalism – laissez-faire; government responsive to the people.

Limited or unlimited government? Led to a dichotomous conflict in liberalism.

Belief system ⇒ Great Depression

Profound confidence in economy shaken; response to adversity by FDR led people to look to national government:

a. Because national problem and because national government is responsive to changes in beliefs.

b. Change in power structure. Masses get right to vote ⇒ welfare state, then Great Depression and federal focus constellation of interest groups pro-welfare state ⇒ federal power.

Historically more power at Federal level vs. state, restoration of power to states strengthens one set of interest groups. Extension, rather than change of values or leads to a new group with power and government becomes more responsive. Government is more readily available as a process of collective choice. Samuels is not sure of this. Nineteenth century government was available at lower levels; control in a few hands, e.g., county sheriff. But 20th century federal government more available? The World Wars, Great Depression legitimized government, and made availability more conspicuous and ready.

3. Increasing and more complex role of government in macroeconomic supervision of the economy. Treasury in 1860s, 1870s had limited activity. Not until 1920s and after, that we have significant government involvement. Fiscal policy, except tax cuts of 1964, 1980/81. Not really adopted for macro consideration ⇒ potentially ad hoc. Most policies cost much ⇒ The Fed. Very hard to quantify this.

4. Greater knowledge leads to the ability to control things (physics, chemistry). Increased ability to control, and our interest in controlling leads to a different attitude toward world. Exploding growth of science funding by government. Corollary: Attitude is that if there's a problem, there should be a solution – then look to the government to fix the problem.

    Carl J. Friedrich [likely in *Revolution*]: Our century and 17th–18th centuries is "greater policy consciousness." More widespread recognition that social arrangements are not given but are a human construction which is a choice, which leads policy. Therefore, all areas are a contested domain. Decisions seen as made by government but increased object of use. Leads to corollary: much traditional anti-intervention talk is conducted to obscure government's involvement, leads to create law takers.

5. Increased perceptions of externalities and public goods. Individuals are
    autonomous only within opportunity sets that are a function of others.
    Public goods are activities or products; cannot exclude. Marginal cost of
    increase = 0, therefore there is a wide range of circumstances for applica-
    tion. Last two centuries, growth of cities lead to an increased necessity
    of recognizing public goods ⇒ because of germ science theory. Problem
    now is that infrastructure is weighing out conflicts with population's
    desire to decrease government spending.

6. Now have situations where income elasticity of certain goods > 1.
    For example, government goods with increase in income, Engel's
    Law.

7. Psychology of government. Not incorrect to see historically two views of
    government (but impossible to measure).
    a. Authoritative father figure
    b. Big brother
    Pragmatic, mechanical treatment of government as a means to get things
    done is not the same as the metaphysics of a, b decreased because wider
    range of access.

8. Risk: social living requires dealing with risk ⇒ people's attitude.
    Government collectivizes and shares risk; share costs of risk – risk of
    war, economic insecurity. Makes government a more active tool. Basic
    theory is that the welfare state is the analog of security of property – old
    age, health, etc. Government = more conspicuous today ⇒ vehicle or
    arena of social power play:
    1. Insecurity
    2. Policy consciousness
    And this draws more people in. The process is workable: if conflicts, one
    formula is to convert from zero-sum to positive-sum game by spending
    on all parties. Programs are adopted because original plan is extended to
    include everyone (poor and middle class) but who pays?
    a. Conflicts that are dramatic have risk solutions eclipse funds.
    b. Hiatus between decisions to spend and decisions to raise taxes
        (Wicksell).

9. Difficulty in terminating government programs. Programs are adopted
    because particular interest group, then after adopted, the beneficiaries
    support the program (Tullock).

10. Demographics. Enormous population growth; increased longevity (by 15–20 years), increased population under 20 and over 60.

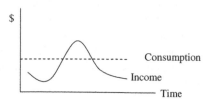

Lifecycle hypothesis ⇒ need programs increased for under 20, and over 60 without a change in power or a change in ideology, e.g., Reagan and California and increased funding.

11. Lessoned capacity of individuals to care for selves in impersonal, urban world.
Failure of nuclear family = consequential insecurity. This has led to an increase in private sector institutions.

12. Technical factors. Economics of scale in public goods in an organization sense, e.g., highway system, NASA (which the federal government organizes and finances). This leads to government as a programmer of collective action. Urban renewal is an example of a plan that did not succeed.

13. Production of private goods that required government funds. For example, automobiles required highways, police, courts – complimentary relationship.

14. Tendency within government to expand (empire building, etc.) Pressures exist to expand from within.

15. All else equal, economic growth leads to increased tax revenues that lead to increased government programs. Twentieth century ⇒ increased revenues with growth, therefore not to have increased taxes to spend more. Fractionalization of spending vs. taxes budgetary decisions leads to log-rolling quid pro quo.

16. Logic of politics is promising things to voters. Peacock and Wiseman (1961) have a study of behavioral public finance.
    a. That public officials like to spend more because this leads votes.
    b. Citizens want more public goods.
    c. Citizens do not like more or higher taxes.

The first two combine to spend more, the third leads to a lag between spending and taxes $\Rightarrow$ increased government debt. People want free lunches.
Factors relevant to growth of government, continued. Demographics, logic of politics. Other factors:

17. Certain activities of government are not expensive, but very important – e.g., courts, legislatures. Some rights are expensive – environment regulations. This leads to a costliness of rights.

18. Greater opportunity to levy taxes.
    Revenue and technology, money economy; educational levels, income in a subsistence economy, self-employed. Property tax is about owner-ship of property; if at issue then it is difficult to levy taxes, therefore increased market economy, employers, decreased extended economy are tax hurdles, therefore public sector larger in industrialized countries.

19. Ratchet effect post-WWI, WWII. Wars overcame tax resistance; lasted after the war, but rose during wars; falls after, but not to preceding level.
    Long list of factors; nonideological, relevant, complex, which are not easy sound bites. The problem is the degree to which spending is posi-tive, and the degree to which spending is normative, but no necessary reason why is absolutely positive or normative, e.g., demographics $\Rightarrow$ increase in older people with an increase in political power. Conclusion: no simple answer why government expenditures have increased.

Adolf Wagner (1880s)

Theory of Wagner's Law: law of rising public expenditures; share of government spending to GNP increased.

Still debated and controversial. Wagner states that public expenditures will increase:

1. Law and order activities are necessary to have markets, compare capitalist and precapitalist societies; need increased government in terms of basic economic institutions, contracts enforcement, and this costs money.

2. Modern economy requires infrastructure expenditures: roads, transport, communications, scale economies.

3. Social economic activities, including education, banking, and the post office.

From standpoint of 1885, this is a new world. Urban, industrial, needy ⇒ public production of goods. But Wagner's Law bugs people. Seems right so far: government spending to GNP has increased from 3% to 5% to 35% in the United States, in Europe up to 45%. Data seems to confirm this; but more than this is involved, e.g., defense, war, transfer payments. The expenditure elasticity >1 relative to tax revenue; true between developed and underdeveloped countries, but each has a big range.

Explanations of Wagner and supporters

1. Interconnection between public and private sectors.
    Increased in the private ⇒ Increase in the public, they're mutually reinforcing.
    e.g., automobile industry, cars ⇒ roads. This is all associated with increased urbanization, increased population growth, which leads to building more roads. This leads to the specialization of labor, large scale of production ⇒ cumulative causation.

2. Increased centralization of power in government at all levels especially at the federal, central level, and also centralizing power in private sector ⇒ concentrated power acts in a symbiotic fashion; "pressure for social progress" leads to people demanding social progress and they will use whatever institutions are available (public and private), therefore modernity leads to change and progress, of which governmental activism is an inherent characteristic.

3. Law applies independent of political system. Imperative, cumulative causation of public and private sector growth. Political science, see Dye. Conclusion that political system variables are unimportant, which is controversial and open to judgment.

4. Social stability. In a modern world this is increasingly a function of government. It's more complex, insecure, expensive because of increasing complexity, atomization, concentrated power, public good-externality societies.

National Tax Journal, Abizadeh and Grey (June 1985)

Major comprehensive analysis: compare growth of government expenditure to an index of measures of economic development, including

  - Real per capita gross domestic product (GDP)
  - GDP from agriculture as a fraction of the total
  - Total commercial energy consumption
  - Foreign trade importance
  - Financial intermediaries (M2)

Wagner's law applied to those in process of development and not at other stages. Discriminates: developing (law is demonstrated), poor (law is not demonstrated), developed (reverse is true). Problems of limited time and data, exogenous international events.

Studies on Attitudes

– 1963 study of US families conducted in 1960 and 1961:
  1. Income = little effect on regard to taxes
  2. Income influences preferences for participatory programs
  3. Increased willingness to pay taxes with increased education
  4. Party identification insignificant

– 1967 study of 1959 data (Detroit):
  1. Preference for tax type dictated by self-interest (most significant are income and home ownership).
  2. Education tempers the effect of income.
  3. Political party or union identification is significant.

– 1974 study of Swedish tax payers in 1969:
  1. Percent report that taxes unreasonable relative to benefits increases with income.
  2. 50% tax rates are not too high, given benefits.
  3. Dissatisfaction of government falls as education increases.

– 1979 UK study (only men):
  1. Reliable predictor of attitudes is income.
  2. Progressive taxes found but less as increased income.
  3. >50% taxes unreasonable.
  4. Party identification is not significant.

Wagner's Law? Claim seems to be correct; forms which growth takes are not unreasonable, but do not exhaust explanations. Therefore, empirical and sensible explanations. Critics claim:

1. Correlations only and not causation.
2. What happened is not because of law, but because of policy decisions: Some is attributable to mixed feelings, e.g., demographics: law requires social security or disability funds but pressures have created and are expected because some organization of government and society.
3. The law implies only to takeoff and not preindustrial or postindustrial societies.
4. Many variables are difficult to treat: social, cultural, political.
   Status of Wagner's law is mixed $\Rightarrow$ brilliant, original, accurate analysis confirmed empirically. But people are uncomfortable with it; runs counter to ideology of Western civilization, nuance of inevitability, which is strong and rubs many the wrong way.

Peacock and Wisman argue (1961):

1. Government prefers to spend more rather than less because of special interests, pet projects.
2. Citizens prefer to pay less tax rather than more.
3. Government must give some attention to citizen preferences.
4. Citizens want more public benefits rather than less.

Some predictive value: explains the Reagan years. Increased sources, decreased taxes $\Rightarrow$ huge deficits.

Solomon Fabricant (Fabricant & Lipsey, 1952): study which attempted to explain increases in public spending:

1. Economic growth
2. Population increases
3. Technology that leads to increased income, urbanization, and industrialization
4. Changes in the value system

This is a broad study. Robert Wood does this at the municipal level using econometrics. Turns out that 96% of variance is explained by the following variables, with the first three being most predictive.

*1. Size
*2. Level of industrialization

   *3. Density of housing
   *4. Average population age
    5. Extent of low income
    6. Residual affluence
    7. Level of land reserves

Suggests technical factors, but is Wagner's Law a law or a policy? Middle ground = operative technical factors; demand for goods and public goods ⇒ what to discuss?

War power renders both eminent domain; police powers ....

Six quarters – answer all six on final ⇒ understand argument and rhetoric as it is. Not to let extreme positions define a problem. Issues of relative risks, costs, and who bears the costs, e.g., FDA and drug approval – no solution to the problem; no criteria for decision. Rule of thumb in computers: don't buy the first version because bugs and delay vs. haste in company decisions.

Questions
Epistemology and ontology: Ultimate nature of things is not objective or subjective. Samuels sees as subjective in the manner of Kant. Qualifications or credentials of knowledge? Theories that have to do with ultimate nature.

Marxist: The State is an instrument of ruling class ⇒ element of superstructure. The function of state is to reproduce the system. Reproduce the capitalist system by creating capital ⇒ state autonomous or part of superstructure? Bob [Robert] Solow articles in the *Journal of Economic Issues* on modern development of Marxist (1970s). Capitalism: science and nature journal.

[Bertell] Ollman's *Theory of Alienation* (1971): Part of the story. Yes, alienation from participatory politics because the state is run by plutocrats who are law makers. Marx talks about alienation from each other, from work, from self. Participating in politics was not central because at that time, only 10% could vote.

[Adam] Smith relied on

    1. Moral values
    2. Markets
    3. Legal rules

Various interpretations; many ignore economic role of government in Smith. Smith is not laissez-faire; not lots of rules or activism. Last week's *Newsweek* magazine article by [Paul] Samuelson: Smith has been appropriated by supply-siders. Smith ['s work] is richer than ideologies tend to make out, e.g., social-biology. It seems to affirm modern social Darwinism. History of economics is a tool for interpretations.

Coase: Can't say why didn't respond. Market-driven notion of economy. Coasians carry logic of externalities to a logical conclusion; Pigou says sure, but that's not the real world.

Review Day

Positivism 1   Positivism 2

IS X is a useful means to achieve Y

I am sitting here   What is necessary to achieve an end?

IS $\Rightarrow$ means $\Rightarrow$ ends

Coase – Probably accepts cost minimization but not a major function $\Rightarrow$ wants competitive market economy.

Posner: 1.   Wealth maximization
          2.   Focuses on cost minimization

$\Rightarrow$ What he recognizes as costs: form of society. "Land of society" or "social/public purpose" as a mechanism to resolve choice. Where we want to draw the lines for forming society? $\Rightarrow$ Economic develop and the [Max] Weber thesis. It explains American north and nondevelopment of French Canada and South America. However, now south is looking to take off for economic growth. Eminent domain leads compensation (takings clause). Historically required compensation.

Equal Protection and Corporations: "person" in the amendment is usually taken to be a biological person vs. acting as a person. Corporation $\Rightarrow$ 1790s England; 1840 in the United States. General in corporation; life in perpetuity, liability.

NOTES

1. Samuels was partial to two examples of relativism. The first is the three blind men attempting to identify an elephant, as each feels a different part of the animal. The second is encapsulated by the phrase that "one man's terrorist is another man's freedom fighter."

2. This quote was paraphrased in class. The correct quote is "Power tends to corrupt, and absolute power corrupts absolutely," Lord Acton, 1887.

3. Karen Danielsen Horney (1885–1952) was a German–American psychoanalyst who challenged a number of Freudian beliefs, particularly with regards to women and sexuality.

4. Rudolf Goldscheid (1870–1931) was a fiction writer and sociologist, whose most important idea was that of the Economy of Human Beings.

5. A. Allan Schmid, Wisconsin, PhD and institutionalist. Schmid is an economist at Michigan State University in the Department of Agricultural Economics.

6. Paul R. Diesing (1922–2011) was a philosopher who studied the social sciences with a focus on rationality, methodology, and ideology in social science research.

7. *Public Finance in Theory and Practice,* 1973, by Richard A. and Peggy B. Musgrave.

8. *Public Expenditure,* 1971, Jesse Burkhead and Jerry Miner.

9. David *Bromwich* in the *London Review of Books,* vol. 18, no. 17, October 1996.

10. Samuels served as a member of the student's PhD dissertation committee. We are unable to identify the specific individual or title of the dissertation.

11. Professor of Law in Residence at the Michigan State University College of Law.

12. Guido Calabresi (1932–) is an Italian–American legal scholar and senior judge on the US Court of Appeals for the Second Circuit. He is considered by many to be a founder of the law and economics movement, along with Posner and Coase.

13. This statement is prescient, as in 2009 Richard Posner published an editorial piece in *The New Republic* titled "How I Became a Keynsian." This piece is indicative of a broader change in Posner's thinking on the role of the state.

14. Classic property rights case that looks to balance the rights of a property owner (of red cedar trees) against a reasonable social policy designed to reduce the spread of disease from red cedar trees to apple orchards in Virginia.

15. Now Lockheed Martin, as the company merged with Martin Marietta in 1995.

REFERENCES

Burger (1974*). U.S. vs. Nixon.* A Supreme Court case.

Coase, R. (1960). The problem of social cost. *Journal of Law and Economics, 3,* 1–44.

Epstein, R. A. (1985). *Takings: Private property and the power of eminent domain.* Cambridge, MA: Harvard University Press.

Fabricant, S., & Lipsey, R. E. (1952). *The trend of government activity in the United States since 1900.* Ann Arbor, MI: UMI.

Ollman, B. (1971). *Alienation: Marx's concept of man in a capitalist society.* New York: Cambridge University Press.

Peacock, A. T., & Wiseman, J. (1961). *The growth of public expenditure in the United Kingdom.* Princeton, NJ: Princeton University Press.

Rawls, J. (1971). *A theory of justice.* Cambridge, MA: Harvard University Press.

Sax, J. L. (1971). Takings, private property, and public rights. *Yale Law Journal, 81,* 149.

Sen, A. (1992). *Inequality reexamined.* Cambridge, MA: Harvard University Press.

Simon, H. A. (1983). *Reason in human affairs.* Stanford, CA: Stanford University Press.

NOTES FROM WARREN J. SAMUELS'S 1999 COURSE ON THE ECONOMIC ROLE OF GOVERNMENT

Edited by Brady J. Deaton, David Schweikhardt, James Sterns and Patricia Aust Sterns

Economics 819
The Economic Role of Government
Professor Warren J. Samuels
Michigan State University
Fall 1999 (Note: the last time Samuels taught this course.)

COURSE SYLLABUS [We do not replicate the portions of the syllabus identical to that published in the 1996 notes, but do publish the readings lists as they differ.]

Texts added to the 1999 course readings list:

Nicholas Mercuro and Steven G. Medema, *Economics and the Law: From Posner to Post-Modernism.* Princeton: Princeton University Press, 1997.

Warren J. Samuels, "An Essay on Government and Governance."

Warren J. Samuels, Steven G. Medema, and Nicholas Mercuro, "Institutional Law and Economics," for Boudewijn Bouckaert and Gerrit De Geest, eds., *Encyclopaedia of Law and Economics.*

Documents on Government and the Economy
Research in the History of Economic Thought and Methodology, Volume 30-B, 267–317
Copyright © 2012 by Emerald Group Publishing Limited
All rights of reproduction in any form reserved
ISSN: 0743-4154/doi:10.1108/S0743-4154(2012)000030B008

Warren J. Samuels and Steven G. Medema, "The Economic Role of Government As, In Part, A Matter of Selective Perception, Sentiment and Valuation: The Cases of Pigovian and Paretian Welfare Economics."

Warren J. Samuels and Nicholas Mercuro, eds., Editors' materials from *Fundamentals of Property and Government* (1999).

Warren J. Samuels and A. Allan Schmid, "The Concept of Cost in Economics," in Warren J. Samuels, Steven G. Medema and A. Allan Schmid, *The Economy as a Process of Valuation*. Lyme, NH: Edward Elgar, 1997. pp. 208–298.

Warren J. Samuels, "The Concept of 'Coercion' in Economics, in Warren J. Samuels, Steven G. Medema and A. Allan Schmid, *The Economy as a Process of Valuation*. Lyme, NH: Edward Elgar, 1997. pp. 129–207.

Warren J. Samuels, A. Allan Schmid, and James D. Shaffer, "An Evolutionary Approach to Law and Economics," in Richard W. England, ed., *Evolutionary Concepts in Contemporary Economics*, Ann Arbor: University of Michigan Press, 1994. pp. 93–110.

Warren J. Samuels, "The Growth of Government," *Critical Review*, vol. 7, no. 4 (1993), pp. 445–460.

Warren J. Samuels, "Reader's Guide to John R. Commons, *Legal Foundations of Capitalism*," *Research in the History of Economic Thought and Methodology*, Archival Supplement 5 (1996), pp. 1–61.

"History of Economic Thought and the Economic Role of Government," pp. 39–43, in Warren J. Samuels, "My Work as a Historian of Economic Thought," *Journal of the History of Economic Thought*, vol. 18 (Spring 1996), pp. 37–75.

Warren J. Samuels and Steven G. Medema, "Ronald Coase and Coasean Economics: Some Questions, Conjectures and Implications," in Warren J. Samuels, Steven G. Medema, and A. Allan Schmid (eds.), *The Economy as a Process of Valuation*. Lyme, NH: Edward Elgar, 1997. pp. 72–128. [D]

LECTURE OUTLINE

I. Introduction to the Study of the Economic Role of Government: Alternative Approaches to Law and Economics

    A. Course Objectives
    B. General Approach/Introductory Comments
    C. Introductory Points

II. Fundamental Legal-Economic Processes: The Legal-Economic Nexus

    A. First Model: Value Diagram
    B. Second Model: Opportunity Set Model: Inter-agent Relationships
    C. Third Model: Policy as a Function of Power, Knowledge and Psychology Variables
    D. Fourth Model: Problem of Order
    E. First Paradigmatic Case Study: Pollution
    F. Second Paradigmatic Case Study: Pregnancy Leaves
    G. Third Paradigmatic Case Study: Red Cedar Case, 1928
    H. The Legal-Economic Nexus
    I. Some Fundamental Points

III. Law and Economics in the History of Economic Thought

IV. Of Law and Rights

    A. Law as Language
    B. Constitutional and Legal Juxtapositions and Conflicts
    C. Complex Intertemporal Characteristics of Law
    D. Law
    E. Rights
    1. Rights in General
    2. Property Rights
    F. Some Principal Points or Conclusions
    G. Some Legal-Economic Fundamentals

V. Ronald Coase and Richard Posner: The Coase Theorem and Wealth Maximization

    A. Introduction
    B. Coase and the Coase Theorem
    C. Posner and the Maximization of Wealth

VI. Regulation and Deregulation
VII. The Compensation Problem

LECTURE NOTES

    I. <u>Introduction to the Study of the Economic Role of Government: Alternative Approaches to Law and Economics</u>

The focus of this course is on <u>fundamentals</u> of the economic role of government, or the legal-economic nexus.

Focus is on a <u>positive</u> – that is, non-normative approach. Want to focus on the <u>process of working things out</u> – examined in a non-normative manner. This approach has no ability to solve problems. It will help understand what is going on, not on what should be done.

Focus is on various approaches to law and economics.

What this course is about:

1. Law as social control – control of whom and for what purposes?
2. Changing law as social control – changing the whom and/or the purposes.
   • A key concept is "How things are worked out".

For example, consider the graph below. What is going on in this graph?

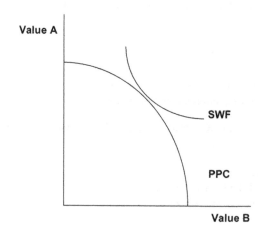

• Determination of values on axes
• Determination of shape of Social Welfare Function
• Determination of shape of PPC

Includes weighting of values

Identification of preferences

Language is used to justify each of these

Government's inevitable role – promotes, protects one interest over another, whether we like it or not. We must distinguish between description (what is going on), explanation (how and why it is going on) vs. justification (why it should go on).

Joseph Spengler on the "Problem of Order" (see Samuels' article). [Three] dimensions for every society to work out:

1. Freedom vs. control
2. Continuity vs. change
3. Hierarchy vs. equality

Every society must have a process for working these out.
What is emphasized in understanding this process?

1. Legal – economic reality is constructed by mankind, even when it is not recognized as such. There is no natural economy, no natural polity. It is a socially constructed legal-economic nexus.
2. Closure, certainty, clarity, vs. ambiguity. Social control provides closure, certainty, and clarity.
3. Law vs. policy. Law traditionally viewed as having the standing of "a given," while policy is often viewed as mutable. But this is not true – law is a function of policy decisions. Law is policy and the two are not as different as commonly assumed.

[Charles] Lindblom: "muddling through" is done through partisan mutual adjustment. This is a form of "working things out" or social construction.

False dichotomies in political economy:

1. The polity (the political system) and the economic system. These are two aspects of the same thing. Example: Is property an economic concept or a political concept? Samuels – it is both; polity and economy are inseparable – it is a product of the political/economic nexus. Locke and

Smith both wrote that the main role of government is to protect the property of the rich from the poor.

2. Non-interventionism (or laissez-faire) and reform. The term "intervention" suggests that government is being introduced into an area in which it was previously absent. This is false. Government is always present – the question is whose interests will government protect and promote? Another way to view: There is no area of life in which government does not have a law.

If there are areas in which there is no recognized law, conflicting parties will bring different parts of law to defend and promote their position. Changing circumstances (e.g., technology) may create situations in which the law is not clearly defined, but the conflicting parties will force a clarification of the law.

Who are law-makers, vs. law-takers? Law-makers see the law as made by people and the important issue is who will make the law. Law-takers take the law as a given that cannot be changed. Governance is not simply a matter of who holds a given political office. It is a matter of who holds power, including those who do not hold political power.

**A central issue: Most of economic theory deals with positive sum games – achieved through exchange among individuals. Most of the difficult issues – most of the problems that government must deal with are not positive sum games. Government must choose among conflicting interests – must decide whether a given interest is consistent with some conception of public purpose. There is an inevitable conception of public purpose that underlies law.

Key terminology: First dichotomy – take a phrase – "pure, liberal, democratic society." What might this mean? What are specific combinations of freedom and control, what institutions exist, what things change and how are they changed? Example: What is "freedom of information" vs. "right to privacy?" depends on working out the details. Freedom vs. control is a first dichotomy.

Second dichotomy: Pure abstract markets vs. actual markets. Pure markets are a-institutional – without need for institutions. Actual markets operate through institutions. Coase – Firms "create" markets by their decisions – markets do not operate independent of firms. "Optimal" solutions only arise within an institutional setting; there are no prices or costs independent of institutions. Markets are not neutral. Property and markets are not independently given.

Third dichotomy: "Non-intervention" or "laissez-faire" vs. "activism" because government is inevitably active and engaged. The question is which interests will government support. "Regulation vs. deregulation" – these are <u>not</u> different. We shall see that these are analytically equivalent. Government is an instrument available to whoever can control it. This is what has to be worked out.

<u>Introduction to the Study of the Economic Role of Government</u>

Major points:

1. Political and economic systems are not independent, self-sufficient structures. They are made and remade by man.
2. There is a political/economic nexus.
3. Much of what is said about the economic role of government serves as "psychic balm" or social control.
4. The terms "law" and "policy" are often treated as being different. This is false.
5. The making and remaking of the economy are a <u>process</u>. [Charles] Lindblom calls it "partisan mutual adjustment" – it is bargaining among interest groups. The issue – who gets to participate and on what terms?

A framework for understanding material:

1. Abstract notion of the economy and the economy as it is actually institutionalized. Economy as institutionalized changes, regardless of whether abstract ideas of the economy change.
   Similar to the abstract concept of "liberal democracy" vs. the reality of actual "liberal democracy."
2. Abstract notion of property vs. actual definitions of property.
   The market, democracy, [and] property are not given to us – they are social constructs. Critical question is not "whether to have government" but "which interest will government serve" – it is a tool of whoever can control it. The most fundamental "competition" in society is <u>not</u> among goods, but among those who would control government.
3. Government is both an instrument of the powerful and an instrument by which the power of the powerful can be checked.
   Laissez-faire vs. intervention: This is not a description of reality or has any objective meaning – it is instead an attitude.
4. Polity and economy are not separable. They are mutually determined. They are product of same legal/economic nexus.
5. Governance: The making of decisions that affect other people.

6. The idea of "public purpose." Government is inevitably involved in resolving the conflicting claims of Alpha and Beta. Public purpose is not a given – it must be worked out.

Paradigms in considering these issues:

1. The productivity paradigm: To have income is to be productive, but to be productive is to have income. A tautology.
2. The exploitation paradigm: To have income is to have exploited someone to get it. But we have no objective way of saying what someone's income would have been if they were not exploited.

Both have a reassuring function:

- Productivity – people have what they deserve
- Exploitation – people don't have what they deserve

3. The appropriation paradigm: People get what they get, however they get it. The question is how do they get it? By stacking the deck? By stacking the law? What are the conditions that permit someone to get what they get?

- See David Ellerman in Samuels and Mercuro on contracting.

This is all an amplification of a point: The legal-economic structure is a social structure that is constructed, not given.

Different Approaches to the Study of Law and Economics

1. Neoclassical approach (see Hirsch text): Major characteristics: (1) the market is conceived of in pure and abstract form – without reference to specifics. The market is seen as independent of all other social processes. (2) Has a particular research protocol of how research is to be done. Produces unique, optimal, determinate solutions. Unique – there can be only [one] solution. Optimal – defined in Pareto-optimal terms. Solution is in equilibrium – there would be no further gains from trade, no other changes without some outside force affecting the system.

Posner argues that the neoclassical approach is related to wealth maximization. Other neoclassicals say that the approach is related to utility maximization, which may not be the same as wealth maximization. Posner's approach: The law itself is a wealth-maximizing process. Others approach: The law is given; the major research question is what will be the impact of the law on the economy? Posner would argue that most government institutions are obstacles to wealth maximization; others would say that we cannot conclude that, we can only analyze the impact of alternative laws.

Pigouvian approach: Welfare maximized when MSC = MPC and MSB = MPB. If not equal, under-/overproduction of goods may occur. A second Pigouvian approach argues that welfare can only be maximized when marginal utility of money is equal across individuals.

Pareto approach: Welfare maximized when gains from trade are exhausted. If trade is occurring, it must be that such trade exhausts gains from trade. If no trade occurs, there must be no gains from trade that can be accomplished.

2. Institutionalist approach: Focuses on factors and forces that work to determine whose interests count. Law establishes respective market positions that determine who gets what gains from trade.
3. Critical legal studies: A movement among law school professors. Now emerging in law schools among younger in profession. Examines law in a class context, gender context, racial context, [and] social construction. This is a marriage of Marxism and the earlier school of "legal realism." Legal realism was a reaction against analytical jurisprudence (AJ). AJ says that all law is a matter of deriving conclusions inevitably from premises. Legal realism says that law is a matter of experience, not simply of logic. Thus, there can be multiple interpretations of the law – law is an inductive process, not a deductive process.

Marxism: Government is a part of the superstructure that represents the ruling class. The state allows the ruling class to exploit the ruled class. State also facilitates the accumulation of capital and protects the system against attacks. Critical legal studies combine Marxism and legal realism.

Samuels: All of these three groups share an instrumental view of the state: The state is a tool that is available for the capture and use by those who can acquire control of it. These groups have different values, different views of reality, and different attitudes toward capitalism. Each of these also contains an affirmative approach or agenda for government – each has important fundamental roles that government must play in the economy.

Some differences: (1) Neoclassicals focus on resource allocation. Others do not. (2) Neoclassicals see economy as independent and self-sufficient. Others do not.

(3) Neoclassicals see the economy only in terms of markets. Others see economy in broader terms of institutional framework within which markets operate. In general, neoclassicals prefer to abstract from institutional details, others want to focus on these details.

Approaches to study of law and economics (see Medema and Mercuro):

1. Neoclassical approach: There are several versions. One type: What econometric variables explain outcomes? Another version has: (1) there is an abstract model of the economy that exists and that has nothing to do with any particular set of institutions. And (2) search for a unique, determinate solution.

Laden through this is the notion of optimality. For example, Pigouvian welfare economics – MSB should equal MPB, and MSC should equal MPC. This implies reform – these conditions are optimal, and deviation should be corrected.

Or Pareto optimization – there are gains from trade. Trade should take place until gains from trade are exhausted.

Or the notion of productivity – People get what they produce. Samuels: But this is not what "causes" productivity. This is a condition, not a cause.

Emphasis in neoclassical approach is a search for a unique, optimal, determinate solution.

2. Institutionalist approach: Institutions are both a dependent and an independent result.
3. Critical legal studies approach: Many are influenced by Marx and by "legal realism." Analytical jurisprudence – law is a set of precedents from which legal decisions can be deduced. Legal realism – law must be based on experience, not deductions from basic principles. Thus, judges are fundamentally activists, even when they say they are not. Often combined with an emphasis on exploitation paradigm.
4. Marxist approach: Government is a tool available to whoever can control it, and will be used for purposes of exploitation. An instrument of class domination. A function of government is to protect the ruling class.

What do all approaches have in common? Each sees the government as an instrument used by someone. Each has an affirmative theory of what government should/should not do.

These are each modes of discourse, The "Hermeneutic Circle." Choice of theory defines elements of problem and therefore solution.

Every term – for example, property – has a history, and therefore multiple meanings. Example: What is "an institution?" Veblen – a common, settled habit of belief. Commons – collective action in control and liberation of individual action.

How can we think of these? What is the network of topics with regard to the issues that are the fundamentals of government?

What is important in understanding schools of thought regarding the economic role of government?

- Think of a matrix of issues
- What are their positions on these issues?
- What are their views of others on these issues?
- What issues do they exclude?

Neoclassical Approach (NA)

Postulates that there is a pure, abstract, market system. Assumes there is an independent economy that exists.

NA has a research protocol. All research is supposed to yield unique, optimal, determinate solutions – a "right" answer.

Is based on methodological individualism and rationality.

Methodological individualism (MI) – Only way to study economy is to study behavior of individuals. Only they exist.

Methodological collectivism (MC) – Only way to study economy is through study of institutions, collective action.

Normative individualism (NI) – Only individual preferences should count.

Normative collectivism (NC) – Only collective preferences should count.

Samuels: These are all fundamentally wrong and misleading. For example, markets are a collective phenomenon. They cannot be studied only through either MI or MC. NI – to say that preferences are self-chosen ignores that individuals are socialized, which affects choice. NC – the concept that there is "a public interest" ignores the many conflicting interests and their stake in an issue.

All of these ignore: "Which individuals and within what structure?" Any action is a function of both of these.

The issue of structure vs. results: Samuels – this is the foremost question of policy analysis. Some will focus on structure, others will focus on results. Sometimes debates center on structure, other times on results.

The NA focuses on "the market" – different markets, governed by different sets of institutions, yield different results. What do we mean by "the market" – there is a market in both cases:

Power Structure1 $\Rightarrow$ Rights Structure1 $\Rightarrow$ Market Structure1 $\Rightarrow$ Allocation Outcome1

or

Power StructureN $\Rightarrow$ Rights StructureN $\Rightarrow$ Market StructureN $\Rightarrow$ Allocation OutcomeN

So "market will always work." It works within a rights structure. So if AO is "efficient," that is circular – because AO is a product of PS and RS – AO is "efficient" only within its PS and RS.

Neoclassical economics has a term called "a good" (or output or commodity). But this is an empty term. Is it a "homogenous" good? But quite diverse sets of goods can have high cross-price elasticities – fur coats and Caribbean vacations can be substitutes – or part of the same "market." This begs a fundamental question – what is "the output" of a police department (absence of crime? number of criminals captured?).

The terms of "positive" vs. "normative."

Samuels – positive describes "what is" – in terms of who, what, how, why.

Normative – describes what should be. Contains a "choice element."

An "ought" cannot be derived from an "is" proposition alone. Requires an additional normative premise. See Samuels article – "What is is and ought to be."

Two types of positivism:

Positivism 1 is described above – based on definition, description.

Positivism 2 – "X is what has to happen to reach end Y." It assumes a normative end. [Glenn] Johnson – this is conditional normativism.

Samuels (and Friedman): Does end justify means? Yes, always so. But this is an empty question. Real question should be "what ends are justified?"

NA has right (Friedman) and left (Skitovsky) versions.

Institutional Analysis (IA)

Whereas neoclassical analysis depends on an abstract, ideal market, institutionalism focuses on the actual forces in the economy. Based on same chain:

Power Structure $\Rightarrow$ Rights Structure $\Rightarrow$ Market Structure $\Rightarrow$ Allocation Outcome

But also adds: Control of government as part of the power structure.

IA sees question of "who uses government" as a central issue.

Leads to "the ubiquity of law." All aspects of life have a body of law that governs who has what rights, who is exposed to actions of others, etc.

Whenever a "new situation" arises, people react – they draw parallels to existing law or they call for a new area of law.

In either case, however law is defined, some set of laws will be found to apply to the new situation. Even government decision to "do nothing" establishes the law that applies to the new situation.

Government is deeply involved in determining how the economy is institutionalized. Statement of "get government out of (an area of the economy)" ignores that the decision of "getting out" is an unavoidable act of "re-creating" the economy. Such statements are an attempt to channel policy. The real issue is: To what interests will government lend its support. "The Economy" and "The Polity" are not given – they emerge together from the legal-economic nexus. There are two things going on:

1. "The working out" of solutions (which depends on structure)
2. "The working out" of structure (which determines solutions).

Economy = f (polity, i.e., law)
Law = f (economy)
Another way to say:
Public = f (private)
Private = f (public)

"Private" rights are determined by "public" decisions. Property is property because it is protected. It is not protected because it is property. Adam Smith – Government exists to protect rich against poor. Samuels: How did they become rich? By use of government to protect property.

Spengler: The problem of order. We must resolve [three] conflicting issues:

1. Freedom (or autonomy) vs. control
2. Continuity vs. change
3. Hierarchy vs. equality

Samuels: This is a positive description of the problem. Law affects each of these. Law is a function of all of these [six].

Selective perception: All of the above are subject to selective perception. Samuels: In "the process of working things out," everything can be subject to selective perception. Pareto: Society is a system of mutual manipulation of perceptions. Samuels: What we perceive as "freedom" and what we see as "control" [are matters] of the marketing of ideas. Similar for "regulation" vs. "deregulation."

What are differences in "schools of thought" on law and economics? Differences in definitions of "law," of behavior, of relevant variables, of paradigms.

Harmony models vs. conflict models: Neoclassical is typically a "harmony" model, while many non-mainstream models are conflict models. But note: Smith, Ricardo, et al., are filled with recognition of conflicts. Much of mainstream economics – externalities, game theory, etc., can be based on conflict.

Free will vs. determinism: Underlying free will is philosophical realism, or scientific realism – that there is a "real" economy that exists and is to be studied. Scientific realism relies on data collection and hypothesis testing to study a "real" economy.

Free will is exercised within constraints. People attempt to change these constraints. Rules of a game [and] rules of the economy are not a transcendental matter. Thus, the "deterministic" nature of the economy is not given as neoclassical approach assumes.

The role of legitimation: We often selectively legitimize (or delegitimize) that which we want (or don't want). We need to consider what is legitimized/de-legitimized by theories of what is or what ought to be.

We should be aware of:

1. Selective perception
2. Inevitable role of choice
3. Process of working things out

Are we discovering social reality when we study it, or are we defining it? If only discovering, there is no role for choice, free will – we only discover that which exists.

Law can have variety of roles: (1) psychic balm – laying of minds at rest, (2) social control.

How do we decide what law is? If we agree with Constitution, we appeal to "Founding Fathers." If we disagree, we appeal to constitution as "a living document." This is all a matter of interpretation and selective perception, manipulation of rhetoric as a means of defending/challenging the constitution.

Law has a body of theory embodied in words that are used to define reality. The "fallacy of misplaced concreteness" assumes that the use of term demonstrates its concreteness.

II. Fundamental Legal-Economic Processes: The Legal-Economic Nexus

The legal-economic nexus and the fundamental nature of law and economics.

Refer back to "the value diagram." What is going on? It is a working out of

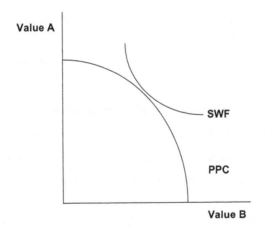

1. Values on agenda
2. Trade-offs
3. Preferences
4. Weighting

Values: What issues and alternatives define the agenda of choices? True in any legislature or any court.

<u>Trade-offs</u> of the PPC: This is somewhat understood in "guns and butter" case, but is much less understood in political case. Can be affected by "withholding power," other means of achieving influence, etc.

<u>Preferences</u>: Depends on how issue is framed, rhetoric deployed, socialization processes. Formation of preferences is influenced by same processes that define values.

<u>Weighting</u>: Different people have different weights, but weights are also formed by same process of values and preferences.

There is a simultaneous working out of all four variables. There is a joint determination and definition of all four.

<u>A second model</u>: The opportunity set (OS) model.

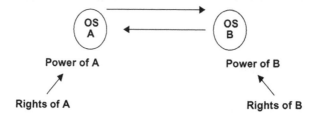

Opportunity Set of A = f (Power of A) <u>and</u> Opportunity Set of B = f (Power of B)

Power = Participation in decision making or the basis of that participation.

But OS of each is also a function of the choices made by the other party.

Each can go to the court or legislature in an attempt to change his own OS and the OS of others.

Power: Either or both – participation in decision making or the basis of decision making. These bases are fluid and "up for grabs."

Key principles:

- Power is necessary to achieve desired ends.
- The quest for power is partially derived from desire to achieve particular ends and for its own sake – for identity reasons.
- The reciprocal nature of power. A's power is influenced by B's power, and the reverse is also true.

The interesting cases are those of conflict – Alpha and Beta are in the same field of action and the choice to grant power to one also exposes the other to the consequences of the other's decisions.

- Tendency of powerful to seek further power. For desired ends or for identity reasons.
- Power seeks to provide its own rationalization.
- Pluralism as a goal requires the division of power as a check on power in order to diffuse power.

    1. This guarantees that conflict is inevitable between parties seeking to check one another.
    2. All are parts of government – legislature; courts are all parts of government.

Dualism of power: Decisions are a function of the power structure <u>and</u> power structure is a function of decisions.

Ex: Legislative apportionment changed in [the] 1960s.

- Working rules of law and morals govern the distribution and exercise of power, <u>and</u> vice versa.
- Values depending upon the decision-making process, <u>and</u> vice versa.
- Distribution of income and wealth <u>and</u> vice versa.

<u>A third model:</u>

Policy = f (Power, knowledge, and psychological variables)

Knowledge: What people accept as true and are willing to act upon. Witte – what matters is not what <u>the case is,</u> but what people believe is the case.

Psychological variables:

Karen Horney – people have [three] forms of behavior – aggression, compliance, withdrawal.

What is important is people's identity – what is important to them.

Each of these is a heterogeneous variable. There is also interdependence among these variables.

Any proposition that can be made about one variable can be made about the others – that is, any phenomenon can be interpreted in terms of any one of these variables.

See Samuels, *Pareto on Policy*, for a view of this by Pareto. Pareto – political choice is a matter of mutual manipulation in which capacity to manipulate is unequal.

Samuels: Again, we selectively perceive terms like freedom, coercion, government, power.

Herbert Simon: We call government "democracy" when we like it; we call government "politics" when we don't like it. (Simon – *Reason and Human Affairs*, p. 99). Simon – this is an obstacle to solving problems. Samuels – this is just how we solve problems, often without recognizing the selective and normative elements of what we do. Also see Samuels and Mercuro critique on rent-seeking theory.

Samuels: What is the role of the expert in the policymaking process? The medical parallel – go to different doctors, will get different treatments.

[Allan] Schmid – Expert should identify alternatives and consequences. Is policy a matter of subjective choices or technical issues? Samuels – it is both. Choice of both means (subjective) and ends (technical) are at stake. See correspondence of Oliver Wendell Holmes and Harold Laski: Laski – what is the public interest? It is what we each claim it should be.

Samuels: The alternatives/consequences approach is still selective. Judgment is inevitably involved. What is important is to escape an absolutist position in which that which is "proven" is in fact assumed.

Knowledge: Samuels – our definition of reality (what is going on, how it is going on, why it is going on) and our values.

Ex: Differences arise in defining "what is the problem?" Once you define the problem, you have prefigured the solution.

What is a "problem" – what exists, what is desirable, and what is possible.

Different understandings of what will be taken as given. Again, by defining what is taken as given, we are predefining what solutions are available.

Choice of alternative models/paradigms also predetermines solutions that will be reached.

Pareto: Beliefs are non-logical/experimental, which cannot be tested in a logical/experimental manner. Logical/experimental beliefs are testable. Said that most of what we believe most of the time is non-logical/experimental – myths, ideology, symbols, untested beliefs. Michigan legislator's comments to Samuels on how to vote on legislation:

1. Ideological litmus test
2. Logrolling with others
3. Immersion into analysis of alternatives/consequences

Samuels: What people believe is what they choose to act upon. There is also mutual manipulation of information as a means of manipulating psychology (This was Pareto's view.)

Treatments of power in public finance. How do you treat unequals equally? By treating them equally or unequally? There is not clear solution. Second issue – taxation policy is a matter of transferring taxes "from me to thee."

Pigou – Smith's invisible hand does not operate outside of government, but within a system determined by classes who seek to determine its operation.

Schumpeter – Taxes are "a handle" that can be gripped to control the system.

For references – See Samuels, Land Economics.

Samuelson – *Newsweek*, January 7, 1974, p. 58; politics is economics by other means.

Three Fundamental Points

1. It is important to see that economy is not simply a system of freedom. It is a system of both freedom and control – for Alpha to have freedom, Beta must be controlled. Freedom, like coercion, is in the eye of the beholder.
2. One of the fundamental questions is about the power structure.
3. Continuity and change are not polar opposites, but are closely related concepts. Every system has modes of change. Choice is among modes of change permitted and their consequences.

First Preliminary Paradigmatic Case Study

Consider a river with a steel plant (ST), and downstream a shrimp plant (SP), a flower producer (FP), and a swimmer's beach (SB). Steel plant wants to use river to dump waste. This affects the shrimp catch. The flower plant can be damaged by steel waste, but can gain if shrimp plant adds nutrients to water. Beach swimmers [are] affected by pollution.

If ST plant has right to pollute, then SP, FP, and SB (or government on behalf of swimmers) must bear the cost of cleaning the water. Government has [two] choices – permit ST to pollute and distribute costs among SP, FP, and SB, or refuse steel permission to pollute and distribute cost to steel plant owners and/or its consumers.

The costs are not created by the law – the law only determines the distribution of costs.

Pigouvian model: MSC should equal MPC via a tax or subsidizing of steel plant pollution equipment.

Rights are reciprocal: ST has right to pollute or SP, FP, and SB have no right to water, or SP, FP, SB have right to water and ST has no right to pollute. Thus, externality is also reciprocal – it is imposed on ST by others or on others by ST.

Coase: If market is well defined and transaction costs = zero, then rights are allocatively neutral – trades will always result in the same allocation. Samuels – there are many reasons beyond TC why it is not allocatively neutral.

The shrimp plant produces effluent with nutritive value to flower producer, but is a cost to beach users. Raises the Pigouvian issue of whether MSB = MPB because of external benefit.

Coase and Stigler (his price theory book) are quite different. Stigler – there is no externality problem because of the Coase theorem – rights are allocatively neutral. Coase, properly understood, is that rights are dual in nature.

Determining rights does not create costs – it determines the distribution of costs among stakeholders.

The status quo point is the existing system of rights, and the realized set of externalities, and costs. Change the system of rights and you will change the distribution of externalities and costs. Note: If I dump in river, it may be legal; if I dump on neighbor's land, it is illegal. Status quo is not always clear – not always clear who has what right. The right in place may simply be a de facto right that government must yet decide.

See Samuels and Schmid on costs: All of the past theories of cost are useful in some sense. They add the notion that rights are what give registration and valuation of interests. Cannot register demand in the market if you have no right.

Different distribution of rights will yield different Pareto-optimal outcomes. Coase, properly understood, shows that rights are not allocatively neutral.

See Samuels and Medema on Coase, and Medema's book on Coase.

Some people claim as a rule that whoever bears the smallest total cost should be the one to bear the cost.

In the Red Cedar case, we see that government has to choose. If there is a market and rights are allocatively neutral, then there is no issue for government. But these are often not true, so people appeal to government to assign the rights and thereby distribute the costs.

Second Case Study – pregnancy/parental leaves for mothers/fathers

How does one get the right to a maternity leave? Through private contract? Through company policy? Through legislation? Through litigation? This demonstrates how rights get generated. They do not simply exist.

All discussions of law and economics hinge on the issue of rights. Some have said this is a false basis for discourse.

Third Case Study – red cedar/apple growers' case

Red cedar fungus lives on cedar trees, and kills apple trees within a given radius. Cedar fungus exists in nature – cedar owners did nothing to create the fungus. Apples were an industry, cedars had aesthetic value. In absence of statute to the contrary, red cedar owner imposes cost on apple tree owners, apple owners eventually got a statute passed, state entomologist given authority to identify trees, destroy, and offer some compensation.

So, two choices: No law – protects red cedar owner. With law – protects apple owner. The state of nature defines this to be true. Cedar owners claimed government was taking property for benefit of someone else. Went to Supreme Court – Court admitted that in either case, government must choose which property owners' rights would be defended.

1. Look for Hayek list on Internet.
2. Look for Posner book on impeachment.

IV. Of Law and Rights

Law as language:

1. Law and rights are matters of language. Terms must be given definition – cost, commodity, etc.
2. The complex, intertemporal nature of the law. Law that appeals to precedent uses past to justify. But law defines the future and its future

consequences. Constitutionalist law and common law is ex post facto law. When we begin a case, we do not know what the outcome will be.

3. Public good nature of law: Has a high cost of exclusion – when a court reaches a decision, it applies not only to that case but also to others.

Judges rarely have their decisions reversed.

All law requires interpretation – every clause of the Constitution requires interpretation (see Edwin Corwin, *The Constitution and What It Means Today*). Common law also requires interpretation and application of law to specific cases.

The term "police" has a long history – to Adam Smith, police power referred to policymaking power.

Term "taking" must be interpreted also. Does a regulation requiring that [two] persons be on duty all night at a convenience store qualify as a taking (it increases cost of store owner)?

Sovereignty: The modern state is a descendent of a feudal state – operated by the king, who was sovereign. Where is sovereignty in the modern state? The people are sovereign. So when can the government be found to be liable? In *Kawananokoa v. Polyblank* in 1907, Holmes says that there can be no legal right against the government which writes the law determining whether it is liable. If the government is instituted by people, then the people are sovereign.

What is sovereignty? Is it a particular locus of decision making? Where in government? Government is not a singular thing – it has many dimensions, many points of entry.

Sovereignty can be viewed as a balance of forces – produced by pressure, negotiation, withholding of approval. It is a process of "working things out." Holmes: Every ultimate source of power has a realm of power beyond which it cannot go because the people will fight. Locke extolls the virtue of the legislature over the king, but insists that the right of revolution is a necessary check.

Did the English have the power to legislate for the American colonies? They said so, but people fought.

Governance can include private holders of power (see Samuels' article on government vs. governance). Corporations, for example – a creature of the law – are able to influence the law.

What is government? Some say it is a monopoly on legalized violence. True, but not a central issue. The central issue is that government has the authority to define its own rules, functions, and liability. It is the working out of these that matters most. The issues that reach government are the pejorative issues – when "crap hits the fan," it inevitably reaches government. Only the difficult issues reach government.

Are courts part of government? Holmes – on this there is no argument. Samuels – but this is the issue – who declares that the courts are part of government – the government does so. The question is also remaining – if "the people" are the sovereign, then which people? This must be part of the process of working things out.

Monsanto – attempting to protect its property through terminator, other genetic protections, but their ability to do this is also a matter of public opinion about their right to do so.

Example: New York Stock Exchange claims that it "owns" price data from the stock market. News services claim they have the right to broadcast without paying for the data. NBA has claimed it owns scores of games in progress. Samuels – researchers claim the same when they say that a work in progress or review should not be quoted without permission. If this is followed, how do we review or discuss research?

The concept of law as a primitive, undefined term. Law is ubiquitous – there is or soon will be a law governing every situation. Common law vs. civil law. Common law – common in the sense that it comes from "the people's courts" rather than "the king's courts." Intended to be based on "reasonable common practices" – but if there was a common, accepted, practice, there would be no need for a lawsuit to arise.

Civil law systems – dominate in Europe (except Britain) and in Louisiana. Claims that courts are to employ a code adopted by a legislative body. Judge is to simply apply the code.

Samuels: Notwithstanding the rhetoric in both systems, judges in both systems are "making law" through their interpretation.

Law has [four] domains:

1. Common law
2. Constitutional law
3. Statutory law
4. Administrative law

Three conceptions of law:

1. Divine law – generated by God
2. Natural law – derived from the nature of thing
3. Positive law – created by man

Divine and natural law takes law as something given and preceding man. Not usually applied to "right turn on red" issues, but is often invoked as part of moral issues. Is part of the realm of metaphysics. Even when there is agreement on divine or natural law, there is often disagreement on the details.

Locke: Earth created by God for mankind in general. People earn their property by labor using the earth, so long as one takes no more than can be used (not wasteful). Later, Locke says that despite this divine right, the law is what the civil law deems it to be. Also says that by agreeing to the use of money, we have implicitly agreed to permit the accumulation of wealth beyond that permitted in his earlier definition. He ultimately favors the hegemony of property owners, acting through the legislature, relative to the king. Supports property, protected by legislature, as a tool of business class.

Law is made, not found. The notion that law is "found" is both psychic balm and a matter of legitimation. Creates a sense of certitude.

What is "politicizing" the law? It is making explicit those aspects of the choice about law that were always political in nature (but perhaps obscured).

Running through all of this is the "naturalistic fallacy" – attributing to nature, or to a "natural order of things" – that which is actually a matter of social choice. Laws of property, often taken as "natural," ignores that law is socially constructed.

What is a "right?"

[Three] forms

1. A claim – if A says he has a right to do X, it is a claim.
2. Result of an adjudicated conflict – by some social process, a right has been granted to a specific party.
3. Sanction that can be brought to bear to enforce a right. Without sanction, a right has no meaning.

What is "law?"

The concept of law has many meanings. (This is "court law" not statutory law.)

1. The decision – Alpha gets X and Beta gets (or pays) Y.
2. *Ratio decidendi* – the reason, or basis of the decision.
3. The precedential sequence – what series of cases that serve as precedents upon which the *ratio decidendi* must rest. Note: In any case with multiple decision makers (ex: Supreme Court), there may be many precedents and

ratio decidendi cited by decision makers. They may not agree on <u>why</u> they reach a conclusion.

4. An overarching legal principle or rule which is applied to (1) to (3) above. There may be multiple principles that can be applied. Natural law and divine law can be a part of such principles. Such principles tend to be "projections" of idealized society – they might or might not bear a resemblance to existing society.

Natural law – some believe there is no such law, that it is only a justification. Others believe that such law does exist. Others may believe it exists, but disagree what the natural law is.

Legal realist approach – law is "what courts do." There is the law as written, and the law as used in reality. The use of law involves the use of discretion by judges, prosecutors, etc. Holmes, Stone were legal realists.

<u>The sources of law:</u>

1. Custom – where there is a set of established customs, these customs may be absorbed into the common law.

The customs of business law were absorbed into commercial law. Much of the "consumer movement" of [the] 19th and 20th century has been an attempt to override much of this law.

As one group, and its customs, rise in power, it will attempt to replace the prevailing customs in law with their customs.

2. Morality – law based on moral or ethical principles. On any issue there are many moral or ethical principles that may apply. St. Thomas Aquinas – for any problem, there must be not only general principles, but also particular principles.
3. Public policy – law based on political principles.
4. Statutes – laws established by legislature.
5. Force – the will of the sovereign. It is the interest utilizing force that is the source.
6. Precedent – past legal decisions.
7. Opinions of experts – authorities' opinions regarding the law or its interpretation. The concept of a "relevant market" in antitrust is an example.
8. Legal theory – all legal theory has a system of logic, definition, and reasoning.

Truth vs. validity: Truth – descriptive accuracy or correct explanation. Validity – the correct application of logical reasoning. The fact that a model is valid does not mean that it is true. It can be valid, but might not be true. The conclusion of any system can be valid but that conclusion is not necessarily true. To determine truth, one must ask: Who holds what premises? What are those premises? Controlling the terms of a model to be followed is a means of controlling the conclusions of a model and assuring its validity.

Thus, law is both logic and life, but it is especially life. Validity does not equal truth or desirability.

See book – William Empson – *The Seven Types of Ambiguity*.

Rights can be seen in many contexts:

1. A claim
2. An affirmation of a claim
3. A means of affirming a claim.

"Rights" play an important role in American discourse. The term "rights" is used when we really mean "claims."

[Wesley] Hohfeld wrote much on rights, including concepts of "right to" and "right from."

In an opportunity set model, rights enter as the basis for power.

Consider the statement "X has the right to." This has many meanings, depending upon who says it.

1. When said by a court, it is an "is" proposition, but it is also an "ought" proposition.
2. It is a way of structuring power in decision making "X has a right, and Y does not."
3. Court is also trying to legitimize its decision – to convince that X should have the right.

If a participant in the decision-making system says "X has the right to," it could be an "is" proposition, or it could be an "ought" proposition, or it could be a claim or it could be an affirmation of the claim.

4. If one who sits in judgment of the law (from the legal philosopher to the man on the street) says "X has the right to" can be is or ought.

5. If a logician says "X has a right to," he may be judging its consistency from a logical perspective.
6. Any right is relative to other rights. It is also relative to social control in general (which includes other rights). It may also be inconsistent with other principles and constrained by other principles. (I own this baseball bat, (a right) but I may not hit you with it (not a right)).
7. Every right is relative to other rights and has meaning only relative to other rights.
8. A "de jure" right is recognized in law; a "de facto" right is not yet recognized or enforced by law. If legal rules do not exist, then moral rules or other rules can become de facto rights.
9. On the one hand, it is accepted that rights govern economic performance. Opportunity sets, which are defined by the initial set of rights, determine the available Pareto optimal set of solutions. Some claim that economic analysis should determine rights – rights should go to that party that maximizes income. But there is a tension here – market analysis depends on rights, but now rights are to be based on market analysis.

Consider the Pigouvian analysis in the graph:

Pigouvian Analysis

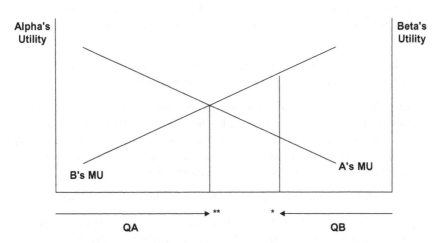

From point *, utility is maximized if we move from point * to point **. But this assumes (a) we know people's utility functions and (b) utility maximization, and MU = MU is desired objective (or equal marginal utilities, not equal income is the objectives), and (c) there are no disincentive effects (if transferred from A to B, neither will reduce their effort or output).

What we have in the neoclassical paradigms is a tension that rights determine results, but results determine rights (or at least welfare maximization advocates would do).

What are property rights?

See Mercuro and Samuels, first and last chapters.

The notion of property rights evolved from land as property. The term "property" was later applied to other forms or property – securities, rights in a contract, market value (takings).

Property is the name we give to certain protected interests. Property interests are given higher status than other protected interests.

Property rights are rights related to a form of property – "sticks in the bundle."

What is the nature of property rights? Same as rights in general, but more privileged. Ownership of property is power and establishes the basis for participation in decision making.

Is property an absolute or relative thing? Property is relative to other rights, relative to law, relative to government decision making that defines property rights.

We often think of rights as a "private right," but rights also have a public nature. They come about from public processes and enforcement.

Property rights are problematic and contingent. They are exposed to "forces of creative destruction," they are affected by the actions of others, subject to legal change. Return to red cedar case – an inevitable necessity to choose. A question of pragmatism: If we all accepted an alternative metaphysical scheme, what difference would it make? Not much – we would still have to choose.

Rights are the basis of power – that is, participation in decision making.

Property rights – property is power – rights in property are a protected interest that defines participation in decision making. Property is "a bundle of rights." Rights are not absolute – must be relative to other rights.

Property rights are not intrinsic – they are contingent upon the outcome of the market, the decisions of government, etc.

Property, government, and law co-evolved to transform the definition of property. This transformation arose out of conflicts – conflicts among property owners, of property owners and non-owners. Essentially similar to Schumpeter's process of creative destruction. As conflicts arise, old values are destroyed, new values arise.

Key point: There is an inevitability of non-compensated lawsuits (losses). When rights are not antecedents, but are the product of government decision, there will be winners, losers in any case.

Property, like government, requires an inevitability of choice. Details about whose interests will count are not given – they must be worked out within the legal-economic nexus.

Property is whoever's interests are protected by law. It is not protected because it is property; it is property because it is protected. Like any government decision, it requires the inevitability of choice. Key question is always: Whose interest will be protected? Whose interest will be exposed to the actions of others? Which interests will government support?

"Night watchman theory of Government" – Government's job is to protect property. This begs the question of whose interests will be protected. Government is a source of power for those who control it.

The relationship of property and neoclassical economic analysis. If you have property system 1 and trade, you will get optimal outcome 1. If you have property system 2, you get optimal outcome 2. There is no single optimal solution. Allocation of resources and distribution of income are a function of the initial distribution of rights. Distribution of rights is a matter of government, and government is a matter of conflicting interests' attempts to control government and have their interests protected. Government and property are a co-evolving process of determining whose interests count.

Several points to be made:

1. Government is ubiquitous, important, and inevitably activist. It is fundamental to the processes of the economy. Ideology often clouds this reality. "Protection of property" or "minimizing government" both obscure reality of the true role of government. Economic role of government cannot be measured by dollars of spending. These are attempts to use selective perception to obscure the inevitability of decisions.

2. What does a model exclude as well as include? Any model that excludes government's role of choice cannot say anything about the true role of government.
3. Rights are of a dual nature. If Alpha has a right, Beta has a non-right. To say that "everyone has rights" begs the question.
4. Do you treat unequals equally or unequally? Treating unequals equally may reinforce inequality.
5. Selective perception runs through all of this.
6. There is always a relevant body of law that applies to a given situation (or soon will be). The central issue is: how that law is to be changed/preserved?
7. The nature of the status quo point. Status quo defines distribution of rights, and an array of outcomes and externalities. It is subject to interpretation and selective perception.
8. Only places where there is "an absence of government" are in truly new areas created by technology that differ from existing situations. There soon will be a law in any such areas, however, when conflicts arise.
9. Business is the most radical element of society. It is what causes greatest change in markets. Politics are an alternative to economics.
10. There is a conflict over the control of government and whose interests will be protected. Government is both a tool of power and a tool to limit power. Both Pareto and Knight recognized this. Knight referred to "useful fictions" – these fictions give conclusions that we find acceptable.

What is "government"?

Many things:

1. An arena of power and power play. Politics is about quest for and exercise of power.
2. Articulation, clarification, juxtaposition, and choice of values. A value choice process. It is a process of deciding whose values count, but this phrase can be an oversimplification in that people don't just "have values." Values are learned and chosen as part of a larger social choice process.
3. An institution of collective action. It is an institution through which society acts.
4. It is a collective bargaining process. A matter of negotiations, of trading one person's perception of interests for another person's perception of interests through vote trading.

5. Government is politics, and politics is government. The alternative is dictatorship.
6. Government is a process. It is a continuing process of becoming, not a final, completed status.

Property: Is the term "property" a descriptively accurate category? Samuels – no, it is not. What is "public" vs. "private" ownership of a means of production? Property is the right to make decisions about acquisition, utilization, and disposition. If this is true, there is no such distinction of public vs. private ownership. Most of the means of production are owned by corporations or government. These cannot be described in terms of ownership decision making. Managers, not owners, make decisions in both of these. Owners of a corporation cannot make decisions about the company they own. In both cases, there are people who are able to make decisions, not by virtue of their position as owners, but by virtue of their appointed positions.

[Milovan] Djilis's book, *The New Class: An Analysis of the Communist System,* book in [the] 1960s argued that Soviet Union was ruled by "A New Class" that was appointed. [Joseph] Schumpeter's *Capitalism, Socialism, and Democracy* and his essay, "The March Toward Socialism," and [John Kenneth] Galbraith's *New Industrial State* all reached the same conclusion, as did [Adolf] Berle and [Gardiner] Means's, *The Modern Corporation and Private Property*.

If the basis of power is the ability to make decisions, then power and ownership can be separated.

Since there is more than one person involved, an important issue is how these interact.

What is "the market?"

What does the term "the market works" mean? The market always "works." There will be a solution for each structure of rights within which the market operates.

The market is a function of the law and of business decision making. Modern liberal thought was a reaction to and rejection of monarchical thought and control of the economy. This obfuscates the inevitably activist role of government. "The market" will work out differently depending on the structure chosen.

Samuels: Government operates within market, and market operates within structure of government. Both "government" and "market" are independent variables and dependent variables. We obfuscate this to avoid the reality that such choices are political. In order to deal with the simultaneity of these two, we may use selective perception to make certain variables "given" and to deny the inevitability of political choice.

There are two things going on within this domain: (1) the process of determining and redetermining decision-making structures and (2) the process of working out Pareto optimal results within that structure. Each structure yields its own Pareto-optimal result.

Rationality: Perhaps the most important concept in economics because it colors all models we use. Economic rationality vs. others (legal, administrative, social rationality). Each has its own basis for making choices. Economic rationality – people seek their self-chosen goals on the basis of means that are also self-chosen. Or – people pursue their self-interest. But this is not a given – how do people choose their self-interest? And how do economists define self-interest?

Economists typically refer to profit maximization or economic welfare maximization. What does this mean? Stigler – not until [the] 1960s did economists begin the widespread use of utility functions in a wide range of problems. How do people learn their preferences that define their self-interest? What are the ends and what are the ends-means relationships?

Whatever we can say about peoples' goals/means decisions, it is true that people act using constrained maximization within their opportunity sets (which are a function of law). This gives rise to the distinction between law-making mentality and law-taking mentality. Law-making mentality understands that law is subject to change and a matter of control. Law-taking mentality accepts law as given.

Uncertainty: Risk, according to Knight, is calculable and insurable, uncertainty is incalculable and uninsurable. The current dominant framework is rational expectations, which assumes away much of the problem of uncertainty.

All statements of "fact" carry a subjective element of uncertainty.

Rationality implies a form of deliberateness. But Smith, Hayek, and others have said there is also non-deliberate decision making – tradition, customs, and habits.

Bounded rationality: Decisions are based on "sufficient knowledge," not "perfect knowledge."

Principle of unintended/unanticipated consequences: All social actions have unintended consequences. Raises question: How can you know your interest if there is radical indeterminacy, bounded rationality, and unintended consequences? We should be wary of any model that proposes optimal solutions–based rationality. Given BR, UI, and RI, how can we know what policy to choose?

Side note: For over a century, the most honorific title in Western intellectual circles was the title of "science." This had many meanings, but increasingly in the 20th century, physics became the standard by which "science" was defined. Economics developed in this context and in the image of [the] 19th century physics. This was important, because economists wanted to hold the status of science – with "laws" and determinate solutions. This also gave rise to a desire for apolitical knowledge – knowledge above politics, above values. This combined with a denigration of politics and a desire to remain removed from politics. This gives rise to [three] domains: (1) the pure individual as an abstract concept; (2) the structure independent of the individual; (3) the web of values and beliefs. In order to pursue the scientific agenda, economists have sought to abstract from (2) and (3) and focus only on (1). End of side note.

Deborah Stone: Rational model is flawed in that it ignores structure, values, beliefs, and (in Samuels' terms) the process of working things out in politics. Political science has imported rational choice theory to become the dominant paradigm. There is a counterrevolution against rational choice on the grounds that it leaves out too much. A crucial issue in the debate: Why do people vote? Rational choice theory says that voting is irrational, but people do vote. So why do they vote? End of side note.

Are issues of policy a technical issue or a subjective issue? [Richard] Musgrave's economics of public sector: Size of public sector is a technical, not a subjective, issue. But Burkhead and Minor say there is no definitive rule to determine the size of the public sector.

The role of the expert: Is it to advise on ends, or only on the means to achieve ends? The role of the expert is a matter of social power. See book *The Intellectual as a Man of Power* (or a similar title).[1] Goal of economics was to be an objective source of knowledge on means to achieve ends.

Can we resolve the conflict of technical and subjective approaches? Consider "technological externalities" (smoke as pollution) vs. "pecuniary externalities" (effects on prices due to certain actions or policies). Some say technological externalities should be addressed; pecuniary externalities should be ignored. (Though Coase theorem says you can ignore technological externalities if transaction costs are zero and trading is possible.) Are these a matter of technical solutions? Yes, it can appear to be technical and objective, but it can also be viewed as ideological. Choice of terms and categories leads to results.

Buchanan/Stubblebine view of Pareto relevant and Pareto irrelevant externalities: If people value enough to trade/negotiate, it is Pareto relevant. If not, it is Pareto irrelevant.

V. Ronald Coase and Richard Posner: The Coase Theorem and Wealth Maximization

[Richard] Posner's view: Objective is to maximize the value of output, so there should be a market for everything. See *Economic Analysis of Law* and his attempt to define a market for rape. Also advocates a market for babies. To what degree is his view based on technical considerations, and to what degree on ideology? May be difficult to distinguish.

So are questions of the economic role of government a technical matter or a subjective matter?

See book by Garry Wills – *A Necessary Evil*. On fact and myth of founding of U.S. government. See *New York Review of Books*, November 18.

If we fail to recognize the dual nature of rights, then "deregulation" looks very attractive and any "reform" that changes the existing structure of institutions looks very threatening. In 1954, Knight's review of Lionel Robbins' book, Knight says "Robbins is seeking to develop propaganda for a free society." Also see Samuels' book of 1966 *The Classical Theory of Economic Policy*. Buchanan does the same – says he is building a fortress of the market. Buchanan/Stubblebine later introduced the notion of "Pareto relevant" externalities (those on which people trade or buy each other off) and "Pareto irrelevant" (in which no one trades and no action is needed). How is this done? Structure a model that includes only the variables that lead to the result desired and omitting variables that dispute the result desired.

What is at issue, in part, is the desirability of market solutions. Some people prefer market solutions. Stigler, Buchanan, [and] many Coasians are attempting to build an ideology of free markets. Economists don't like to be seen as ideologues, rather than scientists, but their views are heavily value-laden.

There are many levels at work – the propaganda level, the technical level, the level of utility maximization as a description of reality vs. a methodological approach, the level at which wealth is defined by social institutions.

Posner: Often seen as the father of mainstream law and economics movement, and an alternative to Coase. Contends that the function of courts is to maximize the value of output, and they do behave in this way. Believes that judges play an activist's role (see his "potted plant" article). Samuels – Posner's view is tautological – the court always determines a maximum wealth within the chosen structure of rights. There is no measure of output maximization that is independent of the chosen rights structure. See Samuels and Mercuro analysis of Posner's judicial decisions – he never says "I am reaching this conclusion to maximize wealth."

VI. Regulation and Deregulation

Issues of regulation and deregulation: It is incorrect to think of regulation as analytically different from deregulation. Property rights are defined by regulatory statutes and decisions. This is so because of the reciprocal nature of rights. Will Alpha be exposed to Beta (under "regulation") or will Beta be exposed to Alpha (under "deregulation"). Regulation is fundamental, it defines property rights and who may do what to whom. Regulation is fundamental and not epiphenomenal. Analytically, the two are identical – in each case, one interest is exposed and one interest is protected.

Case: Microsoft – Is Microsoft a firm that gained its position by way of its successful, rivalrous behavior? Or by way of behavior that defines the structure of the market by way of its behavior? The questions of what rights a firm has, or what constitutes competition are open questions, not given. The nature of antitrust regulation is such that by definition it is about determining the structure of markets. Judge cited behavior as Microsoft's violation; Microsoft says its behavior is competitive. At the bottom is a question of power – if you see power in the private sector that requires checks to prevent coercion, then government must do the checking. Or if government action is seen as coercion, then government must be checked. But in either case, government's role is the same – it defines behavior that is acceptable.

What are the potential systems of regulation? (1) Government, (2) morality (especially evident from the 1300s to 1800s, when some business practices that are now common were seen to be immoral), and (3) market. How is the market a regulatory system? Management has sometimes created "markets" via internal competition within the firm – divisions within a firm may compete for resources or they may compete against "outsource" firms for some resources.

What is a market? Economists often use this as a primitive, undefined term. Sometimes it is defined in terms of a group of producers and consumers. Others would define as a group of goods with high cross-price elasticities. "Efficiency" as a standard for a "market working" is only relevant within a preexisting system of rights.

VII. The Compensation Problem

The Compensation Principle

Assume an airport exists and desires to expand by adding a runway and increasing its volume of business. This increases the number of people exposed to over flights. Until [the] 1930s, a person's property was conical – a "cone" from the center of the earth, then a tube into space – property rights included all space above a piece of land. Could not fly over without owner's permission. In a 1930s case, a court called this illogical. Airlines are permitted to fly over property without compensation.

If the airport expands, should it have to compensate landowners? In general terms, should the change in the behavior of one actor be considered a taking by another party? There is no formula that can determine when government should and should not compensate for losses. If government creates windfall gains, can it take it back? (Constitution ignores this.) This all gives rise to "a language of conflicting expectations." Samuels – such losses are ubiquitous, but the question of loss compensation is very unevenly applied.

There is no single rule that can define when there is or is not a taking. The courts have used a variety of rules.

Eminent domain [ED] – Arises from need for government to acquire property for government use. In this case, it is a physical taking. Some companies – such as public utilities – may have the right to exercise eminent domain.

ED and the takings issue [are] now applied to non-physical takings – actions that leave property physically intact but reduces its value.

Police power – authority of government to act in some interest. This conflicts with ED. Policy power might not require compensation, but ED requires compensation. [Richard] Epstein (University of Chicago) contends that property is absolute and diminution of property value requires compensation.

The desire to say that "the courts will work this out with a set of final rules" is simply not achievable.

Examination of Compensation Rules

[Frank] Michelman's utility rule: – A highly logical approach, but not self-dispositive – judges must still determine whether conditions are met (or "which box a given situation fits into").

Saks [Joseph Sax?]: Focuses on "non-conflict creating spillover effects" – says in these cases there should be no spillovers. But this ignores the most important problems. In spillover cases, he wants to maximize output "of resource base." But what is the resource base?

[Lawrence] Berger: Stresses fairness (what accords with community sense of fairness) and efficiency. Wants to minimize sum of (a) nuisance costs (externality), (b) prevention costs, and (c) administrative costs. Also affirms "first in time" – If

[two] lawful activities conflict, then the second to arrive should compensate first to arrive, so as to protect the expectations of the first property owner.

[Richard] Epstein: Very narrow police power, very broad eminent domain power – any change in rights must be compensated. Wants to extend eminent domain to cover much of the range of police power so that the compensation principle applies more broadly. Wants community custom to dictate in such cases – but how is this determined? Judgments must still be made. In the end, Epstein wants to prevent legislation by making compensation costs apply to any change.

[Lawrence] Bloom and [Daniel] Rubinfeld – Case for compensation is strongest where risk of loss is large relative to individual's wealth. This also contains an element of judgment.

In all of these, there is a broad range for selective perception and subjectivity. Whenever the court uses any of these principles, it is creating property and rights. The court makes what property is whenever it decides who has rights and who is denied rights.

Very few ask "what is going on in the application of the compensation principle?" Donald Black did so. Observed that compensation principle has largely been applied to protect an individual from a large organization (including government). Another way of saying this is to say that strict and absolute liability is usually only applied to large organizations. Black also said that compensation varied directly with "social distance."

Mercuro/Samuels: View externalities as ubiquitous and consider the reciprocal nature of rights and exposure. Question is whose rights will count and who will have an established right (the right to be compensated). They want to deal at the "rights determination level." Rights have no intrinsic value – value is based on economic and non-economic variables (expectations). So the capitalized value used to determine compensation is based on assumptions of these variables. Key question is not on compensation, but is whose interest will be protected[.] No matter whose interest is protected, someone will suffer an uncompensated loss. This is often selectively ignored – ignores that when we recognize a right (or compensate) we impose a loss (on payer). This is the process of constructing/ reconstructing the economy. There are opportunity costs to either choice.

So what is the role of the compensation principle? Some say to protect property – but Mercuro/Samuels say this cannot be true – it is more fundamental in determining property.

Some see compensation principle as a mechanism for limiting power of legislature, but this ignores the inevitable necessity to choose (red cedar case).

Compensation principle can also serve as psychic balm, as a means of making reality simpler, more acceptable, by establishing a principle that satisfies the losers, that is a check on legal change that also legitimizes legal changes that do not provide compensation, and that itself provides a form of social control.

The demand for compensation is a part of the broader demand for rights.

Case: Lucas [*Lucas v. South Carolina Coastal Council*] compensation principle case.

Lucas Case: Souter's dissent – nuisance focuses not on property, but on conduct, and regulation limits that conduct. Said court should not have taken the case as an appropriate case on takings.

Again property is a status given to interests.

The normative question is "Do we want to freeze the law of property and freeze the protection of existing interests?" Samuels – we have never done so – we have had continuing change.

New Topic: The "Rule of Law" and the Equal Protection Clause

Rule of law: The notion that law should rule, not personal whim, and there should be one law for all people. Questions: Does the rule of law apply to procedural questions – so that when certain procedural issues are addressed the rule of law has been applied? How are procedures to be changed and why? Who determines the law and is it to be subject to change? How can equal protection be provided when there is inequality in the substantial law?

"Rule of law" is often invoked to prevent the use of discretion by decision makers. But all actors in the process inevitably use discretion. There is discretion used in classification – to what laws do certain facts apply? Which law will apply when laws (or principles) conflict?

Equal protection clause of [Fourteenth] amendment: "Nor shall any state deny to any person equal protection of its laws." What does this mean? School financing case – school funding can be very unequal across school districts. In many cases, an attempt to treat unequals equally is to treat them unequally. Similarly, to treat Alpha's interest "equally" may treat Beta's interest unequally.

What is the role of "Universal Rights?" Right to be free of coercion, free of hunger, etc? If this is a "right," against who should the coerced or the hungry bring a case to defend their rights?

Inequality and poverty – inequality is particularly offensive in the face of great wealth. Some are concerned with outcome, others are concerned with the mode (or "game rules") of distribution.

Some would say that "institutionally produced inequality is wrong." But this ignores that each institutional arrangement has its unique distribution.

Affirmative action: If some have been discriminated against, how does one deal with past unequal treatment? Locke and Smith – function of government is to defend the rich against the poor – but the rich already control government. Bentham – wanted greatest happiness for greatest number – but this has an insoluble dilemma – should we increase happiness of more people somewhat, or of fewer peoples a great deal?

What is the objective of government? Only one objective is promotion of equality. Other objectives may conflict. The equal protection clause must be worked out within a system with inherent inequality.

What is the role of equal protection clause? A means for seeking redress of grievances and a lever to promote change.

<u>Growth of government</u>

Why has government grown so much in past century? Samuels – this is a poor question – government "size" or "role" cannot be measured by spending or share of GNP.

It is difficult to reach a conclusion about this question.

Adolph Wagner and Wagner's law: It is inevitable that government share of GNP will increase.

Ballard Campbell – *The Growth of American Government* (book). Early period – he calls "The Republican Period" – government had no power of direct taxation. Agriculture dominated (1780s–1870s). "Transitional Period" (1880–1920s) – industrialization required support and infrastructure. Regulation of industry through antitrust, food and drug laws, labor laws, etc., followed the creation of new conditions that arose in this era. There was also an increase in government expenditures and new forms of taxation. There was also a complex, but largely cooperative relationship of state and federal governments. 1930s–1970s – "The Claimant Period" – with roots in great depression. Involved distributional objectives, macroeconomic stabilization, civil rights, labor and consumer protection, rise of federal mandates to states. 1970s–1990s – "The Period of Restraint."

Side note: Voluntary vs. volitional. When is an act voluntary? Volition has to do with an ability to choose within an opportunity set ("Your money or your life" is a choice). Voluntary involves a choice of the choices from which one chooses. Most choice in economics is volitional, not voluntary.

Campbell continued: What are the causes of the growth of government. There is no single case that explains all growth in government. (1) Industrialization (he says this is the largest factor). With national or regional markets, need for infrastructure, role of government increases. (2) Pressures from interest groups. (3) Partisan politics – parties provide new programs as a means of competing for votes. (4) Self-interested activity of politicians, bureaucrats, etc., who provide programs to specific blocks of voters.

Why is all this so complex? Campbell – the continuing impact of "republican impulse" – the view of government as a threat to individuals and an ideological predisposition to be suspicious of government. This prevents government in the United States from developing coherent, long-term policies.

This creates a continuing ambivalence – on the one hand, people are suspicious of government, on the other hand, people are pragmatic in the use of government. This is a major factor in the role of government in the United States. When a problem becomes seen as national in scope, then people turn to government.

Another factor adding to complexity is the interdependency of local, state, and federal governments. This adds complexity to any issue that crosses jurisdictional lines. The growth of spending has been faster since World War II at the state and local level than at the national level.

Another factor is growth of use of government to reduce risks of living in a modern, interdependent world. [Michael] Polanyi – *The Great Transformation* – the shift from tradition to industrial market society required government to provide forms of security that traditional arrangements could no longer provide.

Another factor is that different groups have been able to capture benefits that were intended for a wider group. Samuels: many welfare programs have been adopted only when benefits were provided to a broader public other than the poor.

Samuels: There are interpretative questions in understanding the growth of government expenditures. Is this a normative or a positive question? Is the growth of government expenditures inevitable or is it a matter of policy choice? It is probably not entirely inevitable nor entirely an issue of policy choice.

Another issue is the meaningfulness of differences in economic systems. How do you compare expenditures across systems? Do terms "capitalism" and "socialism" have any explanatory value? Does Max Weber's term "political capitalism" have a meaning?

Another issue deals with the particular roles of government. If government has role 1, role 2, role 3, and role 1 is a long-standing role, then is new role 2 truly a new role or is it merely an extension of role 1? If government's fundamental role is the protection of interests and rights, then how does one distinguish among these roles? Is a "new" function truly new, or is it merely another example of protecting interests?

Another issue: In order to define the level of government spending, several factors must be understood: (1) power and power play (2) belief system and ideology. Example – How do you explain the New Deal? (or Reagan Revolution) Is it a matter of power – a shift in who holds power? Or is it a shift in belief systems and ideology? (3) Psychological variables – view that U.S. system is unique and of value but we also see it as intrusive. These can be manipulated by those with power or using ideology. (4) Technological imperatives – Galbraith and others – the technological imperatives determine government expenditures. (5) Population growth – Thomas Malthus really had [three] points – population will grow faster than food supply; quality of life will decrease as population increases; society will be forced to rely more on social forms of control and less on tradition. As population density increases, interdependencies increase. (6) Average level of income affects capacity to tax. (7) Distribution of wealth.

The difficulty in explaining the growth in government expenditures is that these often cannot be separated as explanatory factors.

Another difficulty is that "government" is not homogeneous. Different parts of government operate differently and with different rates of growth.

Another issue is the definition of output. Quality of goods changes over time. This makes comparisons difficult over time. What is the output of the public sector? Is it particular activities or particular outcomes? How do you evaluate the outcomes of schools, for example? It is not clear how to measure these, so spending becomes the proxy of outcomes.

Another issue is the identification of the consequences of public spending. Example – if there is a low level of fire protection, owners will pay more for fire insurance, which would result in lower capitalized property values. Or good schools may result in higher capitalized property values. So consequences of policy and spending may affect property values. If two jurisdictions have different levels of spending, is this a reflection of different demands by citizens, different levels of professionalism and quality of output, or "empire building" by politicians and bureaucrats? In national defense, how can a citizen or a legislator make decisions about defense spending and defense systems?

Does participation matter? [That is], do people gain some benefit by their mere participation in government decision making? Does this explain the growth of government in some way? If so, does it explain the willingness to use government?

Are supply and demand interrelated? Do people begin to demand a public service once it has been supplied and they experience its benefits?

Issues in decision making – free and unwilling riders, role of decision making – affect collective decision making and must be accounted for in any explanation of the growth of government.

Definition of social welfare function – [Charles] Lindblom argues that SWF only be known after the fact – after decisions have been made and participants experience consequences.

What are explanatory factors in growth of government spending?

1. Growth of war and costliness of wars. Measured as cost per casualty, cost has increased. Various factors – increased cost of technology, cost of internal repression, role of military industrial complex (in which supply creates its own demand).

2. Change in the value system. Values regarding individualism and use of government have changed. There might not be a change in values – but there might be a change in whose values count. Any shift in political power may appear as a change in whose values count. Would this affect government spending?

3. Macroeconomic role of government. Government has assumed a greater role in the macroeconomic supervision of the economy.

4. Growth of knowledge in physical/social sciences. May have increased our desire to control as well as our ability to control. Example – growth of knowledge about health leads to greater desire to control health.

5. Greater, more widespread knowledge about policy. Political scientist Carl Frederick says that 18th century marked the beginning of greater understanding of the role of policy and recognition that policy is a matter of choice.

6. According to Engel's law, different goods have different income elasticity. If income elasticity of demand for government goods is greater than 1, then there might be a growth in demand for government goods when income increases.

7. Greater access to government by a greater number of people. Likely to be a greater use of government.
8. Psychological attitude toward government. Does one look upon government positively or negatively? Or schizophrenically?
9. Attitudes toward risk, especially risks that could be collectivized. Bismarck – to younger groups, he gave control of military. To masses, he gave welfare state. To business, he gave the creation of the corporation. The creation of the corporation was a means of collectivizing risk and limiting liability.
10. Government has become, increasingly, an arena of social power play. It has always been so, but with greater access this is more obvious. Government becomes an arena for redistribution.
11. Difficulty of eliminating government programs. Governments do not change easily. "Sunset" laws attempt to deal with this. Why is this so? Beneficiaries will seek not only to defend but to expand programs.
12. Changes in society – extended families disappearing – functions performed by these institutions may be declining – the "safety net" of family may be judged to be insufficient.
13. Economies of scale permit government to produce some goods that cannot be produced by private sector. May cause growth of such spending.
14. Changes in technology – automobiles in particular – give rise to spending on complementary goods – roads.
15. Fractionalization of budgetary decision making. There has traditionally been no connection between revenue bills and budgetary bills. Only in past 30 years has there been a more direct connection.
16. Quid pro quo decision making – logrolling – in decision making.
17. The logic of politics. Incumbents offer constituents benefits as a means of gaining re-election.
18. Demographic changes in population. Aging of population leads to demand for services by these groups.
19. Increase in expenditures that are labor intensive – and thus expensive – and expenditures that are capital intensive (military) and thus expensive.
20. Revenue sources of government – with introduction of income tax it became easier to raise revenue. Prior to the rise of the money economy, it was only possible to tax property and exports/imports. By [the] end of [the] 19th century, a large share of people worked for someone else and most goods were produced for sale in the market. Thus, it was possible to tax sales and income. Musgrave – the number of "tax handles" has grown with the growth of the money economy.

21. Post-war threshold effect. Following each World War, government spending remained at a level higher than before the war. Had a ratchet effect on spending.
22. Government has underwritten many businesses and institutions.

Conclusion: There is no simple set of factors that explain growth of government spending.

Adolph Wagner (1880s): Wagner's law – government spending would increase (taken to mean that government share of GNP will increase). Also, government spending would increase faster than other components of GNP. His explanation has [three] parts: (1) Law and order – capitalism was becoming more complex and markets required more policing. (2) Public production – industries with high capital requirements and economies of scale would require a role for government – especially transportation and communication. The United States used land grants to fund development of railroad, but Europe could not do this and had more direct financing. (3) Socioeconomics of government – education, banking, and postal services. Wagner missed some elements (military) but clearly identified major factors in growth of government.

Wagner's explanation: (1) There is an interrelationship between the growth of the private sector and the growth of the public sector. There is increasing centralization in both the public sector and the private sector. It is an inherent characteristic of industrial countries. (2) The growth of government is true regardless of the nature of the government or the economy – capitalist or socialist, democratic or non-democratic. Some political scientists agree with Wagner, others disagree. (3) An emphasis on social stability – government is called upon to provide public safety, welfare assistance, [and] other functions required in a more complex, urban industrial society.

See 1985 *National Tax Journal* – study of 1963–1979 for cross section of countries. Used measures of level of development to examine Wagner's law. Found that Wagner's law did not apply in poorest countries, did apply in countries in the process of development, and did not apply in developed countries.

What is role of people's attitudes and preferences for public expenditures? Some studies in [the] 1960s found that income did not affect people's attitude toward public expenditures, but did affect attitudes toward specific spending programs. This and other studies found that education level did affect attitudes toward spending. Party affiliation often found not to be important. A study of Swedish voters found that percentage of persons dissatisfied with government increased as income increased, but decreased with higher education. These studies were in [the] 1960s and 1970s.

What does all this mean? Wagner's ideas were insightful. Does it apply better within some ranges of the development process than other ranges of the development process?

Related concepts:

"Social Overhead Capital" – or social capital. Wagner would say this is a part of the public–private interrelationship.

"The Displacement Effect" – or "The Treasury Doctrine." If government spending increases, it will crowd out other private spending.

"The Inspection Effect" – During a period of war time, problems that would ordinarily be ignored are identified and addressed.

[Alan] Peacock and [Jack] Wiseman [NBER publication, *The Growth of Public Expenditures in the United Kingdom*] – [four] propositions: (1) Governments prefer to spend more rather than less. (2) Citizens prefer to pay fewer taxes rather than more. (3) Governments must pay some degree of attention to citizen preferences on taxes and spending. (4) Citizens prefer more government spending on specific programs rather than less (Samuels adds this). The combination of these is what contributes to a tendency toward deficit spending.

[Solomon] Fabricant: Study of growth of government spending. Growth of government spending was a function of (1) income growth, (2) population, (3) technology, [and] (4) value system. Robert Wood compared municipalities – 96% of variance in level of spending could be explained by community size, housing density, population age, and industrialization.

Aaron Wildavsky focused on the fragmented nature of the budgeting process, combined with quid pro quo voting, explained spending growth.

Colin Clark: "Critical Limit Theory" – Once government spending exceeded 25% of GNP, there would be adverse effects – less resistance to inflationary finance.

Summarizing the Course

Samuels: In any course he took as a student, he would ask "what is the most fundamental question involved?" What is the most fundamental point of this course?

When looking at an issue, focus on who has what rights, what rights are and could be in place. Does not focus on finding a "right" policy, which is presumptuous. There are many ways of looking at the economic role of government.

We have sought to explain what the economic role of government is all about: Has not been about prediction of outcomes or about what are the "correct" policies. The issues involved in understanding a problem can be applied to all problems.

What else do we need to know about "the process of working things out?"

1. Need to understand "the process of working things out that determines the process of working things out" – the rules for making rules.
2. How do people participate in the economy – what is the role of the shaping of the brain – internal and external forces – that influence decisions? This is the field of cognitive science.
3. More sophisticated understanding of politics, involving psychology. [Amartya] Sen's work is also insightful – others doing work that shows political factors are primary cause of famines.

What is role of ideology? See Samuels' chapter in Sidney Weintraub's book on *Modern Economic Thought*.

Modes of Doing Policy Analysis

1. Identification of policy alternatives and potential consequences under varying conditions (Schmid).
2. Identification of "optimal" policies (Hirsch).
3. Systems analysis vs. incremental analysis. Most mainstream analysis is incremental. But systems approach can be complementary.
4. Take peoples' various definitions of "a problem" (e.g., "the farm problem") and conduct analysis based on each of these assumed definitions of the problem.

SAMPLE EXAM QUESTIONS

Economic Role of Government, Spring 1994, Final Exam

Answer all of the following questions, clearly and directly to the point and in such a manner as to indicate your mastery of the materials relevant to each. Answers will be evaluated in part on the basis of the level of sophistication. Avoid duplication of answers; use cross-referencing. All questions count equally.

1. In James W. Ely, Jr., *The Guardian of Every Other Right: A Constitutional History of Property Rights* (Oxford University Press, 1992), the author

says that the U.S. Supreme Court likely will "continue on [its] present course of incrementally extending protection for economic liberties against arbitrary or excessive regulation" (p. 154).
   a. On the basis of what theory of property does this view of property make sense?
   b. Critique that theory of property on the basis of what you have learned in this course.
   c. What is the social role of that theory of property?
2. How does the concept of the "dual nature of rights" affect conventional *economic* thinking? Be specific.
3. Assume that you are Werner Hirsch and have accepted the task of providing a critique of this course. What would you say?
4. What have you learned in this course concerning the use of words in conducting analysis of the economic role of government? Give examples.
5. One view is that the market allocates resources. Another view is that markets are formed by and give allocative effect to the institutions, including the legal institutions, which form them. How do you assess/interpret the significance as *knowledge* of these two views?
6. "The legal system is a microcosm of the larger society; the conflicts and preconceptions which characterize the latter also are present in the former." What is all this about, and what is its significance?
7. Answer all of the following:
   a. The neoclassical approach to law and economics emphasizes "efficient solutions." What is meant by "efficient" and what are its strengths and limits?
   b. How is it possible that law can simultaneously constitute freedom and coercion? Of what significance is this?

Economic Role of Government, [Fall 1996, Final Exam]

Answer all of the following questions clearly and directly to the point and in a manner which demonstrates your mastery of the relevant materials. All questions count equally, except that no. 1 counts twice.

1. a. Some or much of the lectures and readings dealt with a positive (in the sense of non-normative) approach to the economic role of government. State, in a series of propositions, the major arguments comprising that approach.
   b. Some or much of the argument emphasizes the importance of government and may appear "statist" and to contradict, even to deny

the meaningfulness of, the ordinary "conservative" or "libertarian" arguments for "non-intervention." State, in a series of propositions, the arguments which the foregoing approach contradicts.

  c. Given the approach taken in the lectures, how may one present the conservative or libertarian position in a manner that recognizes and gives effect to the major positive (non-normative) propositions advanced in the lectures?

2. a. Identify the principal components of the neoclassical approach to law and economics.

  b. What are the assumptions of the neoclassical approach, and, separately, what are variables excluded or finessed by those assumptions?

3. You have had readings and some lectures on the social, or sociological, study of law. How does the law in practice *both* resemble and not resemble the abstract notion of law treated in jurisprudence and in economics?

4. The compensation or takings problem has been given three kinds of treatment: (1) normative efforts to affirm the exclusive domain of the eminent domain principle; (2) normative efforts to articulate principles by which compensable takings can be distinguished from non-compensable takings; and (3) positive (non-normative) efforts to analyze the compensation/takings problem, its role in legal-economic affairs, and how it works out in practice. Summarize carefully these three approaches and their respective arguments and/or findings.

5. a. Identify, in a series of propositions, the Marxian approach to the economic role of government.

  b. Identify the positive (non-normative) elements in the Marxian approach.

  c. Identify the subjective or normative elements in the Marxian approach.

6. a. State and explain the basis of the Coase Theorem.

  b. State and explain the basis of Coase's own position.
      Or is it not possible?

  c. Consider the view that "the critical issue is not 'government or not government' but legal change of the interests which government is being used to support."

      i. What is the argument which supports this conclusion?

      ii. What is the Paretian view of the conclusion?

  d. What does *laissez-faire* mean, assuming it has meaningful analytical content?

7. Much has been made in lectures of the concepts of "process" and "working things out." What is meant by them, for example, in relation to the several paradigmatic models given in class? What are the limits, or limitations, of these concepts? What, precisely, has to be "worked out" and through what "process(es)?"

8. a. State five propositions concerning the economic role of government that you are willing to accept.
   b. Apply those propositions to the Fifth Amendment taking clause and its application.

9. Much has been made in lectures of the relevance and importance of fundamental epistemological and ontological positions. What does that mean? Why relevant and important? Illustrate with two or three examples.

Economic Role of Government, Optional Midterm

Answer at least [6] and no more than [10] of the following questions. Avoid duplication of answers; you may cross-reference between answers.

1. Compare and contrast the approaches to law and economics taken by Hirsch and Samuels, respectively, with regard to the questions asked and not asked and the answers given. Do not evaluate them.

2. a. The neoclassical approach to law and economics emphasizes "efficient solutions." What is meant by "efficient" and what are its strengths and limits?
   b. Define social in relation to private cost.
   c. Does regulation which assigns the right to clean water to the former polluttee create social costs? Why, or why not?

3. What precisely is the connection between the dual nature of rights and the reciprocal character of externalities with the question of whose interests are to count? Why is this important?

4. Consider the statement: "We want government to do as little as possible to interfere with private choice and in the allocation of resources." Consider also the statement: "Government should promote the interests of all the people, and not those of a select few." Critique the logical coherence of these statements on the basis of the legal-economic fundamentals studied in this course, without evaluating them normatively.

5. a. Are "law" and "rights" philosophically realist or nominalist phenomena? Of what consequence is the answer?
   b. What is "private" about "private law?"
   c. What are the principal issues in constitutional law?

d. Consider the statement, "Law is not about something given (and therefore not subject to any test of 'truth') but about desirable policy, for example, the desired behavior of people or the desired future of society." What is involved in this statement?

6. Consider the questions, "What do judges do – and what most fundamentally do they accomplish when they do what they do?" Present two very different answers to these questions.

7. Present a neoclassical critique of institutionalist law and economics.

8. Present an institutionalist critique of neoclassical law and economics.

9. Consider law and legal-economic analysis as systems of language or of discourse.
   a. How do they appear differently from the presentation in Hirsch?
   b. To what other questions given above does this question relate, and why and how?

10. What are the most fundamental issues or problems of the economic role of government?

11. a. How is it possible that law can simultaneously constitute freedom and coercion? Of what significance is this? Or is it not possible?
    b. Consider the view that "the critical issue is not 'government or not government' but legal change of the interests which government is being used to support."
       i. What is the argument which supports this conclusion?
       ii. What is the Paretian view of this conclusion?

12. Consider the view that "the lectures in this course reflect the nihilist if not socialist views of Robert Lee Hale." Present evidence both in support of this view and against this view.

13. Consider the phrase "the economic approach to law." What does this mean? What are (a) the preconceptions and (b) the limits to its coherence? What specific issues are involved?

14. Critique the proposition, "private property is not protected by government because it is property but it is property because it is protected by government." What does this mean? What are its assumptions, and how may they be critiqued? To what other questions given above does this question relate, and why and how?

15. Much has been made in lectures of the concepts of "process" and "working things out." What is meant by them, for example, in relation to the several paradigmatic models given in class? What are the limits, or limitations, of these concepts?

16. Consider the opportunity diagram and the value diagram. What positive principles are illustrated by each?

17. It is widely felt that (a) law should keep government off of our backs, thereby preserving (*inter alia*) a sphere of private autonomy, and (b) law should facilitate efficient solutions to allocative problems.
    i.   What is the problem, according to the lectures with each of these positions?
    ii. Are these [(a) and (b)] different points? What is their relation to each other?
18. Which three of the foregoing questions approach the same subject from different angles? What is that subject? What is the underlying argument being raised?

NOTE

1. As indicated in the notes, Samuels apparently did not recall the exact title of the "book." No "book" by this title could be found. However, a publication by Paul Potter entitled, "The Intellectual as an Agent of Social Change" does exist. Potter was elected president of Students for a Democratic Society in 1964. The publication was a seven-page pamphlet published by the SDS. Potter argues that (a) intellectuals had become isolated, powerless, and frustrated in the university system, (b) those intellectuals who had been involved in government had been servants of the status quo establishment rather than dissenting voices for social change, and (c) intellectuals could and should gain the power to achieve social change by partnering with the various emerging social movements of that day. Given Samuels' discussion of the role of the economist as policy expert and the technical or subjective and power-laden nature of such a role, it appears that Samuels was referring to Potter's publication. The Potter publication is available at http://alexanderstreet.com/products/sixties-primary-documents-and-personal-narratives-1960-1974.